PRAISE FOR

John Stark Bellamy's

THE MANIAC
IN THE BUSHES

and More Tales of Cleveland Woe

"John Stark Bellamy II is the historian your mother warned you about. . . . He offers bad guys and wanton women, unspeakable tragedy and murder most foul. . . . Morbidly fascinating and wickedly entertaining. . . . Strange? Yes, you can certainly say that about a lot of the tales Bellamy includes in his second (and, one can only hope, not his last) collection of Cleveland crime and catastrophe stories. Strange, but awfully entertaining."
— *The Plain Dealer*

"Fascinating reading." — Les Roberts, *Currents*

"John Bellamy II has turned crime into an art with the second of his books on local crimes and disasters. . . . [He] is a thorough researcher and has mined so much definitive material, you almost believe you are reading and reliving the stories of a current crime. The characters come alive with well defined narrative strength and you are swept up in their lives."
— *The Times Of Your Life*

"Bellamy . . . [is a] Homer of our homicides, wandering through dark places and remembering."
— *Free Times*

THE MANIAC IN THE BUSHES

And More Tales of Cleveland Woe

*True Crimes and Disasters from
the Streets of Cleveland*

John Stark Bellamy II

GRAY & COMPANY, PUBLISHERS
CLEVELAND

Gray & Company, Publishers
1588 E. 40th St.
Cleveland, Ohio 44103-2302
www.grayco.com

Library of Congress cataloging-in-publication data
Bellamy, John Stark.
The Maniac in the Bushes and More Tales of Cleveland Woe
/ by John Stark Bellamy II.
1. Crime—Ohio—Cleveland—History—Case studies. 2.
Disasters—Ohio—Cleveland—History—Case studies. 3.
Cleveland (Ohio)—History. I. Title.
HV6795.C5B45 1997
364.15'23'0977132—dc21   97-33939

This book is the second of several planned volumes on the Cleveland of yesteryear. Narrative slide shows chronicling some of the chapters are available for a fee and additional slide shows are under development. For more information or bookings, contact John Stark Bellamy II via e-mail (jstarkbII@aol.com) or by mail via the publisher of this book.

ISBN 1-886228-19-1

Printed in the United States of America

10 9 8 7 6 5 4

To my mother,
Jean Dessel Bellamy,
with thanks for her inexhaustible love,
unfailing support, and lifelong patience

CONTENTS

CONTENTS, *continued*

PREFACE

"I really liked your book, but why didn't you write about . . . ?"

Believe me, that was the last question I expected to hear as I emerged two years ago, my hands figuratively dripping with gore, with the manuscript of *They Died Crawling and Other Tales of Cleveland Woe*, my first collection of Cleveland's historical horrors. But so it was: virtually everyone who liked the book enough to say so also added a complaint like "Why didn't you write about the Kingsbury Run Torso murders?" Or "Why isn't the Collinwood School fire in here?" Or "Aren't you going to tell what happened to Beverly Potts?" It is partly to assuage such grievances—not to mention my own continuing morbid curiosity—that I have once again committed authorship. And, for those inquisitive souls still unsatisfied by the absence here of their favorite local bloodbath (e.g. "Why isn't the Beverly Jarosz case in here?"), I can only plead the sober reality that I must husband my finite stock of horrors for yet further installments in these ongoing annals of Forest City misery.

I sometimes like to speculate about what the audience for my stories is like—and I am willing to endure the charge of solipsism in concluding that my readers are probably a lot like me. By and large, they are Clevelanders "of a certain age" (as the French say) who have had a lifelong fascination with the melodrama of their city's past. More particularly, they are delighted by the exotic social customs and antiquarian manners exhibited in recountings of Cleveland disasters and murders of yore, and, moreover, they are continually conscious of the impact such crimes and misfortunes have had—and continue to have—on the face and character of the metropolis they inhabit. Like me, perhaps, they recall the *frisson* of fear that echoed through childhood summer evenings, when their parents uttered grim words of caution to them as they fled toward childish pastimes: "You'd better get home before dark—you don't want to end up like Beverly Potts!" Maybe, they're the kind of people who can't help feeling a jolt of superstitious anxiety whenever they hear the words "Kingsbury Run." Or maybe it's just that they get tired of the bored look on their children's faces when they interrupt a drive down East

152nd Street to say "That's where all those little kids died in the Collinwood school fire because the exit doors opened inward . . ."

In a word, my readers, like me, are seduced by the romantic allure of past unpleasantnesses in and about the Forest City, and they are fascinated by the behavior of our local ancestors under life-and-death stress. Readers of this volume will immediately note the serial format used to tell the story of the Kingsbury Run Torso murders. There are a number of reasons for this approach. Chief among them is the sheer bulk of the material: stretching over five years and at least a dozen corpses, its details constitute virtually an entire book. My conviction is that these serial murders are best related in serial form, lest readers weary of prolonged exposure to what is, essentially, a body parts inventory lacking strong human characters. The other reason for chopping up the Torso story is its intractable nature: Eternally unsolved and with almost all of its victims anonymous, it blatantly lacks two elements vital to a good Cleveland murder story—well-defined characters and clear motives. Readers may also note that *The Maniac in the Bushes* has a somewhat darker tone than *They Died Crawling*. This is due to the fact that—I realize more in retrospect than by conscious intent—so many of its chapters are narratives of almost incredibly unlucky or desperately unhappy women. Four of the stories—those of Mabel Foote and Louise Wolf, Janet Blood, Beverly Potts, and Clara Ziechmann—deal with innocent females stalked to violent, bloody deaths. Another two chapters— the story of hammer murderess Velma West and the tale of Medina poisoner Martha Wise—chronicle the deeds of terribly unfortunate women quite capable of evoking considerable sympathy and pathos despite the unspeakable cruelty of their crimes.

One additional word about why I like to write and speak about such criminous Cleveland matters. Many years ago, when I was a puny, bespectacled second grader on the playground of St. Ann's School in Cleveland Heights, I used to fork over my lunch money every day to a burly bully, in return for his not beating me to a whimpering pulp. I can still remember the humiliating shame of handing over the money, day after day. And I can still remember the moment—twenty-one years later—when I picked up the morning's *Plain Dealer* to discover that this same extortionate bully, now grown to thuggish manhood, had just been convicted of first-degree murder for his part in the killing-for-hire plot that took the life of Judge Robert Steele's wife, Marlene Steele, in 1969. I will always remember the feeling I had as I put down the paper, looked up, and said, "You know, life just doesn't get any better than this!"

My debts to many people for their involvement in the creation of this book are profound and unpayable. As ever, I have been inspired and influenced by the writings of George Condon and Peter Jedick; if you haven't read their books, you haven't read about Cleveland. And, more specifically, I wish to thank Steve Nickel for his pioneering research in *Torso: The Story of Eliot Ness and the Search for a Psychopathic Killer* and Edward Kern for the information in *The Collinwood School Fire of 1908*. Thanks also go to Margaret Lynch and her family for alerting me to the Janet Blood atrocity.

As has been the case with all of my literary endeavors, I could not have written this book without the love and support of my mother, Jean Bellamy, a former screaming-bloody-murder Hearst journalist herself. And, once again, I must give special thanks to my brother Stephen Paul Bellamy and his wife, Gail Bellamy; without their love, skill, and support, this book, like its predecessor, would never have happened. Not to mention the personal debts owed to my fellow employees at the Cuyahoga County Public Library, who have endured my peculiar enthusiasms and sometimes unappetizing lunchtime conversations for an embarrassing number of years. They include Avril McInally, David Soltesz, Mary Ann Shipman, Scottie Oblak, Mary Erbs, Judy Vanke, Holly Schaefer, Karen Rabatin, Geli Gricar, Mary Ryan, Nancy Pazelt, Vicki Richards, John Lonsak and Madeleine Brookshire. They have only themselves to blame for encouraging my morbid preoccupations; their unsuccessful efforts to keep me humble have not gone unnoticed. Particular gratitude is due to Ruth Rayle, who bravely booked my first Cleveland Disaster slide show.

My institutional research has been much aided by the knowledge, professionalism, and kindness of these individuals: William Becker of the Cleveland Press Collection, Cleveland State University Archives; Joan Clark and the staff of the Photograph Collection at Cleveland Public Library; and Ann Sindelar and Barbara Billings of the Western Reserve Historical Society. Special thanks are also owed to *The Plain Dealer* for permission to reprint material from more than a century of its copious columns. And very special thanks go to Gwen K. Petechik of Dodd Camera in Fairview Park, who has done a swell job in developing my sometimes alarming photographs during the past year. All errors of fact are mine and are due to sheer ignorance. Lastly, it is a particular pleasure to thank my beautiful wife, Laura Serafin, for her love, support, patience, and participation in my ever-deeper adventures into the Cleveland past. F. Scott Fitzgerald said there are no second acts in American lives; she has certainly proved him wonderfully wrong in my case.

John Stark Bellamy II
May 5, 1997

THE MANIAC
IN THE BUSHES

And More Tales of Cleveland Woe

The Mystery Begins

Beulah Park, September 5, 1934

With the possible exception of the 1954 Marilyn Sheppard murder, Cleveland boasts no bigger or better "signature" crime phenomenon than the baker's dozen of "Kingsbury Run Torso slayings" that terrified Clevelanders and puzzled lawmen during the latter part of the 1930s. It is Cleveland's greatest and most malevolent mystery and hardly a year goes by without a renewal of media interest in this serial saga of Depression-era killings. It is no small irony, therefore, that when the "Torso" killings began on a gray morning in September 1934, there was no thought—much less a mention—of Kingsbury Run.

It's even questionable whether it is proper to begin the Torso melodrama in the 1930s, much less in Kingsbury Run, the topographical remnant of an ancient stream that once fed the Cuyahoga River south of the Flats area. Headless torsos have ever been an attractive resort for killers with inconvenient corpses on their hands, and the first historical mention of a headless body found in the Run appeared in the *Cleveland Leader* on November 13, 1905. A poor woman scavenging for saleable refuse in a Case Avenue dump came upon the body of a man who had been fatally shot in the chest, decapitated, and dumped in the Run. No suspects were forthcoming, and the unsolved homicide was soon added to a roster of fascinating contemporary mysteries, like the brutal killing of Anna Kinkopf in Payne's Pastures and the locked-room mystery of Minnie Peter's hammer murder. Questions regarding the chronology of the Torso murders become all the more confusing when one discovers that for decades Cleveland police refused to acknowledge the Kingsbury killer's first undoubted casualty—a headless human female washed up on the Lake Erie shore near Euclid Beach on September 9, 1934—as one of the fabled serial murderer's hapless victims.

No one was thinking of Kingsbury Run in the late summer of 1934, least of all twenty-one-year-old Frank La Gossie of Beulah Park (a residential development just west of Euclid Beach Amusement Park) as he walked along the Lake Erie beach adjacent to his street that cloudy September morning. It was about 8:00 a.m., and La

Gossie was up early collecting driftwood and cleaning up the beach area when he noticed something that didn't look right sticking out of the sand. And it wasn't right. It was, La Gossie soon realized, the lower half of a human torso. Neatly severed at the waist between the second and third lumbar vertebrae, it was still attached to the thighs, but its missing lower legs had been cut off at the knees. La Gossie ran to the house of his friend Charles Armitage at 12 Lake Front Drive, and Armitage telephoned the Cleveland police, who took the torso to Cuyahoga County coroner Arthur J. Pearse at the Lakeside morgue.

Examination of the torso that afternoon by Pearse and his assistants disclosed all that was ever to be known about the mystery corpse. It was a female, most probably in her mid-thirties, five foot six, with a projected weight of around 120 pounds. The woman's uterus had been surgically removed at least a year before her death, and the discoloration of her skin indicated that some kind of chemical—probably chloride of lime or calcium hypochloride—had been used on the corpse. (Coroner Pearse theorized that the presumed killer had tried to destroy the body with something like quicklime but had mistakenly used slacked lime, which preserved it instead.) Nothing else could be ascertained from the torso, except that it was not waterlogged, suggesting that it had not been floating in the lake for very long. No other clues to the dead woman's identity were found, and police began sifting through the sixty-odd files on women reported missing in Cleveland between January and July of 1934.

The mystery now shifted thirty miles away, far from Beulah Park and even farther from Kingsbury Run. Madison handyman Joseph Hejduk, after reading newspaper accounts of the murder, reported to Cleveland police that he had found some human remains on the beach near North Perry two weeks before. Previously he had informed Melvin Keener, a Lake County deputy about it, but Keener had concluded the remains were animal and persuaded Hejduk to bury his find on the North Perry beach. Extensive digging eventually unearthed Hejduk's fleshly find on September 7: part of a shoulder blade, a partial spinal column, and sixteen vertebrae (twelve dorsal and four lumbar). All the pieces found in Hejduk's beach burial matched the Beulah Park torso perfectly. They also revealed similar exposure to a lime-based chemical preservative. The next day, two brothers, Denver and Brady Fleming of Evergreen Street in Beulah Park, found a compatible collar bone and shoulder blade while digging in the sand near the original torso discovery.

In the wake of Cleveland newspaper headlines about these myste-

GHOSTLY HAND SEEN IN LAKE, BONES ON SHORE DISAPPEAR

Two Trunks Examined by Experts Also Cast Aside as Means of Solving Crime; Coroner Scouts Tufverson Link

Cleveland Press headline, September 8, 1934.

rious lakeside finds, less useful discoveries were also made by the curious. A clerk working in the Cleveland prosecutor's office recalled an incident six weeks before at a Lake Erie beach area near East 238th Street in Euclid. A fourteen-year-old girl had run screaming out of the water, crying that she had stumbled over a pair of human legs about fifteen feet from shore. The legs had not been located, nor the "ghastly hand" that another Cleveland girl had espied "waving" from the Lake Erie waters a week before Labor Day. The latter girl's father corroborated his daughter's story and further averred that he had actually stepped on the ghostly hand . . . but he had become too distracted by other matters to tell the police about it at the time.

The police would soon begin to lose patience with the growing number of torso clues, including a "gray mass" thought to be a human brain, found by two boys at the foot of East 256th Street (it proved to be suet); a steamer trunk found not far from the first torso find by two boys from nearby Bonnieview Drive (it, like a small box unearthed from the North Perry beach by a young boy, proved valueless in the search for either the killer or the identity of his victim); and a sensational report out of Painesville that a woman's liver had been found on Lake Road near Willoughby (this lurid news was not even investigated by weary Cleveland sleuths). Nor did any concrete clues emerge from a fruitless search for a skull made after two fishermen reported snagging strands of blond hair in their lines off the shore by West 58th Street.

The police and Coroner Pearse did the best they could, having little forensic or circumstantial evidence to go on. Miles of odoriferous neighborhood sewers were searched by detectives, and hundreds of

MORE OF MYSTERY TORSO DUG UP ON BEACH 30 MILES EAST OF CITY

Cleveland Press headline, September 7, 1934.

residents of the Euclid Beach and North Perry areas were quizzed for clues. But without the unknown woman's head or an unequivocal match to a missing person report, it was impossible to say who she had been. One baffled detective confessed, when asked by a reporter whether it was a perfect crime: "No, but so close to being perfect that we don't know what to do next."

Lack of conclusive evidence, however, did not dissuade Coroner Pearse from theorizing about the how and why of the mystery torso to avid reporters. Pearse's initial judgment was that the body was dismembered by someone with professional medical skill, although he qualified this judgment in light of later evidence that the presumed killer had cut straight through the shoulder blade instead of around it. Pearse was probably correct in his conjecture that the body had been cut up and placed in three separate packages, which were then dumped into the lake from air, water, or land—possibly even from as far away as Canada. The grisly parcels then simply floated until the containers disintegrated and washed up at various locations on Lake Erie's southern shore. It was even possible, Pearse allowed, that the body was that of a suicide that had been later churned to pieces by the propeller of a passing ship. After consultation with authorities at local universities, the possibility that the body had been the result of some medical-school prank was ruled out.

Even Cleveland's newspapers were somewhat at a loss to properly contextualize the appearance of the autumnal torso at Beulah Park. Old-timers recalled the Pearl Bryan case, a macabre 1896 murder in which a headless, and indubitably pregnant, torso was eventually identified by means of some unusual shoes. Younger reporters resurrected the tale of the "Battersea Body Mystery," the 1925 discovery of a red-headed male corpse—with its face beaten to an unrecognizable pulp—on Lake Road. (Ten thousand Clevelanders had viewed that corpse at the county morgue in a vain effort to identify it.) More historically mindful souls wondered whether the torso belonged to Betty Gray, the still-missing star witness at the first William Potter murder trial in 1931 or to Miss Agnes Tufverson, a well-to-do lawyer who had disappeared shortly after her marriage to Captain Ivan Poderjay, a notorious Yugoslavian bigamist and adventurer. On September 6, the *Cleveland News* offered a $1,000 reward for information leading to the arrest and conviction of the killer. Like all rewards for the Torso killer or killers, it was never collected.

After five days of sensational headlines, the nameless torso—christened "The Lady of the Lake" by romantic copydesk personnel—disappeared from the headlines. The collected remains of the female victim were placed in coffin No. 102/3 and carefully buried in the Potter's Field section of Highland Park Cemetery at 10:00 a.m. on September 11. Clevelanders moved on to other matters and other murders.

No one had yet whispered the chilling name "Kingsbury Run". . .

Chapter 1

"TWELVE O'CLOCK GIRL IN A NINE O'CLOCK TOWN"

The Red Rage of Velma West, 1927

To glimpse a murder from the past is to embark on a time-traveling visit to an exotic locale, and to meet characters—whether victims or killers—who think, talk, and act differently from the way we do. No case illustrates the foreignness of the past better than the 1927 murder of Eddie West in Lake County.

There are lots of ways to view the West murder file. Obviously, no murder is exactly like another. Each and every killing is unique, a product of a particular place, a particular time, and a particular collision of persons inhabiting—if not always sharing—a particular culture. One could look at the gory and scandalous West ordeal as a collision between the baffled, rural America of bucolic Lake County and the jazz-age modernity of Roaring Twenties Cleveland. That's how sophisticated metropolitan journalists saw it at the time: to them, Velma West's brutal hammer murder of her staid hubby was the virtually inevitable consequence of a big-city flapper's imprudent elopement with a small-town stuffy to the maddening boredom of rustic Perry, Ohio. Many contemporary refugees from small-town America agreed, no doubt, with Clarence Darrow's deterministic justification of Velma's bloody revolt against American Gothic rectitude. He had lived in Lake County as a young man and recalled with bitterness its cramped small-town ways:

> It's all familiar to me. I mean the scene . . . I know the village of Perry. That girl was no more to blame for killing her husband than he was for being killed. It was a tragic mistake to take a frail little girl away from the life she loved and shut her away from the things she knew and yearned for . . . She married and went to live in the right-moraled, dull small town . . . Like any other woman who had been brought up in

luxury and independence, she naturally reacted against every one when forced to continue her cramped small town life.

Cleveland Press writer Paul Packard summed up the city–country aspect of the murder more succinctly: "Country people have little sympathy for the mysterious blond girl who is under lock in jail here. City people see reasons why a Twelve o'clock girl in a Nine o'clock town might be driven to use a hammer."

You could also view the Velma West affair as a study in individual psychology. Like Lakewood's Eva Kaber, who had *her* inconvenient spouse murdered in circumstances of unspeakable cruelty in 1919, Velma West had been sickly most of her life. Velma's defense attorneys were quite prepared to reiterate the long litany of Velma's physical calamities when her first-degree murder trial began in March 1928, and that dreary medical catalog included pneumonia, diphtheria, heart disease, and suspected brain damage. Viewed more harshly, Velma was the predictable creation of a family that spoiled her rotten every day of her first twenty years.

The most lurid and, at the same time, contemporary way of dealing with the Velma West story, however, is to treat it as an episode of anguished and misunderstood sexuality. And that is the way that society and the media in Velma's day eventually judged the matter. The shocking disclosure of Velma's "unnatural" passions at the outset of her murder trial virtually guaranteed its outcome and provided a reassuringly simple rationale for a brutal and disturbing crime.

The past *is* a foreign country, and its inhabitants do things very differently there.

It is best to begin at the beginning with the Velma West saga, because its later details are subject to uncertainty and dispute. Velma herself "confessed" to at least three distinct versions of her husband's murder, and it's clear from the conflicting details that not even she quite knew when she was lying. The tale, then, commences with the star-crossed romance of Eddie West and Velma Van Woert in the summer of 1926.

Thomas Edward West was a son of one of the oldest and most respected families in Lake County. A clan of venerable English lineage, the Wests had long lived in the Perry area and had been known for decades as the proprietors of one of the best-known horticultural nurseries in the United States. Thomas Edward, known to his family and friends as "Eddie," was born to T. B. West and his wife in 1901 and was reared to vigorous manhood in the family traditions of

Eddie West, 1927.   Velma West, 1927.

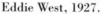

social stability and commercial achievement. Husky and athletic, at about six feet tall and 200 pounds, Eddie was fond of sports, especially baseball, and was never mistaken for the studious type at the local schools he attended in Lake County. But the ever-smiling Eddie was well liked and the special pet of his parents, his brother, and his four doting sisters. In his mid-twenties, he already exhibited welcome promise of carrying on the West family name and business. He relished heavy labor and, because of his size and enthusiasm, took on more than his share of the heavier tasks in the family nursery business.

Then, in the summer of 1926, he met twenty-year-old Velma Van Woert at a picnic at Perry Park.

Velma was certainly an unlikely match for the quiet Lake County nurseryman. The daughter of Bert Van Woert, a Cleveland traveling salesman, and his wife, Catherine, Velma was as completely a product of the big city as Eddie was of the bucolic countryside. Of fragile health since birth, pretty Velma had already survived several serious diseases when she developed a life-threatening ear abscess at the age of twelve. After lingering near death for a month, Velma was saved by a skull operation—though observers would later comment that the procedure seemed to transform the hitherto precociously bright Velma into an intellectually duller girl who had much subsequent trouble with her studies. After finishing her elementary grades at Rosewell School, Velma entered East Cleveland's Shaw High

School but dropped out at the age of sixteen. Little else is known of her formative years except for obvious evidence that her parents spoiled her rotten and indulged her considerable behavioral vagaries. That, and the fact that she liked to hear and play popular music to an almost inordinate degree . . . which would become significant in due course.

Sometime in the mid-1920s, Velma went to work as a clerk at Henry Rothman's notions and hardware store at 6423 Detroit Avenue. She was there for more than a year before Rothman finally felt compelled to fire her. He was particularly concerned about the unseemly rumors swirling around his still-teenaged female clerk: "I told her several times that I wouldn't permit her to do things like that [talking to boys while working], but it didn't seem to do any good. I was trying to help the girl. She wasn't bad, she was a nice young lady from a nice family and I wanted her to behave."

Velma, of course, wouldn't listen, and so Rothman let her go. The loss of her job may not have mattered to Velma, anyway, as she was already engaged to William Chapman, the fifty-six-year-old owner of a restaurant next to Rothman's store. Velma got to know Chapman on her lunch breaks there and began going steady with the restaurateur old enough to be her grandfather. Eventually, their relationship was formalized with Chapman giving her a diamond ring and setting a date for their wedding in July 1926.

The May-December marriage was not to be. Scant weeks before her scheduled wedding to Chapman, Velma met handsome, friendly Eddie West at that fateful Perry Park picnic. A whirlwind courtship followed, and Velma and Eddie stunned family and friends by eloping to Ripley, New York, on July 4, 1926. The engagement ring was subsequently returned to a stunned Chapman by Velma's father.

Love is blind. What attracted Eddie West to Velma Van Woert remains a mystery. Her mother would later claim that initially Velma fiercely resisted marrying Eddie, fearing that she was too delicate to be the wife of such a sturdy physical specimen. But marry him she did, and it should have soon been obvious to both Eddie and Velma—as it was to virtually everyone else—that theirs was a marriage made in hell from the start. They had virtually nothing in common except for their mutual attraction, and, not surprisingly, storm clouds began to gather almost from the moment of their vows. Days after the wedding, a crestfallen Eddie returned to Lake County and was seen begging friends to lend him money. His story was that Velma had thrown him out when they ran out of money on the honeymoon, and she had ordered him to obtain more cash before he returned to her arms. Eddie's parents eventually came up with the money, the honeymoon was resumed, and Eddie and his new bride eventually came home to a Lake County welcome.

Although both Velma's and her husband's families appear to have tried hard, it was a frosty encounter from the start. Giddy, nervous, and often silly, Velma's behavior, with its aura of sinful, big-city temptation and corrupted, frivolous womanhood was a red flag to the staid rural folk of Perry—a mere village of 250 souls—and particularly to the Wests, who were a notably religious family. A *Cleveland Press* journalist later summarized the collision between city and country ways: "There was 'a marked tightening of the lips of the village social censors' after their initial exposure to the irrepressible Velma."

Worse yet, Velma smoked—*in public!*—an enormity almost unknown for women in Lake County and an action liable to stop traffic even in Painesville, the nearby county seat. Under the headline "VELMA SMOKED—AND PAINESVILLE IS SHOCKED," *Press* writer W. R. Crowell put his finger on the obvious moral declension such a vile habit in a woman suggested—just what you could expect from a big-city girl who was not fit to be a wife:

> Velma Van Woert West, bridge-playing husband slayer, doubtless will have her day in court . . . Today, however, Main Street was sitting in judgement on her. While the grosser phases of this case in time may come to rank with Lake County's classic [the incredible Mentor Marsh Murder of 1922] . . . for the present at least street corner gossip hinges on one thing: "Velma smoked a cigarette." . . . What were [the] outside signs the girl displayed that boded ill, reporters questioned. "Why she—she smoked," was the shocked reply.

The connection between the moral depravity of Velma's cigarette smoking and her corresponding wifely deficiencies was further elaborated by a tobacco-chewing deputy sheriff:

> My grandmother smoked a pipe of clay but set a table that would knock your eye out. If Ed had lived he sure would have had to go to the neighbors for his breakfast. The only victuals in the place was a piece of pie and it was sour. Cigarette-smokin' city gals don't have no time for keeping house as a woman should. Ed's wife smoked.

Sob-sister *Cleveland News* columnist Nina S. Donberg echoed the deputy sheriff's strictures, albeit more grammatically: "Even her house tells [the] story. She didn't take a housewifely pride in it. There was no thoughtfully planned, well-filled larder, no boxes of cereal, no can of coffee and tea."

It was soon evident to the newlyweds' families and friends that there was a lot more to the West marital discord than incompatible backgrounds and Velma's notorious defects as a housekeeper. Velma was restless and edgy, and craved the nightlife of Cleveland, thirty-five miles away. Ensconced in a modest white bungalow on the edge of the West family estate (adjacent to the dwellings of both Eddie's parents and his brother James), Eddie and Velma settled down to a routine of slovenly housekeeping and acrid bickering, punctuated two or three times a week with frantic jaunts to Cleveland. Eddie often unwillingly accompanied Velma on these trips, but it was only too clear that he wanted to settle down—and the sooner the better—to a domestic life of family, children, and work. It was equally evident, within weeks of their hasty nuptials, that these were the very goals and values that Velma most despised.

Somehow, a year went by and the unhappy marriage lurched along. The young couple didn't have much money—Eddie's salary in the family business was at most twenty-five dollars a week, supplemented by free use of the bungalow—and Velma increasingly pouted and pined for the luxuries, great and small, she had known as the petted and indulged daughter of Mr. and Mrs. B. L. Van Woert. Local residents thought maybe Velma was finally settling in when she was seen for some weeks at work in the West family vineyards in the summer of 1927. But her grape-picking stint was only to pay for a desperately desired fur coat, the very accessory Velma needed for her frequent trips to enjoy the high life of Cleveland.

Something had to give, and it started giving in the summer of 1927. Miss Mabel Young, 23, of 2111 Willowdale Avenue in the Cleveland suburb of Parma Heights, came to visit some friends in the Perry vicinity, and Velma met Mabel soon afterwards at some social function. The two women hit it off, and very soon Velma was penning passionate letters to Mabel, pledging her undying love. So passionate, indeed, was the correspondence that Velma soon cautioned Mabel to route her own letters through the address of a cooperative friend in Perry. Eddie, it seems, was showing symptoms of jealousy about her female friendships, and Velma became so upset about Eddie's resentment that she complained to Lake County Sheriff Edward ("Big Ed") Rasmussen about Eddie opening her mail. A

The West "murder bungalow," 1927.

well-meaning individual who flattered himself—with some justice—on being a kind of father figure and confidant to young mar-
rieds in the county, "Big Ed" had a chat with both Velma and Eddie
that autumn of 1927 and assumed that the matter was resolved.

It was not. Sometime in late October of 1927, Velma left Eddie for
several days and returned to her parents' apartment in East Cleveland. She said that her marriage was over, but Bert and Catherine
persuaded her to return to her husband. Then, on November 23, the
day before Thanksgiving, Velma showed up again in Cleveland.
Stopping at a barber shop at West 65th and Detroit Avenue to get her
hair bobbed, she retailed her marital woes to barber Valentino Del
Fino: "My husband strikes me . . . he scolds me all the time and over
the littlest thing that's wrong around the house. Only this morning
we had another quarrel and he struck me."

Philip Manacapilli, sitting in the chair next to Velma, subsequently heard Velma telephone Mabel Young from the shop and
heard her tell Mabel that Eddie had hit her. Minutes later, at the Gordon Square Pharmacy, the chatty Velma told pharmacist Albert Edel-
stein that her husband mistreated her and had hit her several times.
But once more, the marital fences were mended and Velma unhappily returned to life with Eddie in the white bungalow.

Only a husband and wife know the real truth about their marriage. And it is likewise true, as newspaper writer Paul Packard argued, that "just what took place in the bedroom of the little West bungalow no one will ever know." But something terrible and fatal for Eddie West indubitably occurred there, and what follows is the fullest account that can be garnered of what transpired.

Sometime on the afternoon of Tuesday, December 6, Eddie and Velma got into their green Hupmobile roadster, and Velma drove them to Painesville to see Eddie's doctor about his chronic rheumatism. They argued bitterly all the way to the doctor's office and left when the wait there proved intolerable. After eating a late lunch at Mrs. J. B. Well's roadside hot dog stand, they returned to the doctor's and got some medicine. They were seen about 5:30 p.m. at a Painesville bank, and Velma later claimed that they argued all the way back home, where they arrived shortly before 6:00. E. I. Skinner, a nearby neighbor, saw a car pull in their drive about that time and then some lights flash on in the house. Skinner could not, however, identify either the car or who was in it.

Exactly what happened next is the big question. We know that Velma and Eddie were still arguing when they got to their second-floor bedroom and that Eddie changed into his pajamas, as if getting ready for bed. Maybe it was something he said, perhaps something nasty about her suspicious friendship with Mabel Young—something, as Velma later insisted, that "riled me, it cut me to the bone." Maybe it was just his adamant refusal to give her the car keys. Maybe he even threatened to divorce and disgrace her. Maybe he hit her, maybe not. In some versions of her story, Velma said she slapped him and that he gave her a bloody nose. In another Velma version, she confessed that she said something insulting and that Eddie, uttering dire threats, started toward her . . .

Whatever words, threats, or actions sparked Velma's rage, we do know what resulted. Velma picked up a hammer, just brought from the basement or fetched previously for a window repair, and hit Eddie in the head with it. She hit him hard, and he probably fell down on the floor, enraged and groping blindly as blood gushed from a terrible wound in his skull. Velma's first confession was her bluntest statement on what happened: "I hit him and he dropped." Eddie probably tried to get up again at least once, perhaps as many as five times. Velma's chief defense attorney, Francis Poulson, would later cross-examine Dr. R. H. Spence, a doctor who examined Velma in jail, in an effort to prove that Eddie was still in a position to retaliate murderously against Velma's continued hammer blows. Poulson's interrogation couldn't have helped his client much:

> Poulson: Did she tell you that after he went down for the fourth time he was still struggling?
> Spence: No, not exactly. It was the fifth time that he was still struggling.

In any case, the evidence on Eddie West's corpse was unmistakable: Velma hit him at least six, perhaps eight times in the front of his head with a heavy clawhammer. After he ceased trying to get up, she pulled a pillowcase over his head and bashed him some more with the hammer; the pillowcase was to cut down on the amount of blood sprayed. Then she rolled the body over and beat Eddie's skull again for a while with a leg from a broken bedroom table. She later said she kept beating him even after he stopped moving because she was afraid he would kill her if he regained consciousness and got up again. Given her state, which she variously characterized as a "red rage," "blind rage," and "wild rage," Velma probably couldn't even remember exactly when and why she did what she did.

Her next actions, however, revealed cautious and sober cunning. Fetching a ball of nursery binding twine, Velma tied Eddie's wrists and legs together tightly. (Her initial claim was that she wanted to make sure he couldn't hurt her, but she eventually confessed she wanted to make the scene look like a burglary gone awry.) She then dragged some of the bloody bedclothes down to the cellar, thoroughly smearing the walls and floors with Eddie's blood along the way. Down in the cellar Velma burned the bloody linens in the furnace, along with her own gore-encrusted garments. She then walked outside and smoked several cigarettes. Returning to the bedroom, Velma fished the car keys (with great difficulty) out of the pockets of her husband's trussed corpse and went downstairs. Leaving the back door wide open, she got into the green Hupmobile and drove thirty-five miles to Cleveland to the house of her friend, Mabel Young.

It was a gala night at Mabel's house. All the members of the Semper Fidelis Club, a group of West Commerce High School alumnae, were gathered there for a bridge party, and many of the members had been anticipating the arrival of Velma West, who was said to be a lot of fun, the life of the party. Which she soon proved to be. Arriving about 8:30 p.m. at the Young residence, Velma went upstairs to freshen up. A horrified Mabel Young later recalled Velma's entrance:

Velma never seemed in better spirits than when she arrived at our home Tuesday evening. The vibrant personality that made her easily the most popular among the younger married girls in our set was never more in evidence. She greeted me at the door with a laugh and went immediately upstairs to "fix up" for the party. If I had known her mission was not so much to use a lipstick as to wash from her hands the blood of Eddie West, what a different party it would have been.

A different party, indeed. Velma soon joined a bridge game in progress and, although new to the pastime, won every hand she played and was high scorer at her table that evening. She probably would have been the highest scorer at the party, except that she periodically interrupted her game to go to the piano. There she regaled her impressed audience with a medley of popular "blues" tunes of the day. Songs like "So Blue," "Tired and Lonely for Home," and, most movingly, "Just Like a Butterfly Caught in the Rain":

Here I am lonely, tired and lonely
Crying for home in vain.
Longing for flowers, dreaming of hours, back in the
    sun-kissed lane.
I know that all of the world is cheery, outside that old cottage
    door.
Why are my wings so weary, that I can't fly home any more.
Here I am praying, brokenly saying, "Give me the sun again."
Just like a butterfly caught in the rain.

Although later, with her daughter facing a first-degree murder rap, Velma's mother would insist that Velma was actually withdrawn and quiet at the Young bridge party, the other girls present all agreed—and testified—that Velma was the heart and soul of the fete, and that her plaintive, bluesy singing was the hit of the evening. The party broke up about 11:30 p.m. and Velma spent the night at the Young house.

Velma arose the next morning, ate a breakfast inevitably described by the newspapers as "hearty," and left Mabel's house at about 9:30. Velma took the streetcar to her mother's apartment in East Cleveland, and then the two of them took the trolley to Public Square. They had long planned a mother-daughter outing to buy Christmas presents, and they sampled the sights, sounds, and merchandise of downtown Cleveland stores like Higbee's and Halle's until mid-afternoon. Velma bought a dozen handkerchiefs "for Eddie," and longingly ogled a scarf "that Eddie would just love," but did not purchase it. Catherine Van Woert and Velma then returned on the streetcar to the Van Woert residence at 1727 Page Avenue.

Lake County sheriff Rasmussen and the East Cleveland police were waiting there for them. Taken into custody as they were walking up the drive, they were taken to the Lake County jail in Painesville for interrogation by Rasmussen and Lake County prosecutor Seth Paulin. They were soon joined by Mabel Young, also picked up for questioning, and Bert Van Woert, who got off a train in Ashtabula when he read the shocking news about his son-in-law Eddie in an afternoon newspaper.

Eddie West had been found beaten to death in the cottage on Narrows Road in Perry. Eddie had not shown up for his 10:00 a.m. nursery shift on Wednesday morning, an uncharacteristic lapse that soon brought his brother James to the front door of the white bungalow. The door was locked, but the back door was wide open and most of the electric lights were blazing. James eventually made his way upstairs, where he started back in horror at the sight he found. His brother Eddie was lying on the floor of the bedroom, with his shoes off and his head beaten in. Some of the bloody bedclothes were wrapped around his body, there was a bandanna around his head, and his hands and feet were tied with twine. James West immediately called Sheriff Rasmussen and Dr. W. R. Carle. Eddie's corpse was removed from the house, a guard was posted to prevent anyone from going inside, and a search was begun for the murdered man's missing wife.

Velma held up well during the first three hours of interrogation. She remained calm, even after being told of her husband's grisly death, and she steadfastly insisted that she had left him in good health the night before and knew nothing about his murder. She remembered Eddie cranking the Hupmobile for her when she left for Mabel's party and then kissing her good-bye. Sheriff Rasmussen, who conducted most of the questioning, was baffled, both by her smooth story and her incredible sangfroid. Finally he said, "I know you're telling me the truth. But why did you leave the back door open?" Velma suddenly slumped forward, recovered, and then said, "All right. I'll tell you the whole truth. I killed him after a quarrel." She then wrote out and signed a 200-word statement, admitting her guilt.

That statement was the basis of the first-degree murder charge eventually brought against Velma, although she added other details—many of them conflicting—in subsequent conversations with the avuncular Sheriff Rasmussen. And, allowing for some differences in language and detail, the story was pretty much the same: They quarreled, Eddie hit her or threatened to hit her, and she hit him with a hammer a number of times. Whatever quibbling Velma did about the details, however, the crux of her intended defense was clear from the beginning. She was an abused woman who killed her husband for fear of losing her own life at his hands. "EDDIE HIT ME, WIFE CRIES," screamed the headline of the next day's *Cleveland News.*

The disclosures of the next seven days furnished material for a first-class orgy of sensationalism, and Cleveland's newspapers did not disappoint. While *The Plain Dealer*, a deliberately staid sheet, concentrated on the details and discrepancies of the investigation, the *Press* and the *News* focused on what their readers really wanted: lurid facts and bizarre psychology. The *Press* obliged with voluminous baiting of the Lake County hicks, whose presumed bucolic folkways and cow-pie culture had driven sophisticated Velma around the bend. After dwelling on the horror caused by Velma's public smoking and bad housekeeping, *Press* scribes caricatured Eddie West as a rude rube, resentful of his wife's polish ("He'd rather play 'Hearts' in the village store than bridge in a Cleveland mansion"). They then dwelt with unconcealed, prurient relish on the girlish garments on display in Velma's Painesville jail cell, in a feature entitled "Pretties in Velma's Cell":

> A blue and gray steamer rug plaided in red has been used to
> cover the bare wooden bench. Soft silk pajamas of delicate
> pink are thrown casually on the lower bunk, and there are the
> other dainty underthings of a modern, luxury-loving girl . . .
> An apple green felt hat with a rhinestone pin, obviously cho-
> sen because of the becoming contrast with the gold blond
> hair, lay on the desk.

The *News* relied on the considerable sob-sister talents of Nina Donberg from the beginning, and her editors weren't disappointed. Donberg wrung every last tear out of the story, and at the same time satisfied her readers' sense of retributive justice with a stance of unrelenting, bullying scorn toward the accused murderess:

> Will the spoiled-child little girl face of Velma West save her
> from the consequences of her revolting crime?. . . It is not a

sweet face, nor is it a pleasing, friendly one. Neither has it the shadows that indicate depths of character. The eyes are a restless blue and look out under droopy lids that make Velma appear sleepy and sullen in spite of her nervous glances. The childish snub nose gives a petulant willful look to the face and the pouting lips over white teeth speak of intolerance and angry moods . . . Daddy's girl has let her temper get the best of her once too often and now she stands accused of the murder of her husband and it is up to daddy to summon all of his life to protect her from her own folly.

For those desiring the veneer of science spread over their prejudices, Cleveland newspapers offered a smorgasbord of half-baked psychologizing and pseudoscience about the alleged killer's personality. As noted above, Clarence Darrow, whose opinion was solicited by the *Cleveland Press,* weighed in with a defense sympathizing with Velma's revulsion to small-town life, virtually excusing it as an understandable incitement to murder. And only a day after Eddie's body was found, David Dietz of the *Press* found a Cleveland psychiatrist, Dr. Daniel A. Huebsch, to natter learnedly, if unconvincingly, about Velma's presumed mental state:

> She is suffering from an infantile fixation which in its turn, led to a split personality . . . To her unconscious mind her husband represented the obstacle which prevented her from returning to babyhood. He was the symbol of present-day reality which cut her off from her dreams. Her unconscious mind had control when she killed him.

Homer Croy, a prominent American novelist, was also recruited by the *Press* to analyze Velma, and his take on her echoed Darrow's disdain for the presumed hatefulness of small-town life. Velma wasn't trying to kill Eddie, Croy argued, she was simply striking out at "everything that tortured her in Perry." It was the inevitable consequence of a husband's trying to constrain his wife's lifestyle with psychological chains. Such repression could only have one result: "But when he first clamps [the chains] on, it certainly means trouble. Pretty soon, the girl finds some sort of hammer. She is not hitting the boy—she is cracking her chains."

Best of all was Dr. H. Del Spence of Painesville, whose statements must have increased contemporary popular contempt for alienists a great deal. When Nina Donberg of the *News* asked if

Velma was insane, Del Spence delivered the goods: "Define insanity for me and I will answer your question . . . Insanity is geographic. Her insanity means non-conformity to the beliefs and habits of her community. Perhaps 200 or 300 years from now or possibly sooner, we will not punish such people as Velma West, but we will treat them as we do the physically sick."

It's a good guess that for most Cleveland newspaper readers there was probably far more resonance to the antifeminist sentiments of "Mrs. E. P.," whose letter published in the *News* drew from the Velma West parable the clear, if ungrammatical, lesson that a woman, "once married, should consider their husband and not pleasure."

Those inclined to give Velma the benefit of the doubt were not aided by Catherine Van Woert, whose appeal for sympathy in the December 13 edition of the *News* painted an unnuanced picture of a spoiled-rotten adult child:

> But even after her marriage, I couldn't think of her as any-thing but her mother's little baby girl. I tried too hard to make everything easy for her . . . She visited me frequently and wanted me to go with her. She wanted me to join with her mood and play with her. But I was too busy . . . I [have] told her that as soon as the world hears her whole story that they will know she never meant to commit a crime . . . What more could any mother do?

Velma wept copiously, smoked many cigarettes, and read the voluminous newspaper coverage of her crime in her jail cell. Meanwhile, her father began to organize her defense. Initially recruiting attorney H. T. Nolan and his son Eugene, B. L. Van Woert soon turned the case over to Richard Bostwick, the twenty-seven-year-old Geauga County prosecutor. Bostwick, the son of the previous county prosecutor, was well known in Northeast Ohio as a "dude," celebrated for his long fur coat and derby hat, and he honed his public persona with comments like this: "I always mean to play the lone wolf in my practice." He soon made it clear, in a comment to a *Press* reporter, that he was going to use a self-defense strategy with Velma: "a physically weak girl-wife who accidentally killed defending herself from a beating she expected and feared from a brutal, husky young husband . . ." Bostwick was soon relegated to second place, however, by the recruitment of Francis W. Poulson to head the defense team. Famous for having helped save Eva Kaber from the electric chair in 1921, Poulson struck a pose of unalloyed bravado

Velma West and Sheriff "Big Ed"
Rasmussen, March, 1928.

from the outset. Asked if he would move for a change of venue, he told reporters, "No, I will be perfectly willing, even, to try the case as I see it now with a member of the West family on the jury." It was noised about for awhile that William J. Corrigan, Poulson's associate in the Kaber trial, was also coming aboard but that proved just a rumor.

The judicial process ground into action on December 8 with a preliminary hearing before Judge Marvin H. Helter at the Painesville Town Hall. After testimony by police officials and witnesses, Velma was charged with first-degree murder and sent back to jail. She maintained her eerie calm until the photographers began to flash their bulbs at her, upon which she became hysterical, fainted, and fell to the floor. Helped to her feet by Sheriff Rasmussen, she made it to the town hall steps before swooning anew, screaming as she fell, "Oh God! Oh God!" Velma's teary travails didn't impress Nina Donberg one bit: "When she left the courtroom she decided to have a tantrum on the stairs and fell to the floor."

Two days later, Velma's late husband was buried after a memorial at the T. B. West residence. There were also services at the Perry Methodist Episcopal Church before interment in the little Perry cemetery near by. Throughout this family ordeal, Eddie's relatives conducted themselves with remarkable dignity, maintaining an almost perfect public silence—except to say that it would have been worse for them if they had been in the present position of Velma's family. Mrs. Van Woert, who apparently didn't know when to keep her mouth shut, commented to reporters that same day that Velma was "lonely" and had wanted to attend Eddie's funeral.

Even as Eddie West was lowered into the Perry graveyard, Richard Bostwick began to drop hints that the Velma West defense might use an insanity plea in addition to the claim of self defense. However gay her behavior in jail—reports were that Velma laughed much, smoked prodigiously, and read a lot of "True Story" magazines—Bostwick gravely described to reporters the fragile mental state of his client at the time of her rash act: "Mrs. West was ill when this murder was committed. She was exceptionally nervous and distracted. She was abnormally irritable."

Velma returned to the Lake County Court on December 12 for another hearing before Judge Helter. Poulson made a motion that the charge be reduced, thereby making Velma eligible for bail, but Helter refused. When Velma heard his decision, she started screaming, "Let me alone! Let me alone!" She screamed and fainted again when she saw the crowd waiting outside the courtroom. It was later explained that she reacted so violently because she was under the impression that Judge Helter had just sentenced her to the electric chair. The deciding factor in Helter's decision to deny bail was probably Lake County coroner O. O. Hausch's description of the wounds on Eddie West's corpse. There was a deep gash on the forehead and another terrible blow that destroyed one eye; either blow would have been sufficient to cause death, but there were also numerous additional injuries all over the face and skull. Meanwhile, at the jail, the theatrical Sheriff Rasmussen gave unsolicited demonstrations of Velma's probable murder technique to female visitors, realistically waving the murder hammer in the air and pretending to fall under its blows.

It was a lengthy interval between Velma's arrest and her eventual trial, but Velma whiled away the time as best she could with cigarettes, magazines, and endless chattering to the jail matrons and "Big Ed." Within seven days of her arrest, she was already receiving hundreds of letters, mostly supportive, from correspondents, mostly female, from around the country. One woman wrote that she was "thoroughly familiar with the life of an oppressed wife and didn't much blame one for rebelling, even with a clawhammer." It was soon reported in the newspapers, however, perhaps after diplomatic hints from her defense team, that Velma was reading the Bible and thinking pious thoughts. In any case, it is a fact that she was baptized into the Perry Methodist Episcopal Church on January 23 by the Rev. E. P. Wykoff, who had conducted her husband's obsequies only two weeks earlier.

There were still a few tidbits left for sensation addicts as Velma's arraignment neared. Scott E. Leslie, a reputed handwriting expert, analyzed Velma's scrawl and found it childish, indicating "a restless and inconsistent nature." The ever-reliable Dr. Daniel A. Huebsch also examined Velma's handwriting and found that it—surprise!—gave evidence of a "split personality." And there was a persistent rumor that Eddie West had still been alive when Velma departed in a huff to Cleveland on that fatal December evening. The gossip whispered around Lake County was that local bootleggers, angry at Eddie's enthusiastic cooperation with the efforts of local authorities to enforce the Volstead Act, had either assassinated him that night, or rather fortuitously come upon the half-dead Eddie after Velma was done with him—and finished the job.

Fifty-one witnesses came before a Lake County grand jury on January 9, 1928, to give evidence in the case. Almost a dozen of them reiterated that Velma was the veritable life of Mabel Young's party the night she killed her husband. Velma's lawyers were very upset that they were not allowed to examine the death bungalow, but Judge Helter's decision stood and would not be overturned. A first-degree murder indictment was duly handed down and trial was set for March 5. Velma's lawyers refused to plead her at a hearing on January 23 before Judge A. G. Reynolds, and so a legally mandated plea of "not guilty" was entered for her.

Velma's long-anticipated trial opened at 10:00 a.m. on March 5 before a packed courtroom audience (estimated at seventy-five percent female). But rumors were already rampant that her lawyers were trying to plea-bargain her case down to a second-degree murder charge. A new element in the case, long hinted at, had finally surfaced during the previous weekend. Suddenly, the two traumatized families involved in the impending trial discovered a common interest in halting the case. Over the weekend of March 3–4, Mabel Young submitted an eight-page deposition to Sheriff Rasmussen. The prosecution was prepared to introduce it as evidence.

Elicited from Young by Rasmussen during a three-hour questioning session between 5:30 and 8:30 p.m. on March 3, Young's statement confirmed in detail what had long been suspected and hinted at

behind the scenes in the Velma West mystery: Velma West was a les-
bian, and it was more than probable that her unconventional sexual
tendencies had figured in her husband's terrible death.

Of course Mabel Young's matter-of-fact revelations caused a sensation in the newspapers. Female homosexuality was a big deal in
1920s Cleveland, a very big deal in ways which cannot be imagined
by contemporary readers habituated to more public disclosures of, if
not always more tolerant views on, alternative sexuality. The *News*
editors were so stunned that they refused to name Velma's sin in public, coyly alluding only to "abnormal sex proclivities similar to those
portrayed in the French play 'The Captive.'" But the *Press* spoke for
a shocked Cleveland public on March 5 when it stated: "The abnormal love that the state charged to Velma West may go unnoticed in
some parts of the world, but in Lake County it was strange."

Mabel Young's eight-page statement was a sad document, and
probably every word of it was true. It told of the friendship that had
sprung up between Mabel and Velma that summer, and Mabel's dis-
quiet when she learned that Velma's affection for her was "not the
friendship of woman for woman, girl for girl." It went on to testify
to Mabel's genuine feeling for the unhappy Velma, and Mabel's hope
that Velma's sexual passions could be straightened out by exposure
to Mabel's wholesome social set. (Hence, Velma's inclusion at
Mabel's bridge party on the night of December 6.) Young's statement documented further Velma's blizzard of letters to Mabel, each
one pledging steadfast love.

The assertions of Young's statement, when put together with other
facts known about Velma or divulged by her to Sheriff Rasmussen
while in jail, coalesced to create a portrait of a sexually tormented
and very confused young woman. Apparently seduced some years
previously by an older woman, Velma had begun dressing up frequently in male attire several years before she met Eddie West. She
liked to have her photograph taken in such attire—it was known to
Velma's lawyers that the prosecution had photographs and was willing to introduce them—and Velma insisted that Mabel address her as
"Val," a sobriquet Velma thought more masculine than her given
name. The whole situation was a recipe for tragedy, as Velma's unre-
quited physical passion for Mabel added a dangerously explosive
element to her increasingly unhappy marriage to Eddie West. No one
will ever know what went on between Velma and Eddie behind
closed doors, but their relations, emotional and physical, could not
have been happy ones. It is even possible that the triggering incident
occurred when Eddie himself began to show an interest in Mabel

Mabel Young, December, 1927.

Young. Velma admitted that she saw Eddie kiss Mabel on several occasions, but Velma insisted that the kisses were at her own request. Velma, in any case, denounced Mabel Young's statement as "lies, all lies!" and swore that she would never forgive her erstwhile friend.

Late on the afternoon of March 5, the prosecution, led by Seth Paulin and Homer Harper, and the defense, represented by Bostwick and Poulson, cut a deal. Velma would plead guilty to second-degree murder, and none of the evidence would be released to the public. Each side continued to posture that it had the winning case, but Poulson was probably right when he argued that the prosecution's intended introduction of a motive based on Velma's alleged lesbianism (that Eddie's death was a murder of removal, so Velma could concentrate on Mabel) would actually have helped his client, because "no alienist could deny Velma was insane if the reported accusations in Miss Young's statements were true." In other words, female homosexuality was considered open-and-shut evidence of insanity in 1920s America, and Poulson knew that the introduction of such exhibits as the photographs of Velma in "mannish attire" would instantly get his client off on an insanity plea.

So the deal was made, although everyone involved, except for presiding judge Jesse D. Barnes, kept up a barrage of belittling remarks.

Poulson, who had actually threatened to sue anyone who suggested that he was ready to plea-bargain, and who had characterized initial reports of Mabel Young's statement as "mere muck," publicly praised the successful plea bargain as a compassionate compromise that spared the reputations that would have been wrecked by the exposures of a trial. Prosecutor Paulin scoffed at Poulson's claims, sneering "Compromise? This is no compromise. Second degree was all I expected to get, anyway, and why not take the quickest and cheapest way?" To which rejoinder, canny Richard Bostwick riposted with the perfect squelch, "You really had a perfect first-degree case." Sheriff Rasmussen, who perhaps had been anxious to reenact his popular pantomime of the murder struggle in court, confessed himself "heartbroken" at the decision, insisting they had the evidence to send Velma to the chair. Velma's parents were indiscreet and ungracious to the last: Catherine Van Woert let it be known that she was very unhappy with the verdict, and her husband delivered himself of one final blast of spleen against the country village that had rejected his petted daughter: "Of course I'm not satisfied. What parent would be? The village is not satisfied either. The people wanted to hear all the dirt and filth of a trial."

Wearing a felt hat, black satin dress, and black shoes and stockings ("an ensemble which proved becoming to the young widow with her pale complexion, slightly reddened lips, blue eyes and golden hair"), Velma stood before Judge Barnes on March 6 to receive her sentence. Permitted to speak, Velma replied, "I have nothing to say." Speaking to the trial principals, the venire of 46 unused jurors, and 200 avid spectators, Judge Barnes noted the weaknesses in the evidence for first-degree murder: "It isn't even an argumentative question. The state couldn't hope for a conviction of anything higher than second-degree." He then turned to Velma and said: "I don't think this is the time for talking. The mandate of the law is the most potent lecture that can be given. This was a horrible, and unthinkable thing. This staid old community has been stirred . . . I have never before been called upon to sentence a woman for an offense of this kind."

Barnes continued, "It is the sentence of this court you spend the rest of your natural life in the Women's Reformatory at Marysville." Velma burst into tears. Judge Barnes's words came exactly three months to the day after Velma took a hammer to her husband's head.

And so what Prosecutor Paulin so drolly and repeatedly referred to as that "little transaction at Perry" came to an end.

Velma left for Marysville the next day after a tearful farewell with

Velma West in "mannish" attire,
summer 1927.

her mother. Her last words to Francis Poulson were a plea to put in a good word for her at parole time; Velma had high hopes of getting out when she first became eligible in 1938 at the age of 31. The car taking her to Marysville followed much of the same route she had taken on her last drive to Mabel Young's house the previous December. As the car approached the reformatory gates, Velma seized Nina Donberg's hand—the *News* columnist had been allowed to share the last ride—and whimpered, "Hold my hand, hold it tightly, please!" (Donberg later reported that Velma had been having nightmares for weeks, during which she repeatedly cried out, "Ed, don't!") Upon arriving at Marysville, she was greeted by Superintendant Louise Mittendorf, and she piously vowed to start a new life, saying, "I am going to get in with the right sort of girls." Perhaps Velma was inspired by the well-known words on the sign at the Marysville entrance:

When you entered here you left your past behind you.
We do not wish to have you ever refer to it.
Your FUTURE is our concern—to determine that, you are here.

Alas, Velma didn't follow through on her resolutions very well. Many days of her early years at Marysville as Prisoner no. 3181 were spent in solitary confinement, owing to her refusal to live by the rules. In violation of regulations, Velma continued to keep her hair mannishly short, using shards of broken glass from electric lightbulbs and other objects to cut it on the sly. She was eventually allowed some duties in the prison art classes—but lost them when she showed an unwelcome interest in one of the other female prisoners. She was often in trouble, too, for smoking, which Superintendant Mittendorf banned for two reasons: "The first is that it is dangerous here. The second is simply that they are women and I don't approve." When interviewed by *Press* reporter Walter Morrow in November 1930, Velma seemed dispirited and gave only listless replies to his questions. Prison officials told Morrow that Velma had admitted to them that she had participated in a "love cult" before her marriage and that she had married Eddie partly to prevent her mother from suspecting her true proclivities. Velma's behavior, they added, had gone downhill after the disastrous Cleveland Clinic fire in May 1929. She told Louise Mittendorf that one of her friends had died there, commenting "What have I to live for now?"

By the time *Cleveland News* reporter Howard Beaufait interviewed Velma five years later, she had settled down considerably. She was still disobediently cutting her hair but seemed healthier from a regime of working outdoors in the flower gardens, vegetable patches, and hayfields of the reformatory. She was interested in news of the outside world, especially Cleveland's newly built Terminal Tower, which she had never seen, and still cherished hopes of getting a parole in 1938.

But 1938 came and went, and there was no parole for still-notorious "hammer murderess" Velma West. Although by now a valued "trustee" at the prison, Velma had begun to lose hope, and her anxiety was increased by mounting fears about her health, especially a heart condition. She also complained of a constant noise in her ears, "like an airplane." In the early morning hours of June 19, 1939, Velma escaped from Marysville with three other inmates, passing through three supposedly locked doors to freedom outside. She left a letter for the new superintendant, Marguerite Reilley, pledging affection and justifying her betrayal:

> Because I must have one little adventure in this dull life of
> mine—Because I am so tortured with pain in this body of

Cleveland News headline, December 12, 1927.

mine that it drives me almost crazy. Because I have lost hope
of getting out as I would like to get out . . . Please don't let
them talk too awfully bad about me after this. I'm not bad—
just frightfully unlucky in life.

Although Reilley initially professed mystification at how Velma
had passed through so many locked doors, the superintendant eventually admitted that Velma had been trusted enough to have access to
some of the master keys at Marysville.

A month later Velma was captured in Dallas. When picked up by
the police there, Velma was allegedly on the way to her room with a
man, although, as Marguerite Reilley commented, "That doesn't
sound like Velma." Velma first swore at the Dallas police and refused
to talk, but reverted to the chatty self of her erstwhile Painesville jail
days when offered a pack of cigarettes by a friendly reporter.

While insisting that her fling had been worth it, Velma confessed
that life on the outside had been pretty hard. It was apparent that the
three fugitives had been able to get so far away only by hitchhiking
and selling their bodies in the most squalid of circumstances. And
when Velma's two companions rolled a customer for his wallet in
Tennessee, the bloody results made squeamish Velma faint. Upon
her return to Marysville, Velma lost her hard-won privileges and was
put in solitary confinement for a few weeks. Her only reference to
Eddie West, her first since coming to prison, was a heartless one: "He
couldn't take it. I hit him playfully on the head with a hammer one
night and that was that."

But the years went by, and Velma began to mellow at last. Sometime before her father died in 1944, Velma got religion and entered
the Roman Catholic faith. During the last decade and a half of her
life, she often entertained her fellow inmates at Marysville, singing
and writing her own, often gospel-based compositions. These

included tunes like "Careless Kisses," My Secret Dream," and "Won't You Spare One Little Prayer for a Sinner Like Me?" About her faith and Eddie, she said, "It may sound corny but this is true. We pray more for others than ourselves. Every time I say communion it is for my husband. If his soul can't be saved, I don't want mine to be saved."

Velma's last years were difficult ones, as she was troubled by health problems, including the heart condition which eventually caused paralysis of her arms. Although considered for parole several times, it was obvious that she had nowhere else to go. She died of heart disease on October 24, 1959, at 8:15 a.m., after wasting away to eighty-six pounds. She was fifty-three. In her declining years, she was known to tell fellow prisoners: "Go straight when you get out. There's still a lot of good you can do in this world."

Jackass Hill, Kingsbury Run

September 23, 1935

September 23, 1935, was a fine fall day in Cleveland. A light breeze made temperatures in the low 70s even more welcome, and it seems unlikely that murder was much on the minds of Clevelanders as the pleasant afternoon waned. No one except the county coroner and the police still gave any thought to the year-old mystery of the Beulah Park torso; most civic attention, from the evidence of Cleveland's newspapers, was focused on the Seventh National Eucharistic Congress, which had opened in Cleveland the day before, bringing thousands of devout visitors to the Forest City.

Murder certainly wasn't on the minds of James Wagner, 16, and Peter Costura, 12, as they played that afternoon amid the bleak waste and rubble of Kingsbury Run near East 49th and Praha Avenue. Crisscrossed by the tracks of the Nickel Plate, Erie, and Cleveland Interurban (Shaker Rapid Transit) rail lines, the Run was a neglected area of trash, weeds, and the debris left by the large population of itinerant men who roamed and dwelt throughout such waste areas. It was about 5:00 p.m. and getting toward dinnertime when James and Peter decided to race each other down a sixty-foot bluff known as Jackass Hill to the bottom of the Run.

James got down there first, and while waiting for Peter he spied some sort of white object in a nearby clump of brush. He took a closer look and seconds later fled back up Jackass Hill, screaming to Peter that there was "a dead man with no head down there." James and Peter ran and found an adult, who called the police.

The first law officers to arrive on the scene were Sergeant Arthur Marsh and Patrolman Arthur Stitt of the Erie Railroad police. They investigated Wagner's find and identified it as the headless, emasculated torso of a young white male. The incomplete corpse was nude except for a pair of black cotton socks. While Marsh continued examining the body, Stitt soon found another nude corpse thirty feet away from the first. It was the headless trunk of an older man, also emasculated, with an odd, reddish tinge to its skin. Unlike the first, relatively fresh torso, the second was badly decomposed.

Cleveland detectives and patrolmen soon joined the railroad detectives, and more discoveries accumulated. Next to an embankment about twenty feet from the first body, the searchers found the two pairs of severed genitals. Nearby, Patrolman Stitt saw some dark hairs sticking out of the dirt; further excavation unearthed a human head that matched the first torso. The other missing head was found buried about seventy-five feet away from its trunk. Near it, the police found some bloody clothes: a white shirt, a blue suit coat with a B. R. Baker label, a checked cap, and some underwear. There was also a piece of rope and a rusty pail containing what looked like motor oil. By now the cliffs adjoining the Run were dotted with dozens of spectators, who watched as railroad and Cleveland police brought forth and catalogued their grisly finds.

The bodies of the two victims were taken to the Cleveland City Morgue at East Ninth Street and Lakeside, and Coroner Pearse conducted autopsies that evening. The first torso was that of a young man, described officially as "handsome," about five foot eleven, weighing about 150 pounds, with a light complexion and brown hair. Its head had been tidily separated from the body between the third and fourth cervical vertebrae with a heavy, very sharp knife. The absence of blood in the heart and the retraction of the neck muscles indicated that decapitation had been the cause of death. There were rope burns on the wrists, which, together with the length of rope found, suggested that the victim, presumably tied up, had struggled violently before being murdered. It was estimated that the victim had probably been dead for only two or three days. Fingerprints from the corpse were soon matched with police records to reveal the identity of the first torso: Edward Andrassy of 1744 Fulton Road.

The second corpse was a far more anonymous affair. It was the body of a male who appeared to be about forty-five years old, with a stocky build, about five foot six, 165 pounds, with brown hair and good teeth. He had probably been dead several weeks, and there were no fingerprints available. The reddish hue of the skin suggested that some preservative had been used on the body, but Coroner Pearse did not make the connection—then or later—with the chemically treated torso of the Lady of the Lake.

A visit to Edward Andrassy's home on Fulton Road quickly exposed the unfortunate lifestyle that had led him to an unseemly death at the bottom of Jackass Hill. Twenty-eight years old, Edward had lived in uneasy domesticity with his parents, Joseph and Helen, and his younger brother, John. They had last seen him leaving their house about 8:00 p.m. on September 19, four days before his body was found. Well known to the police as a drunkard, marijuana user, pornography peddler, gambler, pimp, bellicose barroom brawler,

HEAR OF THREATS IN TORSO MURDER

Police Told Man Ordered One of 2 Victims: "Keep Away From My Wife."

The Plain Dealer, September 25, 1935.

bunko artist, and all-around "snotty punk," Edward had long frequented the dives, brothels, gambling dens, and disorderly houses of the "Roaring Third" Precinct, whose ten square miles of slums and vice stretched south of Prospect Avenue in Depression-era Cleveland. Having once served thirty days in the Warrensville Workhouse for carrying concealed weapons, Edward had a reputation as a fighter who managed to get himself beat up rather often; two months before his murder, a Cleveland cabbie had found him lying in an East Ninth Street gutter with his head bleeding. Helen and Joseph, who claimed Edward's body at the morgue, could only utter the eternal plaint of heartbroken parents at the fatal folly of their young: "Edward lived in continual fear of his life. He always told us to mind our own business when we tried to straighten him out."

Interrogation of Edward's relatives and cronies intensified the image of a degenerate young man to whom, sooner or later, bad things would happen. Edward's parents testified that a man had called at the Andrassy home two months before, while Edward was away, saying he would kill Edward if he didn't stop paying attention to the man's wife.

Further investigation by Cleveland police revealed aspects of Andrassy's life that were even more lurid, at least to Clevelanders of that more sexually innocent era. Andrassy was rumored to be bisexual, and the belief that his death might have been related to his deviant associations was reinforced by the police discovery of "muscle" magazines in his room.

All in all, though, Cleveland police had little to go on. A couple of suspects, one of whom was said to have killed Andrassy's brother in a 1922 fight, were brought in for questioning that proved fruitless. And it was reported in the newspapers that two Trumbull Street men had seen a fifty-year-old man stooping over the bloody clothes later found on Jackass Hill. The suspicious sighting had occurred on Saturday, September 21, but the police had not been informed.

What *The Plain Dealer* characterized as "the most bizarre double murder" in Cleveland history vanished from the columns of Cleveland newspapers within three days. The unidentified second torso was buried in Potter's Field in Highland Park Cemetery, and Cleveland authorities were left to privately mutter their conjectures about the unsolved double slaying. Implications drawn from the evidence included the following: 1) Andrassy and the unidentified second victim had known each other, and the body of the previously murdered second victim had been held until the corpses could be dumped together in some act of private vengeance; 2) The victims had been killed and their bodies washed and drained of blood before being dumped in Kingsbury Run (there was no other explanation for the complete absence of blood around the two bodies); and 3) The pail of motor oil, which revealed traces of blood and hair, had probably been brought with the purpose of burning the corpses. In addition, the neat placement of the bodies suggested that they had been carefully carried rather than dumped at their resting place in the Run, and their castration suggested that some sort of criminal ritual—a Mafia gesture?—was involved in the killings. More than that the police could not fathom.

Soon, as with the Lady of the Lake, Clevelanders began to forget about this latest outrage. It was only later, much later, that anyone would appreciate the uncannily prophetic words of Detective Orly May, uttered to his partner Detective Emil Musil, as they reviewed the details of what they had witnessed at the bottom of Jackass Hill on the afternoon of September 23: "I've got a bad feeling about this one."

Chapter 2

ASH WEDNESDAY FOREVER

The 1908 Collinwood School Fire

There is no more terrible a story in the annals of Cleveland than the Collinwood school fire. News of the disaster was heard round the world when it happened, and it has lost neither its horror nor its pathos in the nearly ninety years since it first stunned Clevelanders with its unprecedented—and still unsurpassed—toll of death and suffering, the most woeful Cleveland story ever. Still echoing down through the years is the cry of a grey-haired, grief-stricken man who, fourscore years ago, fell to his knees on a Collinwood street and cried, "Oh God, what have we done to deserve this?"

Like many an American metropolis, Cleveland grew throughout the nineteenth and early twentieth centuries by gobbling up smaller, less dynamic villages, hamlets, and neighborhoods. In the early 1900s, many Clevelanders were convinced that the natural eastern limit of their city should be Euclid Creek, and so it was that city authorities increasingly focused on annexing the village of North Collinwood as the century's first years unfolded. Acquisition of Collinwood would bring Cleveland to the borders of Euclid Village, and most Collinwood residents, too, thought such an incorporation would happen sooner or later. A railroad town that grew up around the tracks of the Lake Shore & Michigan Southern Railroad, North Collinwood grew from a population of 2,500 in 1890 to about 7,500 in 1908. The village was badly strained by the demands of its growing population, and was increasingly hard pressed to provide even basic services like fire protection and education.

Nowhere was the insufficiency of village resources more manifest than at Lakeview Elementary School. Opened in the fall of 1901, the three-story school on Collamer Avenue (now East 152nd Street) had originally served fewer than 200 students in four classrooms. Surging enrollment necessitated construction of an additional four classrooms in 1907, and by the spring of 1908, 350 pupils were housed in those eight classrooms, with a fifth-grade class in the third-floor auditorium.

After the tragedy of the fire, virtually everyone agreed that the construction of the Lakeview Elementary School was unsafe (it certainly was by modern standards), but no one remarked on its dangers at the time. Certainly not the city fathers, who had to pay for the rather impressive-looking structure of wood and brick. Certainly not the architect of the original four-room structure, John Eisenman. Nor did the architects who expanded the building, Searles, Hirsh & Gavin, comment on its structural perils. In fact, Lakeview was probably no better or worse than most schools of the day—as Cleveland officials subsequently found when fears raised by the Collinwood tragedy highlighted similar dangers in Cleveland schools.

Built on a foundation of red brick and framed with Norway pine, the eight-classroom school was oriented on an east-west axis, with its front exit facing Collamer Avenue. Stairways made of Georgia yellow pine led down from the first floor to front and rear exits, identically constructed with two sets of swinging double doors separated by five-foot-deep vestibules. Although the vestibules were ten feet, eight inches wide, they had two-foot-six-inch-wide partitions on each side—so the total width of the attached swinging doors was only a little over five feet. (All of the swinging doors, contrary to subsequent rumor, opened outward, not inward.) The most dangerous component of the front and rear exits was the area between the bottom of the stairs and the first pair of swinging doors: it was only a couple of feet from the last stair to the inner doors, and anyone exiting had to turn slightly to the right in front of the partition to reach the first set of doors.

The school basement contained a furnace and boiler—located at about the middle of the building, separate washrooms for the boys and girls, and some small rooms for storage. Only the basement, hallways, and vestibules had electric lights; the eight classrooms and two teachers' lounges relied on coal-oil lamps for illumination. The school was maintained and kept clean by janitor Fritz Hirter, a forty-six-year-old immigrant from Switzerland, who himself had three children enrolled there. Much beloved by the Lakeview children, Hirter was also lauded by their parents for the meticulous care he lavished on the school and its grounds.

March 4, Ash Wednesday, began much like any other school day at Lakeview. It was pleasant weather for late winter, a little windy but sunny and clear, with a high of thirty-six degrees expected. About 7:30 a.m., Fritz Hirter walked the three blocks from his home on Collamer Avenue to the school and unlocked the outer doors. After stoking the furnace to make sure the building would be warm enough, he went about his usual routine of sweeping the stairs, rooms, and hallways. Sometime after his arrival, Hirter discovered three girls in the school basement playing hide and seek or tag, and shooed them out. Later he would remember only their first names—Mary, Anna, and Lizzie—and no one will ever know what they were actually doing down there.

About 8:00 a.m., the nine Lakeview teachers began to arrive and prepare for the day's lessons. They included Pearl Lynn, who taught a class of thirty-four first graders in a first-floor room at the southwest corner of the building; Grace Fiske, who taught forty first graders in the northwest corner across from Lynn; Ethel Rose, who taught thirty-nine second graders in the southeast corner of the first floor, and Ruby Irwin, whose fourth-grade class of thirty-eight occupied the northeast room opposite Rose's. Up on the second floor were Katherine Gollmer's fifth-grade class of forty-four in the northwest corner; Katherine Weiler's thirty-nine second graders in the southwest room; Lulu Rowley's class of thirty-five third graders in the southeast room, and principal Ann Moran's taught forty-one sixth graders in the northeast corner room. On the third floor, Laura Bodey taught forty-one fifth graders in the former auditorium, now converted to class space because of the overcrowding.

Fire safety was not neglected at Lakeview. There had been at least three fire drills since September, although Laura Bodey later testified that there had not been one since she had arrived at Lakeview in mid-February, and evidence suggests that there had not been a fire drill since Christmas, because of inclement weather. In the event of a fire, janitor Hirter was supposed to ring a bell in Ruby Irwin's northeast first-floor room that set off bells on the second and third floors. The fire signal was three rings; after that, Hirter was supposed to make sure the sets of double doors at both exits were wide open. At the sound of the fire bell, the children were to arise from their seats, assemble in a double column at the side of each room, and proceed to either the front or rear exits in an assigned pattern. As was the usual custom in schools, the younger grades were concentrated closer to the exits, with all the first graders on the first floor. The classes exiting from the second and third floors were trained to wait on the stairs until the first-floor classes had exited the building. There was also a fire escape on the north side of the building, accessible from some of the second-floor classroom windows. The experience of past fire drills suggested that the building could be emptied in about ninety seconds.

The school day officially began at 8:45 a.m. Janitor Hirter later recalled checking the boiler pressure and adding some coal to keep the heat up just before 9:30; he remembered nothing amiss as the school settled into the day's routine. But at about 9:40, while Hirter was sweeping the basement, Emma Neibert, 13, came down the front basement stairs from the third floor to use the girls' washroom. She had only gotten down a few steps when she noticed a puff of smoke. (Hirter would later describe it as no more smoke than one would see at the end of a cigar.) She halted on the second step and called out to Hirter, whom she could see dimly in the basement, "What's the matter?" She received no reply and called again. A split second later, she saw him run by her and race up the front stairs. Seconds later, he rang the fire bell in Ruby Irwin's classroom, which was the closest to the front stairs, and then ran out to open both sets of front and rear doors. And so the Collinwood school fire tragedy began.

The evacuation began well. Ethel Rose's second graders arose from their desks, formed a double line, and followed their teacher safely out into the hall and down the front stairs, physically blocking the stairs to the basement, where flames were already licking hungrily at the tinder-dry pine risers. All of Rose's pupils escaped safely, and her later memory was that both sets of doors at the front exit were wide open. Almost as soon as Rose's class was out, though, flames began to seal off the front-door exit.

Right behind Rose's second graders came Ruby Irwin's thirty-eight first graders. By this time the stairs down to the front exit were in flames. Irwin ordered her pupils to run through the flames to safety. Some of them did, and they survived the day. But most panicked, wheeled around, and began to run toward the rear-door exit. Within seconds, Irwin was driven back from the stairs by the mounting flames and watched helplessly as most of her pupils dashed for the rear exit. She managed to corral some of them and led them into one of the first-floor classrooms. Opening a window, she lowered the children to the ground, one by one, before leaping to safety herself. Some of her pupils who ran to the rear exit also escaped out of other windows on the first floor.

The fatal nexus of the Collinwood fire developed at the rear (west) exit shortly after the attempted evacuation of Ruby Irwin's class. Some of Irwin's pupils ran into children exiting from both the rear first-floor rooms and the four second-floor classrooms. Someone stumbled at the bottom of the stairs by the rear exit, and within seconds screaming, writhing children began to pile up right in front of the first set of rear school doors. Those doors, like the outer pair, were probably both open at the time—but the space was so tight at

Collinwood school fire, March 4, 1908.

the turn by the stairs that no one could get through the mounting barrier of human flesh.

Laura Bodey guided her third-floor class of forty-one fifth graders down the front stairway. By the time they reached the second floor, it was already filled with smoke. Bodey turned the class around—except for a few who panicked and fled down the stairs to join the fatal congestion at the front exit—and led them into a second-floor classroom. There was a fire escape adjacent to one of the windows there, and Bodey began to evacuate the children, repeating over and over, "The fire escape. Girls first." One by one, Bodey lowered the children from the end of the fire escape, six feet above the ground. Only six of her children died that day, all of them ones who had run to the front exit.

By now, only minutes into the fire, both the front and rear exits had become impassable. Second-floor classes coming down the stairs had collided with panicked children on the first floor, and both exits were blocked with bodies of dead and dying children in the areas between the stairs and the inner sets of doors. Some children survived by hurling themselves from the banisters over the rising pile of writhing bodies. But most of them soon joined the fatal masses by the doors, many of those at the bottom suffocating long before the flames reached them.

First-grade teacher Pearl Lynn got her thirty-four pupils out into the hall in good order. But as they reached the back stairs, some of them panicked, and she was knocked down the stairs toward the first set of doors. Children began to pile up on top of her. She later recalled her descent toward death: "All in an instant I was borne down, caught and held as in a vise. The incredible thing was the awful swiftness of the horror. How I got out I don't know. I must have been pulled loose somehow. By that time every stick of woodwork on the first floor was burning."

It's understandable that Lynn could not recall her escape: by the time she was pulled out her clothes were torn to pieces and she was in a state of near-suffocation. She was rescued by Fritz Hirter and Lake Shore Railroad shopman Frank Dorn, one of the first rescuers to arrive at the school. Risking his life, Dorn pulled Lynn and seventeen others out of the blocked front and rear exits. Lynn's arms were badly burned but she survived the fire.

Katherine Weiler's second-floor class of second graders was doing its arithmetic lesson when the fire bell rang. Weiler managed to lead them to the stairs, but they panicked when they got there and began surging down toward the seething mass of children at the back door. Weiler waded into the screaming mob, saying "Quiet, children. Quiet. Go back to the fire escape." She was still trying to get them to turn around and go into one of the first-floor rooms when she was knocked down the back stairs by the crush of children still pouring down the stairs from the second floor. Her body was never found.

Grace Fiske's first-floor class of first graders was normally routed to the front exit, but when she got them there it was already impassable. She turned them around and led them to the back exit, only to find it blocked from floor to ceiling with dead and dying children. Fiske tried to get children to go into a classroom with her and then waded into the blockage, trying to pull children free. Like Weiler, she was eventually knocked down near the rear exit doors and burned to death with the children she tried to save. When last seen, she was attempting to shelter two terrified children from the advancing flames within the folds of her voluminous skirt.

Lulu Rowley later remembered that when the fire bell rang, she stood up, said, "Partners, quick! Don't rush!" and had one of her third graders open the classroom door. Thick smoke immediately poured into the room, and some of the children broke from their lines and ran down the front staircase. The staircase was already blocked, so Rowley tried to lead the remnants of her class into a first-floor room and out a window. The few that went with her got out to safety.

Rowley then tried to get to the back exit to save more children, but it was hopelessly blocked. She eventually escaped out a back window on the first floor. One of Rowley's pupils, Harold Echelberger, remembered the scene after the fire bell rang this way:

> The boys in my room cried out "False alarm, false alarm."
> Miss Rowley told them to sit still and be quiet. At this time
> the room was filled with smoke and all the children were
> screaming and yelling, and finally they broke away from the
> control of the teacher and rushed out into the hall and down
> the stairway . . . Herbert Grant and I dove head first down the
> stairway over the mass of children who were lying under-
> neath us. I don't know how I got out. Somebody seemed to
> grab us and pull us outside. I saw little children putting out
> the fire on their hair with their hands. They were screaming
> for their parents and teacher while the flames were creeping
> all around them.

Katherine Gollmer got her class of forty-four fifth graders out of their rear second-floor classroom. But she lost control of them as they reached the staircase, most of them charging down the stairs to die at the blocked rear exit. Gollmer managed to persuade some of them to go with her into a second-floor classroom. There she found principal Ann Moran, who had just endured a similar experience with her sixth-grade class of forty-one. Moran could not stop them from fleeing to the fatal staircases, though she eventually managed to drag a few children into a room. Together, she and Gollmer smashed a window with a chair and started lifting children onto the fire escape. Moran later recalled the tragic contrast that emerged as the fire progressed:

> I ran out into the hall and beheld the most pathetic sight my
> eyes have ever seen. The children were marching past the
> door in perfect order, heads up and feet keeping time. Their
> teachers were beside them, keeping the lines straight. The lit-
> tle ones were smiling and happy. They thought it was a fire
> drill. A moment later the vanguard reached the first floor.
> They saw the flames leaping from the basement. They
> screamed, broke ranks, and ran for the front door.

The doom of 172 Lakeview children—about half the enrollment of 350 or so—was sealed within scant minutes of the fire's outbreak.

The blaze, which probably started in a small storage room beneath the front stairs, may have been smoldering for some time before Emma Neibert first saw smoke at 9:40 a.m. Cleveland fire chief George A. Wallace later opined that the wood in the building, tinder dry from proximity to inadequately shielded and spaced heating pipes, had been "cooking" for weeks before the actual fire. In any case, the structure was fully engaged within fifteen minutes, a lost cause within a half hour, and a completely gutted ruin within an hour. Aiding the spread and force of the flames was a brisk northeast wind, which blew like a bellows through the eastern back doors and the many windows opened or broken in frantic escape attempts.

Rescue attempts began almost immediately. They were much hampered by the fact that no one in the neighborhood seemed to have a ladder that could reach the school windows, or an axe to chop away the deadly partitions at the swinging exit doors. John Leffel was probably the first rescuer to arrive. Walking by the school, he saw smoke and began to run. When he got to the rear exit, it was already jammed with bodies at the foot of the stairs. He began pulling children out of the screaming mass and was soon joined by janitor Hirter and several other men. Leffel recalled:

> Some of the children seemed to be half-suffocated. Some were unconscious. I did not stop to look. I seized them by the arms or legs and tossed them out behind. I guess there were others to pick them up and carry them out of the way. The flames were rushing upon us and I knew we had only a few moments left. Many of the children were still piled up in the entrance when the heat and smoke drove us back from them.

One of those trapped children was Edna Hirter, the Lakeview janitor's eight-year-old daughter. As Hirter labored frantically with other rescuers to pull children out of the blocked rear exit area, he suddenly caught a glimpse of Edna, trapped just feet away in an impenetrable mass of children. "Papa, oh, Papa! Save me, save me!" she screamed. But Hirter could not get to her; her feet were hopelessly trapped by the entangled arms and legs, and he watched as she burned to death in front of his eyes.

One of the big heroes of the day was Wallace Upton, a nearby resident and owner of much of the orchard property skirting the school. Upton, badly burned as he tirelessly worked to pry children out from the rear exit, saved eighteen children that terrible day. Today, a nearby Collinwood street memorializes his courage.

Diagram of rear door and partition of Lakeview
School. *Cleveland Press*, March 6, 1908.

Within minutes of the alarm, hundreds of hysterical Collinwood
parents began to converge on the fire scene, soon joined by thousands of Clevelanders who had nothing better to do than congest the
area and hamper rescue efforts with their presence. By the time most
parents got there, however, there was little they could do except
watch, like Fritz Hirter, as their children died right in front of them.
One of the unfortunate parents was Mrs. Clara Sprung, who saw
smoke at about 9:30 a.m. from her Collamer Avenue home just
across the street. Arriving at the school, she saw her son Alvin at a
first-floor window, trapped by the advancing flames. Returning with
a ladder from her house, she managed to climb to the window and
grab Alvin by the hair to pull him out the window. Her efforts were
in vain: the fire burned off Alvin's hair in her hands, and he died minutes later in the flames.

There were dozens of similar scenes as anguished parents

watched their trapped children die just inches from safety at the front and rear exits. One of them was Mrs. John Phillis, who could not reach her daughter Jennie, 15, caught at the rear exit. "Oh Jennie! Please come out!" screamed Mrs. Phillis. "I can't move, Ma. Oh, help me, if you can!" replied Jennie. Mrs. Phillis watched in heartbreak as the flames crept closer and closer to her daughter. As the flames began to burn Jennie's hair, Mrs. Phillis reached in and began to caress it. Trying to keep the flames away from Jennie's head, she stayed and comforted her dying child until a falling piece of debris almost cut her hand off.

Another parent who tried desperately to save his own child was W. C. Schaeffer. He got to the rear exit and discovered his eight-year-old son, George, trapped in a pile of children. He grabbed George's hands and pulled as hard as he could—but he could not free him from the deadly mass squeezed together at the back doors. Meanwhile, the flames crept closer and closer, and soon George's hair began to catch on fire. His father smothered the flames but they soon rekindled George's hair. Schaeffer would always remember the look in his son's eyes as he sank for the last time in the mass of burning flesh at the rear exit doors.

William Davis of Westropp Avenue was another one of the early rescuers at the rear exit of the school. There he saw a forlorn little girl, wedged into a corner by one of the inner doors. "Mister, help me out," she pleaded. Dodging through the smoke and heat, Davis managed to get close enough to grab her hand and hear her say, over and over, "Mister, save me!" A moment later Davis was knocked down by a piece of falling debris, and the little girl was consumed by the flames only seconds later. As with so many of the girls killed that day, her long hair and long dress aided the rapid spread of the fire around her.

Given the speed with which the flames spread, even quick escape from the school was not enough to save some little lives. Ten-year-old Mildred Schmitt jumped out of a school window, her long skirt in flames up to her knees, screaming, "Papa! Papa!" Bystanders smothered the flames quickly but it was too late: Mildred died a few hours later at Glenville Hospital. Other casualties of the flames lingered longer, but the last survivor, Glen Barber, 8, succumbed to his injuries on Saturday, March 7. He had been caught at the rear door and eventually had jumped from the second floor, injuring himself terribly. His last words before he died were "I am standing on a large rock, larger than all the world."

Some of the greatest heroes of that terrible day were the smallest.

Oscar Pahner, eleven years old, escaped out the back exit and, although burned, ran to the Collinwood fire station to report the blaze. He then returned to the school to try to save his sister Edna—in vain. Henry Ellis of Westropp Avenue witnessed another act of sublime heroism when he got to the rear exit, as Ellis recounted to a *Plain Dealer* reporter:

> The fire was creeping up on the children in the rear. I saw one girl, who could not have been more than ten or twelve, protect her little brother, who was not more than six years of age. He cried for help and clung to her hand. She comforted him and covered his head with a shawl she was wearing. The flames were growing closer, and the moans of the children mingled with the crackling of the fire. The little girl drew her brother nearer to her. She saw that there was no help. Together they knelt down on the floor. That was the last I saw. The fire caught them after that.

Another little tragic hero was Frederick Paul. He got out of the school safely but returned to try to save his sister Ruth. Firemen later found them dead together in each other's arms. James Turner, 14, escaped from the first floor by breaking a window and then returned to the inferno to find—and die with—his two little brothers, Norman, 9, and Maxwell, 6. Edna Hebler, 14, also got out alive, only to climb back up the fire escape to find her sister Melba. Edna died in the fire, not knowing that Melba had already arrived home. Janitor Fritz Hirter's ten-year-old son Walter was one of the first children out the school door, but he returned to save his sister Ida, and instead died with her. There were several other documented instances of children who escaped and later perished in the flames when they returned to save siblings or friends.

Collinwood firefighters arrived about twenty minutes into the fire. By now all three floors and the Lakeview basement were in flames, and it is unlikely that any fire department in the world could have saved the remaining children. Some could be seen at the windows of the second and third floors, helplessly trapped and screaming as the flames closed in on them. Some began to jump from the windows. Some survived the fall to the ground, especially those who were caught as they fell by rescuers like A. Hansrath, a local merchant who caught three jumpers. The *Cleveland News* reported that Joseph Neill, a nearby resident, rushed to the school in time to catch twenty children as they jumped from the flames, including his own son,

George. More typical, though, was the fate of Mary Ridgeway, Anna Rolth, and Gertrude Davis, who jumped from the third floor and died on impact as they hit the ground. And perhaps the most terrifying sight of the day was the death of Glen Sanderson, a twelve-year-old boy trapped on the third floor. A fascinated crowd of hundreds below watched as Sanderson, fleeing from the flames that pursued him across the third floor, swung hand over hand across the third-floor auditorium stage, using pieces of scenery to swing himself toward the fire escape and safety. He got about halfway across the stage, missed his grip, and fell into the flames below.

As *The Plain Dealer* subsequently remarked, the arrival of the Collinwood Fire Department might have been a comic sight under different circumstances. A volunteer force of no more than ten men, the fire department was an almost pitiable collection of ancient equipment and inefficient vehicles. Moreover, it was delayed because its regular horses were down in South Collinwood pulling a grader, and two horses had to be borrowed from a nearby merchant. And when the firefighters got to the scene—with one hose truck, one engine, and one ladder truck—it was found that their twenty-foot ladders couldn't reach the third floor, where many of the children had fled as a last refuge from the flames. Worse yet, there was little pressure in the leaky water lines—no more than fifty pounds per square inch delivered from the nearest fireplug, 150 feet away—and the fire-hose streams could not even reach the second-floor windows. The firemen did the best they could, rescuing those children they could find and reach, but in general their arrival proved the final ghastly irony of a terrible day.

There were hardheaded political reasons, of course, for the pathetic state of Collinwood's fire department. For years an intense struggle had been waged between those who wanted Collinwood annexed by Cleveland and those who did not. Shortly before the fire, the pro-annexation forces had won a victory for their slate, including Mayor Westropp, but the anti-annexationists had managed to delay the actual incorporation indefinitely through a "poison-pill" commission. (Annexation would not become a fact until January 1910.) In the interim before annexation, neither side was willing to spend any more money on Collinwood's safety forces, as it was assumed that Cleveland would soon take over the duties of fire protection. Cleveland fire units, sent by Chief George Wallace, eventually arrived at the Lakeview fire scene, but too late to do any good.

The climax of the catastrophe came shortly after 10:30 a.m. As hundreds of spectators watched, many with cameras and even, it was

Cleveland Press headline, March 4, 1908.

said, a moving-picture camera, the first floor collapsed into the basement, followed soon by the second and third floors, burying what was left of more than a hundred children in the smoking rubble of Lakeview Elementary School.

The fire was officially put out by about 1:30 p.m., but firemen and volunteers, many released from the Lake Shore rail yards as soon as word of the fire came, began clearing out the dead and injured as soon as they could safely get into the smoldering wreckage.

One by one the corpses were loaded onto wooden carts, and ambulances from undertakers including Mapes and Shepard helped carry them just south of the school to the Lake Shore Railway Storehouse near Collamer Avenue, which had been turned into a temporary morgue. There, over the next few days, groups of parents—no more than ten at a time—were brought in to identify the bodies. Corpses of at least 165 children and three adults were taken out of the Lakeview ruins. Some were easily recognizable, others were badly marred by the fire, and still others were little more than pieces of flesh, bone, and clothing that had been raked out of the ruins of the school. Some, like George Schaeffer, were identified by a ring or an earring that the parents remembered and recognized. Others, like Hulda Swanson, 11, were identified by the fillings in their teeth. One child was identified after her parents had spent hours searching in vain; her little dog was admitted to the morgue and immediately ran

Cleveland News headline, March 6, 1908.

to the side of his dead, beloved little mistress. It was a horrible business, made more horrible when two sets of parents quarreled over one of the corpses, each insisting that it was their own boy.

Despite vigorous search efforts, the body of Katherine Weiler was never found; presumably it burned to ash in the heat of the rear-exit holocaust, although Barney Reiche of Forster Avenue claimed recalled putting Weiler's body on a stretcher. Also puzzling was the corpse of a young man, at first thought to be Weiler's body and then that of an older boy, until the coroner realized that the teeth were too large. It is likely that it was the body of a man named John Kranjnak of 53 Hale Street. Witnesses saw him run into the burning school to rescue children—and he was never seen alive afterwards.

As preparations for the funerals got under way, the inevitable recriminations began. Many of the bereaved Collinwood parents needed a scapegoat for their tragedy, and they soon focused on janitor Hirter and the surviving schoolteachers. Some of the parents thought it rather suspicious that so few of the teachers had died in the fire, while 172 children, most of them from the second-floor classrooms, had perished. The feeling against Hirter soon grew dangerous, necessitating a guard around his house. Despite the fact that he had lost three of his own children in the fire, it was soon whispered around the village that Hirter had been absent from the school when the fire broke out. Indeed, by the time Coroner Burke got the official inquest under way two days later, Mrs. Julius Dietrich was willing to testify that she had seen Hirter sweeping the porch of his house when she first saw smoke coming from the school and that she next saw him running toward it. There were also repeated allegations by fire witnesses, including several of the Lakeview teachers, that the doors of the school had not been open during the attempted evacuation. These accusations of negligence put Hirter through a terrible ordeal

on Burke's witness stand and an even worse one in the court of public opinion. Driven almost to insanity by the loss of his three children
and the terrible accusations of his neighbors, the badly burned Hirter
could only say, again and again: "Gentlemen, I do not know how the
fire started. If you were to kill me, I could not tell you. I do not know.
I do not know. I do not know."

For the record, there was never any credible evidence that Hirter
was derelict in his duty before, during, or after the fire. Although
some witnesses said the school doors were closed during the fire,
crucial witnesses testified that they were all open at the onset of the
fire, suggesting that the strong wind probably blew them partially or
completely shut as the fire progressed. After listening to all of the
testimony, Coroner Burke went out of his way to exonerate the
beleaguered janitor, issuing a statement on Monday, March 9: "I
want to take this occasion to say publicly that the people of
Collinwood have no reason to blame you . . . You did not only your
duty but you did more than your duty."

Hirter's persecution did not end that day, however. A group of sor-
rowing mothers, organizing themselves as the "Mothers of the
Burned District", attempted to have Hirter fired by the Collinwood
School Board. They carried on their campaign against him for some
months afterward, some even refusing to send their children to Clark
School, where he was reassigned. Hirter eventually went to work for
the Cleveland school system, living into the 1950s and dying at the
age of ninety-six.

The official inquest and the various fire investigations did little
good. Everyone seemed to agree, after the fire, that the Lakeview
School should have been fireproofed and that the exit areas should
not have been curtailed by partitions. Cleveland fire chief George
Wallace asserted that the fire started when a wooden beam in the
basement was ignited by an adjacent steam pipe, which had already
dangerously dried out much of the school's wood construction in the
weeks before the fire. That was also the opinion of the state fire mar-
shals, although no one really knows to this day what set off the Lakeview fire. The final inquest verdict held no one responsible for the
blaze, as no Ohio or local law had been broken.

The worst canard to come out of the Collinwood fire was the
sturdy legend that the exit doors opened inward, the presumed cause
of the fatal pileups at the front and rear. This lie was repeated by at
least one state fire marshal on the day after the fire and repeated even
by principal Ann Moran—despite the testimony of the original
architect, members of the school board, the architects who expanded

the school, fire chief George Wallace, and numerous eyewitnesses of the fatal conflagration. The newspapers picked up the fiction and have repeated it more often than not in the decades since the fire. In 1938, a dogged researcher even dug up the original Lakeview foundations and published archaeological proof that the doors had swung outward. In recent years, other researchers have produced actual period photographs of the exit areas to prove the same point. But the legend endures, and if Clevelanders know only one thing about the Collinwood school fire, it is the untruth that "the doors opened inward."

The funerals of the children began on Thursday and continued through the following Monday. The disaster's impact on the small village of Collinwood was visibly devastating. On some streets, such as Arcade, there was hardly a house without a white ribbon attached to its door knocker, indicating a death. Twenty-three families lost two children each in the fire, and eight families lost three children. Small wonder that some of the parents soon sank into dangerous depressions. Several of the mothers tried to kill themselves in the days afterward. One of the most determined was Mrs. Amelia Robinson of Forest Avenue. The mother of the only black children who attended Lakeview, she lost both her daughters in the fire. Robinson bitterly reproached the surviving teachers, blaming them for her loss, and tried to throw herself out a second-story window. Restrained, she subsequently tried to hang herself with a quilt.

The last funerals were held on Monday, March 9, climaxing in a solemn ceremony in Lake View Cemetery. There, in a mass grave near the Euclid Avenue entrance, twenty-one caskets were interred, nineteen of them containing unidentified dead. The Village of Collinwood purchased the burial site, paid at least sixty dollars apiece toward the cost of all the funerals, and eventually erected a ruggedly handsome stone monument to the fire's dead at the Lake View Cemetery gravesite. It's still there and contains a plaque bearing the names of all the dead.

Malign reverberations from the fire continued for some time afterwards. The Collinwood schools did not reopen until September, and when they did—with police guards to protect Hirter and the surviving Lakeview teachers—some of the grieving parents refused to send their children to the three temporary elementary schools conducted in two former saloons and an ex-church. The Mothers of the Burned District subsequently opposed the erection of a proposed new school, Collinwood Memorial, next to the fire site, and the construction of a memorial garden over the ruins of Lakeview School.

Collinwood school fire, March 4, 1908.

Said Elizabeth Powers, one of the unreconciled mothers: "The site of the burned school is both sacred and horrible. The ashes of the children still lie in its ruins, It is a grave. I would not send my remaining child to study and play where part of his brother's body lies." Sacred ground or not, the garden was eventually built. After subsequent years of neglect, it has been nicely restored. Collinwood Memorial School, a fireproof structure of ten rooms, opened in September of 1910. It has been vacant and unused in recent decades, but may yet be restored and redeveloped.

Some good did come out of the Collinwood school fire. Thanks in particular to sensationalistic newspaper coverage in the wake of the disaster, the Cleveland schools were discovered to be largely unsafe firetraps and were accordingly renovated. The effects of the publicity about Collinwood were not confined to Cleveland: the fire made headlines around the United States and the entire world, arousing and energizing the champions of school-building safety wherever the awful story was told. The most unfavorable comment came from German newspapers, which excoriated Americans for the low value they put on human life—especially the lives of the German-American children who had died in the fire. It was probably a similarly invidious motivation that brought Prince Albert von Wurten, the ambassador from Austria-Hungary, to Cleveland on March 10 to inquire into the welfare of his countrymen living in the Collinwood neighborhood.

Finally, like all significant Cleveland disaster stories, the Collinwood school fire had its quota of touching—if somewhat bizarre—incidents. One of the oddest came after Ruby Irwin finally succeeded in getting most of her children to safety through the flames at the front door. She turned around to see one of her female pupils jumping out a window of her classroom at the northeast corner of the first floor. As Ruby stared uncomprehendingly, the little girl marched up to her, handed her a familiar-looking garment, and said in the most matter-of-fact voice, "I went back for your cloak."

Flo Polillo and the Dog That Did Bark in the Night

2315 East 20th Street, January 26, 1936

The year 1936 rolled around, and Eliot Ness, still wearing the publicity laurels of his celebrated fight against the Capone crime empire, was now Cleveland's newly appointed public safety director, having taken office on December 12, 1935. He certainly wasn't fretting about the "Kingsbury Run Torso Killer"—the term was not yet current—but he was already making headlines with his daring January 10 raid on the Harvard Club gambling den and his vigorous crackdown on police corruption. There was also an almost unprecedented cold snap in Cleveland that blistered that Depression-era month with near-zero or worse temperatures for the better part of a fortnight.

It was probably the cold snap that made James Marco reluctant to go outside his house at 2108 Central Avenue on the night of January 25–26. For some reason his dog started barking at 2:30 a.m.—but he ignored it. Eight more hours went by. Another dog in the neighborhood, named Lady and belonging to Nick Albondante of 2100 Charity Avenue, started barking in the late morning of January 26, and eventually a female resident of the neighborhood decided to do something about it. In an alley behind the Hart Manufacturing Company at 2315 East 20th Street, she found Lady straining at her leash and trying to get at a bushel basket resting against the back wall of the building. After peering into the basket, the woman walked to the end of the alley and met Charles Paige, a neighborhood butcher. She told Paige that there were some "hams" in the basket, and he scurried down the alley, thinking her find might be evidence that a meat store—perhaps his—had been robbed. Arriving at the basket, he reached beneath a burlap sack on top—and pulled out a human arm. Paige called the police, who soon inventoried the remaining contents of the basket: two thighs and the lower half of a female human torso. The right arm and thigh were wrapped in pages of a January 25, 1936, Cleveland newspaper; the left thigh in an August 11, 1935, afternoon edition. (Cleveland reporters would for years contest bragging rights as to which paper the parts were wrapped in; the evidence seems to sustain the claims of *Cleveland News* partisans.) The burlap bags were covered with chicken feathers and ashes, and the human remains bore the evidence of coal dust and coal lump imprints. Near the body, detectives discovered another burlap sack, containing a pair of cotton underwear wrapped in a November 19 edition of a Cleveland newspaper. Late that same afternoon, another burlap sack, bloodstained and containing chicken feathers, was found near by at 1838 Central Avenue.

The body parts were brought to the morgue, and Coroner Pearse soon surmised that the partial corpse belonged to a female who had probably been murdered between late Friday, January 24 and early Saturday, January 25. Within twenty-four hours the mysterious corpse was identified. Without a head the police hadn't had much to go on, but thanks to the efforts of Bertillon expert George Koestle— who looked through more than 10,000 of 12,000 possible matches to the mystery corpse's right-hand fingerprints—it was found to be the body of one Florence Polillo.

Well, sort of. Identity, as Victorian novelists such as Charles Dickens and Wilkie Collins have demonstrated, is a fragile construct, and that of Ms. Polillo proved to be elusive. Reported as anywhere from thirty-five to near fifty years old (she was most probably forty-one), Florence Polillo had assumed many identities in her apparently misbegotten and unhappy life. Thought to have been christened Florence Genevieve Sawdey in Ashtabula County, Ohio, and known later under such aliases as Clara Dunn and Florence Martin, "Flo" Polillo had endured a hard and tumultuous life for at least the last decade of her existence. Married at least twice, she had been divorced from her second husband, Andrew Polillo, in the late 1920s. He now hastened to the Forest City in hopes of claiming a $1,000 insurance policy on his long-forgotten spouse.

Further police investigation disclosed even more notorious aspects of Ms. Polillo's biography. She was no stranger to the police of the "Roaring Third" district and had figured in a number of barroom brawls and vice activities. First arrested for soliciting by Cleveland police in December 1930, Florence next came to their attention on June 14, 1931, when she was surprised in the act of "occupying rooms for immoral purposes." She was later arrested in Washington, D.C., on May 2, 1934, for prostitution and charged in Cleveland on October 3, 1935, with illegally selling intoxicating beverages at 1504 St. Clair Avenue. Florence had found intermittent employment as a barmaid, waitress, and prostitute during the early

David L. Cowles of the Cleveland Police
Ballistics Department examines basket in
which parts of Flo Polillo were discovered.

1930s, but since April of 1935 she had been a client of County Welfare. The word on the streets of the Roaring Third was that the aging,
hideously liver-spotted Florence had been going downhill fast in
recent months: there were several reports of her being beaten in the
months just prior to her death, and she had been seen hobbling on
crutches in early January. She was described as short, pudgy, double-
chinned, with stringy, graying brown hair (dyed chestnut), and a
complete set of false teeth.

Extended police interviews with her landlady, Mary Ford of 3205
Carnegie, elicited a more sympathetic, if not quite well-rounded portrait of the unfortunate Ms. Polillo. Mrs. Ford expressed a genuine
liking for her tenant of eight months, remembering her as pleasant
and unaggressive—except when she drank. When Flo sipped demon
alcohol, it was in bulk, and it did not, Mary Ford related, improve her
personality: "Her only bad habit was that she would go out occa-
sionally and get a quart of liquor—bad liquor, too—and drink it all
by her lonesome in her room. When she was drinking she was
pecky—quarrelsome, you know." When informed of the East 20th

WOMAN SLAIN, HEAD SOUGHT IN COAL BINS

Dismembered Body Identified From Fingerprints of Right Hand

NATIVE OF ASHTABULA

Cleveland Press headline, Jan. 27, 1936.

Street location where Florence's remains had been found, Mrs. Ford exclaimed, "I'll bet that's where she went to get her liquor. It was mean stuff."

But there was also a gentler side to Florence Polillo. She often talked to Mary Ford about her mother, and Mary had driven Florence to her mother's funeral in Pierpont, Ohio, in October 1935 because she felt sorry for her. And Florence loved dolls, possessing more than a dozen, which she had individual names for and dressed very elaborately. She would often allow Mrs. Ford's three daughters to play with them, and it must have been a poignant scene when the cops invaded her room and found her silent companions posed on the bed, chairs, and davenport.

Intensive police interrogation produced the paradoxical conclusion that while hundreds of Clevelanders were acquainted with Flo Polillo, practically no one really knew her at all. She changed her addresses and friends with impressive celerity. Returning to Cleveland in 1934 from Washington, D.C., she lived for some months at a hotel on Walnut Street with a blond, handsome man known as "Harry Martin," who reputedly beat her frequently. Florence had also been spotted with a young Italian several weeks prior to her death. There was a rumor of a barroom fight with a black man on the night of Saturday, January 25, and the police sought the whereabouts of other men linked to her—ephemeral men with intriguing names like "Captain Swing" and "One-Armed Willie." Nothing came of any queries.

Efforts to investigate the physical evidence proved similarly frustrating. One of the burlap bags found at the crime scene was eventually traced to the nearby Cleveland Feather Company at 1838 Central Avenue. A shipment of such bags had arrived there on January 17, and a peddler who had bought some of them subsequently resold them to a junk shop and another peddler. They could be traced no further. Another bag was eventually traced to the William Danches Poultry Company at 854 East 105th Street with equally fruitless results. The presence of coal fragments and imprints on the body parts stimulated a likewise frustrating search of every coal bin in the lower Central Avenue area.

Meanwhile, Coroner Pearse and the police had come to some definite conclusions about Torso No. 4. The first was that Florence's body parts had been placed at the Hart Company plant at about 2:30 Sunday morning, hence the barking of James Marco's dog at that hour. The body had been carved with a very sharp knife, Pearse surmised, but one wielded by an "amateur." No trace was ever found of the outfit worn by Florence when she was last seen alive on Friday night: a black cloth coat with gray collar, a black hat, and brown shoes.

As with the Lady of the Lake and the bodies of Andrassy and his unknown companion, the investigation into the mystery of Florence Polillo's murder petered out, as January waned. The police sweated a truck driver at the William Danches Poultry Company who had not shown up for work on Saturday, January 25—but his inevitable release was only delayed by the inordinate amount of time it took him to sober up. A fifty-eight-year-old dope addict and a suspicious chicken peddler were also arrested, questioned, and released. Three men with improbable descriptions were sought as alleged "lovers" of promiscuous Florence Polillo. And Cleveland detectives puzzled, to no avail, over a written record of payments made by Florence to an unfindable "Dr. Manzella." Interestingly, neither Coroner Pearse nor the police showed any interest—despite press queries—in linking the Polillo murder to the three torsos discovered thus far. As far as the authorities were concerned, they were all still isolated cases.

A break in Cleveland's prolonged cold spell produced new, if ultimately inconsequential, developments in the Torso No. 4 investigation. On Thursday, February 7, Leo Gaebelein, a twenty-three-year-old mechanic, decided to take a shortcut through the vacant lot at 1419 Orange Avenue. Walking by a fence, Leo noticed some human remains lying in melting snow in a pit, the remnant of a filled-in cellar. The police soon arrived to find all the rest—except the head—of Florence Polillo: the upper part of the torso, the lower legs, and the left arm and hand. The condition of the neck indicated either that death was caused by decapitation or that decapitation soon followed death. The torso was cut between the second and third lumbar vertebrae, and the head severed between the fourth and fifth cervical vertebrae. The arms and legs, Coroner Pearse judged, had been "expertly" severed at the shoulder, knee, and hip joints. There was an odd gash in the pelvic area, but it was impossible to say whether it was the gesture of a pervert or a mere slip of the knife by the perpetrator of the dismemberment. Detective Sergeant James T. Hogan was quick to state that there was no connection with the Andrassy & Co. corpses of the previous year.

The remains of the unfortunate Florence Polillo were returned to relatives in Pennsylvania for cremation and burial, and the trail of Cleveland's most famous serial killer disappeared again. No one spoke yet of a pattern or of Kingsbury Run. The last word on Polillo's strange demise came in the February 8 edition of the *Cleveland Press:*

> Sgt. Hogan was waiting, on the advice of doctors, for Captain Swing of 2135 Central Avenue, who had been on a prolonged drunk, to come into a more rational state before questioning him in the murder. Swing (Captain is his name, not a title) jumped out of a third floor window early Wednesday, saying he was "blown out," broke both his heels when he hit the ground, and mumbled things that tended to implicate him in the killing.

The head of Florence Polillo was never found.

Chapter 3

THE MANIAC
IN THE BUSHES
The 1921 Foote-Wolf Terror

Sooner or later, you will have this fear. You may be young, old, or in between; you may be male or female, puny or strong. But there will come a time—if it hasn't already—when you will be walking along some deserted, remote, and lonely way, probably in the dark, maybe in the rain or snow, and suddenly, walking along, occupied with your own thoughts, you will stop and listen. You will stop and listen . . . *because you think you hear footsteps.* The footsteps of someone you cannot see but you can hear. Footsteps that seem to cease whenever you try to hear them again. In that moment you will feel the fear of that formless, unknown bogeyman about to jump out and do you harm. . . *The maniac in the bushes.*

Most of us never actually find our maniac in the bushes, or at least he doesn't find us. We survive our terrors and make our way safely home, privately laughing—later—at our recent apprehensions. But sometimes there *is* someone in those bushes, and sometimes he catches his prey. He caught William Lowe Rice on a warm summer evening in 1910 on a pleasant Cleveland Heights boulevard and shot, stabbed, and bludgeoned that prominent lawyer to death. He found sweet-sixteen-year-old Janet Blood on a winter night at the corner of West 106th and Clifton and shot her just below her heart. He surprised Carl Bernthaler and Clara Ziechmann on a balmy spring afternoon in 1908 near a babbling brook in Cleveland Heights—and shot both of them through the heart. And, Cleveland legend would suggest, he ensnared at least a dozen largely anonymous victims and left their body parts scattered amid the wastes of Kingsbury Run. This, however, is the story of what may be his single most awful and mindlessly brutal deed: the murder of Mabel Foote and Louise Wolf on a lonely Parma road in 1921.

Parma in 1921 was unlike the Parma of today. Although the process of suburbanization was under way, it was still predominately rural, inhabited by small farmers and crisscrossed with inadequate, mainly dirt roads. Population density was low, most folks knew each other, and most families sent their adolescent children to the Parma Rural High School located at Bean (now Ridgewood) and Ridge roads.

By current standards, the high school was then a modest affair. Housed in two temporary buildings, it was staffed entirely by two teachers, Principal Louise Wolf, who taught the eleventh and twelfth grades, and Mabel Foote, who taught the ninth- and tenth-grade sections. Just a few hundred feet away, a new, modern Parma High School was under construction, but the small staff and modest physical plant betokened the fact that Parma's educational needs were still modest enough to be run by the Cuyahoga County Board of Education, rather than village or township personnel.

Louise Wolf and Mabel Foote were good women, well liked and just the sort of pious, no-nonsense, unmarried female schoolteachers desired by the conservative Parma parents of the day. A graduate of Ohio State University, Louise had been principal of Parma High for two years. Louise's life had not been an easy one: one of four siblings, she had tried heroically to keep her family together after her parents, Edward and Frederika, died when she was 13. But she failed, and one can imagine her heartbreak when siblings Katherine, Lottie, and John were sent to the Soldiers' and Sailors' Orphans Home in Xenia, Ohio, and three-year-old Edith was adopted by Mr. and Mrs. Charles Taylor of Cleveland. But Louise had grit, and after taking her degree at Ohio State she came to Cleveland in 1918 and worked as a teacher in Royalton Township and Chagrin Falls before coming to Parma. Louise kept house with Miss Effie Bufel at 4417 Ardmore Avenue and commuted to and from school every day by means of a trolley ride to State and Bean roads, followed by a two-mile walk to the school.

Mabel Foote, too, was a tenacious woman. The daughter of J. L. Foote, a truck gardener on Shaaf Road, Mabel lived with her family, though during this period she was spending her nights at a friend's house nearer to the schoolso she could spend extra rehearsal time with her pupils for an upcoming church performance. A graduate of Lincoln High School, Mabel had wanted to be a missionary from an early age. But she thought she needed teaching skills for her vocation, and so took a teaching degree from Baldwin-Wallace in 1920 and came to Parma High in the fall of 1920, after teaching several years in primary grades. An active and tireless member of the Pearl Road Methodist congregation and president of its Young People's Missionary Society, Mabel planned to leave for foreign missionary work in the summer of 1925.

Louise Wolf.

The routine of Wednesday, February 16, 1921—Mabel Foote's and Louise Wolf's last day on earth—was the same as ever; theirs was a schedule by which Parma residents could have set their clocks. Taking the "dinky" down State Road to Bean, Mabel and Louise disembarked and walked the two miles to school, arriving there well in time to greet their thirty students at 8:30 a.m. School was dimissed at 3:30 p.m., followed by more work for the two women, as they graded papers and prepared for the next day's teaching. At 5:00 they donned their coats, locked up the two school buildings, and began walking east on Bean Road to catch the 5:30 trolley. Dusk was coming on and a cold drizzle was falling. C. J. Ubinck, a nearby resident of Ridge Road, saw them leave the school. They were never seen alive again.

It probably didn't occur to anyone until later, but Bean Road was a perfect place for a murder. With few dwellings alongside it, and none at the murder site, it was flanked on both sides by orchards and farms. The badly rutted dirt road was closed in dramatically a few hundred yards east of Ridge Road by dense woods and muddy ditches on both sides. There, the road grade became markedly steeper, too. On the north side of the road, a raised six-foot embankment with a path and fence rail offered an easier footing than the muddy road below. So it is not surprising that Mabel Foote and Louise Wolf took the raised embankment path and began the climb that would take them to bloody, muddy, violent death.

No one knows exactly when and where the maniac in the bushes caught up with the two women. There was a real-estate allotment shack about 200 feet south of the road in a low gully, and the killer could have been hiding in there as Mabel and Louise walked by.

It was a ferocious assault. Using an array of saplings cut from nearby trees and a piece of the nearby fence rail, the murderer fell upon the two women shortly after they began climbing the embankment path. It was a struggle that lasted some time and must have involved heroic resistance on the part of the two women. Footprints found later, and the evidence of the trampled, bloody grass, indicated that the battle ranged over an area of 600 feet, as the three combatants fought their death struggle, crashing into and through the fence and knocking down posts and rails. Mabel Foote tried to use her umbrella as a weapon, breaking off all its points, and both women used fists, books, handbags, sticks, and stones in a frantic effort to beat off their maddened assailant. Back and forth the contest raged, as the maniac beat one of the women with his various clubs while the other tried to aid her beleaguered companion. It is likely that the two women screamed again and again—but there was no one on the deserted road to hear them besides their assailant.

The desperate struggle may have lasted for a quarter of an hour. Either one of the women could have survived had she been willing to leave the other to a terrible fate. But neither Mabel nor Louise would forsake each other as eventually the superior strength of their attacker prevailed, and they were literally beaten to death. Finally, Louise Wolf fell to the muddy earth, her skull smashed, the bridge of her nose crushed, five deep cuts on her head, bruises on her left hand, and broken knuckles, the latter injury caused by her frantic attempt to ward off death with her fists. Flesh from the murderer would later be discovered under her fingernails. Her pocketbook was found under her, one of her rubbers beside her, the other still on her foot. Several feet away was her black handbag, containing a nightdress and apron. She lay face down, arms stretched above her head, fists tightly clenched. Her garments were torn to shreds, and her watch, its hands stopped forever at 5:15—the probable time the attack commenced—was found 150 feet away from her corpse.

Eight feet away from her lay the body of Mabel Foote. She was probably knocked unconscious first and fell face down near the embankment fence. The murderer continued to beat her after she

Mabel Foote.

fell, and she suffered a twice-fractured skull, facial scratches and bruises, a broken nose, and lacerations all over her body. But Mabel may have initially survived the assault: a trail of blood leading away from the fence toward Louise's body and ending in a pool of gore next to Mabel's corpse suggested that she dragged herself toward her companion and managed to get to Mabel's satchel and use her nightdress to rub the blood off her face. But she soon lost consciousness again and died sometime that night, like Louise, from loss of blood and exposure on the freezing mud path atop Bean Road.

The maniac had finished his work as darkness and a heavy rain began to fall on Parma Township. He leaped from the embankment to the road below and began walking east on Bean Road for several hundred feet. He then turned south into the woods and disappeared. His muddy tracks indicated that he had a high instep and wore a broad-toed, high-heeled shoe.

All that cold, frozen night, Mabel and Louise lay bleeding and dying on that slimy embankment path, and no one came along to save them or raise the alarm. Since both of them often spent the night at friends' homes, there was no reason for their families to worry that they had not returned as the last hours of February 16 crept toward midnight. One can only hope that they soon succumbed to their ter-

Body of Mabel Foote, Bean Road, February 17, 1921.

rible injuries: the brave and selfless sacrifice of their lives for each other merited no less.

As horrible luck would have it, they were discovered the next morning by two of their students. Edward Ritenour, 14, and his sister Edith, 16, were on their way to school at about 8:30 on Thursday morning when they almost stumbled on the two bloody, bedraggled bodies on the embankment path. Initially just curious, they soon became frightened, and ran the quarter mile to school to bring the awful news. Given the dreadful condition of the bodies, Edward and Edith had not recognized the teachers. The first adult they told was Frank Owen, a carpenter, who was working on the new high school nearby. As it happened, he was married to Lottie, Louise Wolf's sister, so the bodies were soon identified. Frank soon returned with the police and curious onlookers, and together they brought the broken bodies back to the school. Owing to the muddy condition of Bean Road, both corpses had to be carried by volunteers the entire quarter mile without use of a wagon.

As might be imagined, both the Parma area and the rest of Cuyahoga County went crazy over this unusually brutal double homicide. Hordes of local vigilantes with shotguns, pitchforks, and even more quixotic weapons stalked the woods and roads of Parma for several weeks, frightening strangers and locals indiscriminately. Local officials obviously lacked the resources to mount a thorough investigation, and they quickly and gratefully accepted the aid offered by Cleveland police chief Frank W. Smith and Cuyahoga County sheriff Charles B. Stannard. And, given the usual tensions between city and county officials, it was probably as vigorous an inquiry as could have been mounted under the circumstances. But the circumstances weren't good: the murders were more than twelve hours old before being discovered, and there were never any significant clues—eyewitness or otherwise—to go on. So local officials, Cleveland detectives, and Cuyahoga County sheriff's deputies did their duty: they rounded up the usual suspects. It was assumed from the beginning that the murderer had some acquaintance with the victims and that he bore some physical evidence—scratches and bruises—of the terrific resistance waged by Louise and Mabel. The overlapping, competitive, and repetitive dragnets lasted several weeks, and they produced inconclusive and sometimes ridiculous results, such as the following:

Gladys Greene of Parma testified that she saw two "roughly dressed" strangers hurrying along Ridge Road at dusk on that fatal Wednesday. Both were hatless, and their clothing was torn and mudstained. Parma resident Fred Haas corroborated Greene's account and mentioned that one of the men had a "discolored" eye.

Cleveland Police Chief Smith and Cuyahoga County Sheriff Stannard gave the third-degree treatment to two men who lived near the murder scene, who were "unable to give a satisfactory account of their actions." They were eventually released.

Virtually every man with a scratched face in the state of Ohio was brought in for questioning. One was picked up on Ridge Road on Saturday, February 19. Another was picked up at a West Side coffeehouse; his companion was also rousted, because he had muddy clothes in his room. They were eventually released.

A report from Gallion, Ohio, brought news of a young man, again "roughly dressed," who had boarded a freight train in Linndale and been seen boasting a prominent facial scratch.

A vagrant was picked up in Marion, Ohio, with a scratched face and forwarded to Cleveland police for interrogation. He was eventually released.

A man in Cadiz, Ohio, was arrested when found wandering by the railroad tracks, muttering over and over, "I didn't mean to do it." He was eventually released.

There was great excitement in press and police circles when a bloody overcoat and five books—one containing the inscription "Present to Miss Mabel Foote, Christmas, 1907"—were found in a barn in Royalton. It was subsequently discovered that the blood came from chickens slaughtered in the barn and that the books had been taken from the Parma school house several years before.

Dozens of Parma men allowed themselves to be fingerprinted in the belief that this would help the police reduce the pool of potential suspects—which, in a way, was a sad confession of just how large and indistinct a pool that was. . .

Ralph Shanks, a stenographer from Detroit, was sent to the Warrensville workhouse for thirty days on April 25 by Cleveland City Court Judge A. Howells. Charged with "disorderly conduct," Shanks had barely escaped with his life on April 23, after frightening a Parma girl on Ridge Road. Pursued by the angry mob, Shanks was chased by an mob, armed with shotguns, through woods and swamp and thoroughly beaten before being rescued by the police. No other charges were filed, no one from the mob appeared to accuse Shanks, and his story was that he was "taking a walk and meant no harm."

And finally, Canton, Ohio police picked up a man with facial scratches on February 23, only to release him when he proved his injuries had occurred in the course of trimming trees.

True, more significant clues were also pursued by the frantic police, albeit with the same empty results. A chicken coop, discovered several hundred feet north of the murder site, furnished evidence that the murderer had hidden himself there after the killings, perhaps even washing away the telltale bloodstains at a nearby water pump. Charles Root of State Road came forward to tell police that he had seen a short, heavyset man, again "roughly dressed," walking out of the woods to the south of the murder site about 6:00 p.m. on February 16. And on February 22, the *Cleveland News* announced a new police probe of two construction laborers at the new Parma High School. They had been fired at 4:15 p.m.—just an hour before the killings!—and investigative officials hoped that they could find a

Murder weapons used by the killer of Mabel Foote and Louise Wolf, February 17, 1921.

motive lurking in their presumably disgruntled frame of mind. There was also a vigorous inquiry into the story that someone had scrawled obscene words on the school blackboard several weeks prior to the murder, but nothing came of that. Nor did a police probe into a rumor that someone at the school had recently stolen three dollars from one of the murdered schoolteachers produce a viable suspect.

It was already evident by the end of February 1921 that the investigation was going nowhere. By that date most of the dozen or so suspects had been released, and no better results were being obtained by taking new suspects to the scene of the crime for third-degree treatment. Cleveland police chief Smith got his hopes up about one suspect—a convicted axe murderer and chronic mental patient—and even announced his imminent arrest on February 28. But Smith's hopes came to naught, as did the brief hue and cry over a "wild man" who was seen peering into household windows in the Parma area as February gave way to March.

The tragedy of Louise Wolf's murder provoked an additional, albeit temporary, heartache in another family. Her sister Edith, adopted by the Charles Taylor family at the age of three, had never been told by them that Louise, who visited her often, was her biological sister. In the aftermath of Louise's murder, the Taylors agonized for days before telling the twenty-eight-year-old Edith the truth. To their shock, Edith calmly informed them that her sister Lottie had told her all about it some years before.

Given the almost freakish ferocity of the murders, it isn't surprising that the ensuing manhunt produced its share of oddities. Charles Foote, Mabel's uncle, haunted the murder scene for weeks by night, stalking the woods and frightening the locals with his flashlight. His activities, according to the *Cleveland Press,* "aroused fear, speculation and talk of a ghostly avenger," but they did not, alas, bring about the apprehension of his niece's killer. Charles, by his own admission, was a devotee of the quaint theory that every murderer must return to the scene of his crime.

Weirder still was the appearance of Mrs. May Patterson at the murder site on February 23. Posing initially as a magazine salesperson, Patterson eventually claimed that she was an operative of a private detective agency and that her efforts at sleuthing were aided by "psychic powers" and spectral visitations from the murdered victims. As Mrs. Patterson modestly related to a sympathetic *News* reporter:

> Each night for a week Miss Foote has come to me and begged me to seek out her murderer! When I close my eyes I can see her battling for her life in that lonely road. I can hear her screams as she tries in vain to beat off the youthful, light-haired assailant. In the visions that come to me nightly the face of the murder is blurred somewhat . . . Often I have closed my eyes and tried to see him distinctly but he is moving all the time.

Lest the admiring news hawk think she was but a one-trick pony, Mrs. Patterson further disclosed, "I write, too."

Probably the most disturbing phenomenon prompted by the double murder occurred on Monday, March 20. Classes at the high school had finally been resumed on February 28 with replacement teachers, and both students and teachers were trying hard to put the murder behind them. On the afternoon of March 20, a tall, dark woman entered one of the classrooms without warning and, seemingly, went into a trance. As the mystery woman described how the murder occurred and shrieked that some of the students present knew the murderer, teacher L. H. Seymour fainted dead away. As terrified pupils rushed forward to succor Ms. Seymour, the unknown

Where the bodies were found, February 17, 1921.

woman stalked from the classroom, never to be identified or seen again.

Even the most unusual murders are not immune to the cultural currents of the times, and the Foote-Wolf slayings were no exception. Both the *Plain Dealer* and the *Press* took advantage of the occasion to fan public fears of an allegedly enormous population of subhuman male defectives (or "half-men," as the *Press* liked to term them), uncontrolled by society and likely to prey upon innocent women and children at any moment. The *Plain Dealer* tried hard to compete with a scare headline ("OHIO MENACED BY IMBECILE HORDE"), but the *Press* carried away the yellow honors with its call for a policy of hardheaded eugenics to diminish the population of predatory morons exposed by the Foote-Wolf slaughter. After implausibly linking this double murder to the 1921 murder of Gretchen Brandt (stabbed through the heart by an unknown hand at her home on East 46th) and the slaying of Elsie Kreinbring on September 27, 1918 (stamped to death with hobnailed boots in her home on East 176th), the unidentified *Press* ideologue concluded that all such murders might well be the work of a genetically defective clan known to researchers as the "Sam Sixty" family:

This family numbered 471. Individuals about whom facts
were obtained numbered 261. Of these only three were of
normal intelligence. The criminalistic number 74. The
immoral numbered 77. The number with court records, 60.
Number in public institutions, 56.

It was hardly a stretch from such ominous statistics to the *Press*
conclusion that "some control by society of the increase of the
human family is imperative."

Whatever the agenda of the police, cranks, or the press, time went
by and no solution to the murders appeared. On March 2, a suspect
was captured in Hudson, Ohio, after a multicounty chase led by the
tireless Charles Foote. When in the custody of Cleveland police, the
suspect was covered with suspicious-looking blood—but even his
captors sheepishly admitted that he might have acquired it at their
hands in the chase. The Cleveland police soon decided that he was
not a valid suspect, and he took his leave of the Forest City with the
pleading words, "Please don't let the farmers get me." A week later
a man picked up by the police soon confessed to the killings. He said
he was the man seen coming out of the woods near State Road by
Charles Root on February 16. But a subsequent lineup before Parma
residents produced no recognition of the suspect, and the authorities
soon decided he had concocted his story from newspaper accounts.
By now, Parma residents and the police were becoming so dissatis-
fied with the investigation that there was even talk of exhuming the
bodies of Wolf and Foote for further clues.

The cops got the big break they had been waiting for on March 31.
Questioned initially for an assault on Mrs. Sophie Wolf of 3328 Poe
Avenue in Cleveland, suspect Arthur Ihlenfeld denied the charge, but
then unexpectedly blurted out: "I entered a house on Bucyrus Road
and I killed the Brooklyn schoolteachers."

Taken to the Bean Road scene of the murders, Ihlenfeld impressively reenacted the events of February 16. He was able to pick the
actual murder weapons—some tree saplings and a length of fence
board—out of a group of similar weapons and he seemed to have an
exact knowledge of the murder circumstances that could not have
been garnered simply from newspaper accounts. More impressively,
he was able to supply for details suspected but as yet unproven by
authorities. When queried as to how the two women could have
walked over the water-covered embankment path, he replied that
there had been no water there when he killed them—a circumstance
verified by local residents. Moreover, his hair matched samples on

the murder weapons, and he was able to explain a puzzling injury to Mabel Foote's hand as resulting from his pursuit of her through some barbed wire.

The problem for the police, of course, was that Arthur Ihlenfeld was the very "half-man" Cleveland newspapers had been blaring scary headlines about for weeks since the murders. A mental child with an estimated psychological age of four, he was unable to tell the same story with any consistency, and he retracted each version of his confession almost as soon as he uttered it. The basic version, however, went something like this:

> I met them on the road. I stopped them and threw back my coat. [The assumption is that Ihlenfeld exposed himself.] One of them said, "Get away, you nasty thing." She struck me and I hit her with a club and knocked her down. The other—the good looking one—ran and I chased her. As she started to crawl over the rail fence, it broke. I picked up one of the broken posts and followed her through the woods and back to the road again. As she was getting through an opening in the fence to get back to the road, her dress caught on some wires and tore and she tripped. I struck her on the head with the club and knocked her down.

Ihlenfeld's memory failed at this point; he could only say, vaguely, "Then both of them went away." The conclusion of everyone who interrogated Ihlenfeld was that he either killed the teachers, witnessed their murders—or came across their bodies in the road soon after.

It is to the credit of Parma and Cleveland officials that they handled Ihlenfeld's "confession" gingerly. He was an obvious imbecile, but the investigation had to go forward, and so it happened that Parma residents were invited to a "lineup" at the Parma elementary school on State Road on the night of April 2. There, two by two, Parma citizens were asked to walk by the suspect and say whether they had seen him in the area at the time of the murders. Three persons identified Ihlenfeld as being in the area at that time. One was Dr. S. O. Bludgeon; the second was Herman Greenwald; and the third was August Fuckow, a trolley motorman who had seen Ihlenfeld on his streetcar during the day of the murder.

The evidence from the Ihlenfeld lineup and official police investigations was turned over by a Cuyahoga County grand jury to Judge Florence E. Allen on April 6, 1921. The grand jury had adjudged

Ihlenfeld insane, and attorney William J. Corrigan—eventually to become prominent as the defender of Eva Kaber and Sam Sheppard—was assigned as his public defender. Referred to Judge Baer's court, Ihlenfeld was quickly declared insane by a jury and committed to Lima State Hospital for the Criminally Insane "until his reason is restored." The verdict came on April 13 on the second ballot after only an hour's deliberation.

And so it was over—or was it? In fact, no one has ever been sure that the right man was caught and there is no consensus yet as to who killed Mabel Foote and Louise Wolf. (Virtually all accounts of the murders for the last seventy years characterize them as "unsolved.") On January 28, 1922, almost a year after the Foote-Wolf murders, Sheriff Stannard announced that two men serving terms in the Ohio Penitentiary had confessed to the dual Parma homicides. These tales proved, alas, to be just more false confessions. Next came an anonymous letter received the following month by County Prosecutor Edward Stanton. Its writer purported to give up the goods at last about the long-sought killer: "I can give you information which will, I believe, lead to the arrest and conviction of the Bean Road murderers. One of them is not far away and the other is not hard to find."

After more coy preliminaries Stanton's correspondent got to the gist of the proposition:

> One: Will you keep my name absolutely secret in the whole matter?
>
> Two: Will you do all in your power to secure me the rewards offered for information leading to the arrest and conviction of the murderer?

A tender-hearted informer, the mysterious letter writer also insisted that Stanton provide a guarantee that the alleged killers would not suffer the death penalty. Stanton, who was convinced the writer was a "well-educated woman," refused to give such a promise. In any case, he never heard from his correspondent again.

In 1927 a prisoner at the Ohio State Penitentiary, apparently inspired by newspaper stories about the killings, attempted to "confess" his guilt. That same year, Parma police arrested a man in Elyria on suspicion of the murders. A woman named Edith Gerity of Bridge Avenue had seen this man two days after the murders and remembered that his forearm was bleeding. Six years went by and then one day she saw the same man in an automobile. She wrote down the license number and the suspect was quickly captured and given the

Parma Tragedy Told by Picture

"Parma Tragedy Told by Picture": sketch of murder scene from the *Cleveland Press*, February 18, 1921.

third degree. Nothing came of that, either.

Eleven years after the unsolved murders, a memorial to the slain teachers was placed and dedicated at the entrance to Brookside Park on West 25th in Cleveland. Using funds raised by the Women's Civic League of Brooklyn, trees and shrubs were planted by a granite fountain and three granite benches. The fountain was funded by the teachers of Cuyahoga County and the Alpha Kappa Sigma Sorority of Baldwin-Wallace College (Mabel Foote's alma mater), and the Gleaners Class of Brooklyn Memorial Methodist Church donated the benches. The fountain is dry today, but the memorial tablet placed there still proclaims its simple message :

In Memory of
MABEL FOOTE AND LOUISE WOLF
Died Feb. 16, 1921
ERECTED BY WOMEN'S CIVIC LEAGUE
OF BROOKLYN
Dec. 1, 1932

Who murdered these two decent, perfectly innocent women for no apparent reason? It wasn't robbery, as neither their rings, cash, nor watches were taken. It was not a strictly sexual crime, as both women were beaten but not sexually violated. The theories of the authorities at the time were probably correct. It was most likely someone who knew the schoolteachers, or at least knew them well enough to know their daily itinerary and the vantage points on the

Memorial tablet in Brookside Park for Mabel Foote and
Louise Wolf.

lonely stretches of Bean Road from whence they could be observed
unawares. The name of that someone will probably never be known,
but surely he was the Maniac in the Bushes.

Birth of a Legend

Kingsbury Run, June 5, 1936

June 5, 1936, was a nice day in Cleveland. It was sunny, breezy, and just that perfect sort of late spring day in the Forest City—the kind natives savor before the city settles into its usual two-month slump of hot, muggy weather. It was also a nice day *for* Cleveland. The Republican National Convention was about to open at Public Hall on June 8, and the thousands of delegates and reporters pouring into Cleveland brightened both the fortunes and the reputation of the Depression-scarred city.

Alum Cheeley, 11, and Gomez Ivory, 13, of Cleveland's southeast side shared the sanguine spirit of that cheerful morning. Which is why, no doubt, they decided to play hookey from their classes at Outhwaite School and go fishing instead. Grabbing their poles, they headed north toward Lake Erie, taking a shortcut by way of Kingsbury Run. It was about 8:30 a.m.

Cheeley and Ivory had gotten about 1,000 feet past where the Kinsman Road bridge passes over the Run when they saw what looked like a pair of pants, balled up and wedged underneath a willow bush. Cheeley and Ivory were only human, so their first thought, as Gomez recalled, was exactly what would have occurred to most kids and a lot of adults: "We see the pants all rolled up and we think maybe there's money in the pockets. So we take a fish pole and poke the bundle and out pops the head."

And it *was* a head: the head of a young, handsome male, with reddish brown hair, blue eyes, high cheekbones, a fair complexion, a prominent jaw, and a nose to match. And the eyes were staring, wide open. According to the next day's *Cleveland Press,* the lads instantly fled the gruesome scene, "their own eyes popping wide in horror . . . all thoughts of fishing forgotten." They ran back to Ivory's house and locked themselves in, cowering for eight hours. When Mrs. Ivory returned home at 5:00 p.m., they told her what had happened. She called the police.

The two patrolmen who brought the boys back to the Run had some trouble finding the head, as Ivory and Cheeley were still so shaken that they could scarcely remember where they had seen it. When found again, it had apparently not been disturbed since morning and was still in the same spot, near the Shaker Rapid Transit tracks and about two-thirds of a mile away from the site of the dual slayings nine months before at Jackass Hill. The pants, too, were still there and proved to be dark brown cashmere, relatively new, and equipped with a zipper. Soon found scattered not far away were three shirts, an old brown cap, a pair of bloody underwear, and a pair of tan oxford shoes, rather worn, with their laces tied together and a pair of socks stuffed inside. The bloody underwear was white with blue stripes and bore a laundry mark variously reported as "J. D. X." or "J. D. A." One of the shirts was a white knit polo shirt with a Park Royal Broadcloth label, ripped and bloody at the shoulders and collar.

A torso matching the unidentified head soon turned up. Two New York Central Railroad crane operators, Louis G. Mackey and Peter J. Fagan, were walking between the New York Central and Nickel Plate tracks by an old freight shed when they encountered a headless corpse lying chest down and partially concealed beneath a clump of sumac shrubs, brush, and leaves. The body was nude but unmutilated, except for six tattoos, and was found only about fifteen hundred feet away from its head. There was no blood on the ground, indicating that the unknown victim had been killed elsewhere and his head and torso then flung into the wastes of Kingsbury Run. A railroad worker's testimony that the head was not in the vicinity at 3:00 p.m. Thursday, and an eyewitness's report of a late-model Cadillac seen under the Kinsman Road bridge about 11:00 p.m. that same night suggested the latter time as the dumping hour.

After examining the head and torso at the county morgue, Coroner Pearse and the police drew some conclusions. The body was that of a well-nourished man in his mid-twenties, about five foot eleven, 155 pounds, and missing six molars. The contents of his stomach revealed that his last meal had been baked beans. Death had occurred late Wednesday, June 3, or early Thursday, June 4, and the physical evidence of the decapitation suggested it had been done while the victim was alive. The head had been cut off between the first and second cervical vertebrae. There was no evidence of drugs or alcohol in the victim's body, and nothing to suggest that he had been tortured or bound before being killed. As the fingerprints did not match any on file, Pearse and the police hoped that the head and tattoos might help identify their unknown homicide victim.

The tattoos, although promising, proved to be a baffling, contradictory dead end. It was almost as if they had been found on six different men. One on the left calf was the character "Jiggs" from the

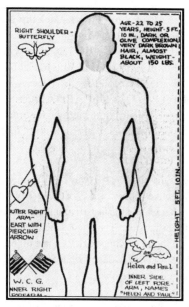

RIGHT SHOULDER - BUTTERFLY

AGE - 22 TO 25 YEARS, HEIGHT - 5 FT. 10 IN., DARK OR OLIVE COMPLEXION, VERY DARK BROWN HAIR, ALMOST BLACK, WEIGHT - ABOUT 150 LBS.

OUTER RIGHT ARM - HEART WITH PIERCING ARROW

HEIGHT 5 FT. 10 IN.

Helen and Paul

INNER SIDE OF LEFT FORE- ARM, NAMES "HELEN AND PAUL"

W. C. G. INNER RIGHT FOREARM -

Diagram of Torso Victim No. 5's tattoos.

comic strip *Bringing Up Father;* on the right calf was an anchor under a superimposed Cupid. On the right forearm was "Helen-Paul" over a dove, with a butterfly on the shoulder above. This orgy of personal decoration climaxed on the left forearm with crossed flags and the initials WCG with an arrow through a heart. Nothing fit together: if the victim's name was Paul, then who was WCG? And how did either of these tattoos fit with the "J. D. X." or "J. D. A." on the bloody underwear? Intensive sweeps by detectives through Cleveland tattoo parlors and laundries failed to turn up any explanatory clues. Nor did circulation of the details of the victim's dental work to area dentists.

You can't say Pearse and the cops didn't try. The day after the torso was found, the head was put on public display at the county morgue in hopes that someone could identify it. Two thousand Clevelanders passed by it Saturday night, churlishly and alliteratively characterized by the *Press* as "many . . . merely morbidly curious," followed by thousands more, until torso and head were buried in Potter's Field at Highland Park Cemetery on June 9. Before burial, Coroner Pearse had ballistics expert David C. Cowles take a death mask of the unknown head. It was subsequently seen by thousands of spectators at the Great Lakes Exposition of 1936–37 and is today exhibited at the Cleveland Police Museum at the Justice Center. No one has ever identified its original owner.

It can be stated definitively that the legend of Cleveland's "Torso Murders"—and the hunt for the "Mad Butcher of Kingsbury Run"—commenced on the afternoon of June 6, 1936, with the bold *Press* headline: "HUNT FIEND IN 4 DECAPITATIONS." In the ominous paragraph that followed, an unidentified writer created the menacing aura of almost supernatural evil and cunning that has graced all accounts of the "fiend" to this day:

> Somewhere in the countless byways of the crowded Southeast Side, detectives believe today, is the grisly workshop of a human butcher who in the last 10 months has carved up and decapitated four persons. The hand which removed from its body the head found in Kingsbury Run last night is the same hand which decapitated two men whose bodies were found in the same gully last September.

The reporter went on to link the three male torsos with the fate of Flo Polillo, and the genie of sensationalistic newspaper hysteria about the Torso killings was out of the bottle, to be kept at large indefinitely by a grateful press corps. Ever after, as Peter Bellamy (the author's father) later noted in an article, Cleveland's population would be "divided into torso suspects, torso experts, torso victims and newspapermen praying to God that the next torso won't show five minutes before edition time."

It didn't much matter to reporters that Cleveland authorities did not exactly agree on the details. (The one thing that they did agree on was that Torso No. 1, the Lady of the Lake, did not count—it couldn't have been the same killer.) Coroner Pearse was rather cautious, stating merely that the decapitations were all seemingly accomplished with a sharp knife. (As if this were a task that someone might possibly undertake with dull cutlery?) Sergeant Hogan, who had previously scoffed at linking the headless torsos together, and still excluded Flo Polillo from his personal torso tally, now told reporters that "a crazed killer with a flair for butchery is at work." Inspector Charles O. Nevel did even better, painting a fearful picture of a stalking killer who espied his latest victim alighting from a freight-car ride and deciding to take a restful snooze in the Run:

> While he was sleeping, this maniac attacked him. First he cut his throat. Then he hacked away at the neck. Then he

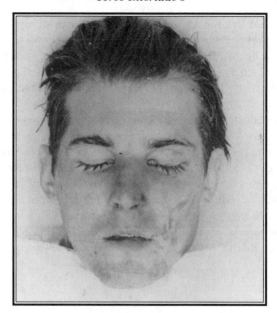

Head of "Tattooed Man," Torso victim No. 5,
displayed at the county morgue and Great
Lakes Exposition.

undressed the victim. After disrobing the man, the killer
wrapped the head and the victim's underclothing and shirts in
the man's trousers, walked across the New York Central
tracks and threw the bundle under a willow bush.

When interrupted by a reporter who wondered just why the
maniac had to undress his victim, Nevel snapped, "That's a maniac's
trick."

Coverage of specific details about the discovery of the fifth victim
evaporated from Cleveland's newspapers within a week, but the hunt
for his killer went on. As the evidence of the tattoos suggested a
naval background, information about the corpse was circulated by
the police to all Great Lakes ports, to no avail. As Cleveland parents
started warning their children to stay away from Kingsbury Run, city
editors started giving serious thought to the possibility of a Cleveland Jack the Ripper. And the professional joy of their reporters at
the arrival of the Mad Butcher was ultimately recorded in the glee-
ful paragraphs of "Mincemeat Marathon," Peter Bellamy's account
of those Depression days when every new headless torso or torsoless

head seemed like the answer to a newspaperman's prayer. Written for a Milwaukee Press Club newsletter. (He would never dare to publish such a light-hearted, sardonic article about mass murders in the town in which they took place!) It's obvious that Bellamy took a jaded view of the Torso-killer coverage, as reflected in the following:

> Opportunity to write color stories about the torso slayings is the answer to a "purple" newspaperman's prayer. There he has the perfect chance to write about "charnel houses of horror," "awful fear," "unspeakable dread," "grisly shambles," "unquenchable bloodlust" and "bloody holocausts." . . . While we will be irritated when the police get excited over a pile of ham bones found in Kingsbury Run and have to write shorts on silly tips and suspects, we won't complain about the Mad Butcher. My God, how that man can sell newspapers!

Chapter 4

"BRING OUT YOUR MAN!"

The 1887–1888 Saga of Bold, Bad "Blinky" Morgan

Charles "Blinky" Morgan died game. He also died hard. Refusing to the end to confess to his innumerable foul crimes, he was calm when Ohio Penitentiary warden E. G. Coffin and his guards came to get him at 1:00 a.m. on Friday, August 3, 1888. All he would say, as they led him to the scaffold in the penitentiary annex, was "This is awful business, Warden." As he stepped to the trap, his hands were bound, and the traditional black cap placed over his head. Dapper to the last, Blinky was suited in black and sported a white bouquet on his lapel.

His hanging was delayed for several minutes while James McGuire, a Columbus saloonkeeper and boisterous Blinky partisan, drunkenly objected to the presence of Detective Jack Reeves of Cleveland, who had sworn to be present when Blinky was hung. After several minutes, McGuire was ejected and the business went forward. At about 1:15 a.m., Blinky stepped forward to the trap and said, "Good-bye, Nellie." A second later the floor opened beneath him, and Blinky fell the length of the seven-foot drop. It wasn't far enough. Blinky had begged Warden Coffin for a nine-foot drop, a distance more likely to ensure that his neck would be instantly broken. But Coffin insisted on only seven feet, and so it was that Blinky survived the initial drop and slowly began to strangle to death in front of the forty-odd spectators.

As his hands had been freed after he dropped, so that doctors could take his pulse, the next few minutes furnished an awful spectacle for the hanging audience. That afternoon's *Cleveland Press* did justice to it:

> The straps slipped down from his legs. He squirmed and writhed for five minutes, making no motion until three minutes after the trap had been sprung. Once he raised his hand towards his throat and it took the full strength of a powerful

man to hold the arm down. Another held his legs to quiet their writhing. All the time his stomach pulsed in and out in his frantic efforts to get air past the rope that closed his throat. All motion ceased at the end of nine minutes but death did not come until 25 minutes had passed.

Blinky Morgan didn't have the last word on his demise. That belonged to Detective Jack Reeves. Hearing Blinky's final utterance—a farewell to his lover, Nellie Lowry—Reeves watched Morgan mount the trap, and, as it was sprung, muttered, "Good-bye, poor Hulligan." That was the best epitaph for both Blinky Morgan and the final act of nineteenth-century Cleveland's most sensational crime. For Blinky Morgan was, as the prosecutor who sent him to the scaffold proclaimed, a "bold, bad man," and readers of his colorful saga are likely to conclude that he got what was coming to him on that Friday morning in Columbus.

It is far easier to say what Blinky Morgan did than who he was. A career criminal and habitual liar, Blinky took great pains to embellish his own legend and promiscuously retailed conflicting versions of his life and misdeeds right up to the last minutes of his life. His real name may have been Charles McDonald. Perhaps it was Charles McDonald Williams. Or it may have been Charles Conkling. Blinky most often went under the name of Charles Morgan, although some claimed to have known him in childhood as Reuben Hazeltine of Farminton Township, Trumbull County. Other accounts said he came from Liverpool, England, or the small hamlet of Brantford in southern Ontario. In any case, he first came to the attention of Cleveland officials on July 9, 1872. Caught pickpocketing on a Cleveland streetcar, Blinky was chased by a Cleveland detective to an orchard, where he heaved a pickax at his pursuer and then opened fire with a pistol as they grappled. It took two detectives ten minutes to subdue pugnacious Blinky, and one of them was so enraged that he subsequently slugged the handcuffed miscreant in the left eye. And so it was that Charles Morgan earned the sobriquet "Blinky," in token of the injured eye which henceforth always looked half closed.

Or was it? Blinky was a champion prevaricator, and when boasting about his unlikely Civil War record would claim that his sinister eye was maimed by a prematurely exploding howitzer during his fourteen-month stint in the naval artillery. He told a more probable story to a *Plain Dealer* reporter on July 3, 1887:

The picture of utter Pickwickian benevo-
lence: Charles "Blinky" Morgan, June,
1887. Photograph taken by James F.
Ryder in the Cuyahoga County Jail.

> My eye was injured by powder. A premature discharge, as
> one calls it. I was blowing open a safe. I had a hole bored and
> powder in it which I had lit, but it did not go off. Thinking it
> had gone out I went up to "arrange" matters when it exploded
> and the flame burst out and hit me in my face.

Like Blinky's bad eye, the truth about Charles Morgan and his
misdeeds was both dim and a matter of perspective. Born in
Philadelphia, Pennsylvania, about 1834, Blinky, by his own account,
turned early to a criminal life under the influence of the media of his
day: "When I was very young I commenced reading dime novels and
read them until my mind was thoroughly poisoned. I thought of all
sorts of wild schemes and when I was sixteen I ran away from home
and went to Texas."

What Blinky did there is obscure, although his boast that he
"made many raids on the Mexican frontier" suggests a lifestyle of
frontier bravado. During the 1850s, he supposedly served some time

in a Mississippi jail before escaping. By 1860, he had become a hardened career criminal, and there was no turning back, as he ruefully confessed to a Cleveland reporter in 1887. "The life I led then had a great fascination for me," he stated, "but in late years it has become a painful necessity."

When the Civil War erupted, Blinky rallied to the North's cause—or so he later said. His most impressive story asserted that he was in Charleston, South Carolina, when Fort Sumter was fired upon, and that he tried—unsuccessfully—to steal a boat and bring fourteen men to its relief. Another entertaining tale (and probable lie) was that he was in New Orleans when the war broke out, and that he patriotically stowed away on a British freighter to avoid living under the Confederacy: "I had no use for the South when rebellion was the issue." His stories of escape from Dixie were as likely as his alleged fourteen-month stint in the Union naval artillery. Major W. T. Wilson of the United States Secret Service averred after Blinky's death that he had known Morgan as a notorious bounty jumper during the Civil War who later served bravely in the army and ended the war as a nurse. All or part of any story about Morgan may or may not have been true.

Blinky's whereabouts and activities in the 1870s came intermittently to the attention of Cleveland authorities. Blinky admitted to living there for about six years, and James Dickinson, longtime Cleveland fire chief, would later recall that Blinky ran a whorehouse on the West Side, presumably when he wasn't getting incarcerated for pickpocketing and resisting arrest.

By the early 1880s, Blinky was a coleader of the infamous and feared Morgan-Lowry gang of the Midwest. His main partner in crime, Martin (also known as "Charlie") Lowry, a notorious and expert safecracker, was married to a woman from Elyria named Nellie; she would come to play a prominent role in the Blinky Morgan story. Nellie was one of seven sisters from an Elyria, Ohio, clan, most of whom were also married to career criminals. Reported by the *Cleveland Leader* to be "a remarkable woman with a fair face and a magnificent figure," Nellie must have been a woman of parts. She must also have been a female of pleasing address and iron nerve. On one occasion she managed to persuade state senator O'Hagan of Sandusky to plead with Ohio governor Bishop to pardon her husband, Martin. O'Hagan's petition, alas, was successful, no doubt because it averred sweet Nellie was "a woman of good character and the wife of a man who had been led astray by force of circumstance."

It is said that Governor Bishop bitterly reproached O'Hagan when he found out the truth . . . but by that time Nellie and Martin had achieved greater things. When Blinky and Martin hit a railway express office in the early 1880s, they escaped with $700 and three watches. But not for long; they were soon shackled and bound in the Mercer, Michigan, jail. Martin faked illness, and a compassion visit by his wife was granted. That was a mistake: Nellie smuggled seven revolvers into the cell, and only three days before trial Blinky and Martin exited Mercer in a blaze of gunfire.

Shortly afterwards, Blinky and his gang went up to New York State to blow a safe. On the way, Blinky quarrelled with a plug-ugly named Nailer, but, professional that he was, decided to wait until the job was done: "We are after money now; when the work is done, I'll settle this quarrel with you." That truce ended with the division of the swag, and when Nailer treacherously violated the terms of an arranged duel, Blinky shot and buried him on the spot.

Blinky's luck ran out in 1883. On August 7 he was arrested in Toronto for shooting and killing a porter in a street brawl. Pursued by Constable Alf Cuddy, Morgan shot at but only grazed him and was soon apprehended. It is recorded that the jury returned a verdict of first-degree murder, but the judge threw it out and sent the jury back until they returned with a five-year sentence, Blinky's punishment for shooting at Cuddy. Sent in October 1883 to the Kingston Penitentiary under the alias of Charles Andrews, Blinky soon made friends with one Matthew Kennedy, alias Harry McMunn. They escaped from Kingston on October 29, 1885, by digging a tunnel under the penitentiary wall.

Sometime in 1886, Blinky gravitated back toward Cleveland. Many of the Morgan-Lowry gang were already there, as was Nellie Lowry. Now the proprietress of a whorehouse on Hamilton Street, Nellie welcomed Blinky back as her man. And why not: her husband Martin was by now doing a twelve-year term for burglary in the East. Also in Morgan's Cleveland orbit was John Coughlin, another career criminal and Nellie Lowry's brother. Probably also hanging around as 1887 loomed were Harry McMunn, Pat Hanley, and a man called William Harrington. Rounding out the gang was James Robinson of Pittsburgh. A professional gambler and small-time crook, Robinson was said to come from a respectable Dayton family. It was hard for reporters to fit him with his uncouth partners in crime, as one *Plain Dealer* reporter noted:

When a reporter of this paper met and talked with him he wore an expensive beaver overcoat, trimmed with fur, a fine diamond glittered on his neck scarf and his apparel was altogether that of a rather loud swell. He is quiet in demeanor and can talk intelligently on almost any subject.

Robinson had reputedly been chastened by the recent death of a fellow safecracker while they were being pursued across a river by deputies. He was said to be thinking of going straight.

All the elements for a criminal tragedy were in place by late January 1887. Toughs like Blinky and his gang could not hang around any place long without finding trouble, and it came soon enough. There had been a growing number of burglaries and assaults in downtown Cleveland under the languid regime of Superintendant of Police Jacob Schmitt, and it didn't take long for Blinky and his men to pick a suitable target.

The crime that ended with Blinky's seven-foot scaffold drop began on a cold Cleveland winter morning. At 7:00 a.m., Saturday, January 29, 1887, Edward Talchan, an employee at Benedict and Ruedy's fur store on the north side of Superior Street just west of Public Square, arrived at work to find the door ajar. Walking into the room, Talchan stumbled over a pile of sealskin sacques (short, loose-fitting women's jackets) on the floor and immediately noticed all the sacques usually displayed on the wall were gone. Talchan telephoned the police, and when a squad of five arrived it was discovered that 356 sacques, valued at $8,000, were missing. Examination of the premises disclosed that a hole had been bored in the front door and a set-screw employed to force the lock catch out of alignment. The hinge knobs on the safe had been removed, but the safe had not been opened.

It was a major humiliation for the Cleveland police force. Benedict & Ruedy's store was quite near Central Station and the conjunction of four patrol beats and two commercial police beats. The heat was on to find the culprits and it soon produced results. It had long been suspected that Cleveland thieves were smuggling their hauls out through the small railroad depots that dotted small towns to the south, west, and east of Cleveland. So when Patrolman Joseph Whittaker spied a horse and wagon plodding down Broadway toward Cleveland at 3:00 a.m., Sunday, January 31, he became suspicious. His suspicion increased when he stopped and questioned the driver, Thomas Story. Story told Whittaker that he had been hired to take some furniture to a house near the Newburgh insane asylum.

When he couldn't find the alleged house for Whittaker, the patrol-man took him in and booked Story on suspicion with $3,000 bail.

During his subsequent interrogation, Story confessed that he had transported two trunks to the Cleveland & Pittsburgh (C & P) rail-road depot in Bedford, but he didn't know any more.

By Sunday evening, Cleveland police did. At 7:00 p.m., John Matthews of Bedford told them that he had seen three men in a wagon drive up to the Bedford C & P depot late the night before. Two of the men had unloaded two heavy Saratoga trunks and checked them through to Allegheny City, Pennsylvania. The same men had later taken the 11:10 p.m. No. 42 train to Pittsburgh, and the wagon and driver had disappeared.

Within hours of Matthews's information, Allegheny City police were alerted. Captain Henry Hoehn of the Cleveland police and C & P Bedford baggagemaster John Kinney left for Allegheny City, where one of the trunks had been traced. Arriving on Monday night, Hoehn got there just in time to be in on the arrest of Harry McMunn, who was living at the rooming house of Annie Smythe, where one of the Saratoga trunks had been taken. There were no furs in evidence there, but Kinney identified McMunn as one of the Bedford men, and he was arrested and booked. The Cleveland police were notified, and Detective William H. Hulligan was sent to Columbus to obtain an extradition order for McMunn. Hulligan took the order to Pittsburgh, and Hoehn and Hulligan left Pittsburgh for the return trip with McMunn in custody late Thursday night, February 3. All three boarded the No. 28 smoking car on Train No. 41, a C & P passenger run routed through Alliance and Ravenna for an early morning arrival in Cleveland.

The two policemen and their prisoner were seated on the left side of the smoker, Hulligan on the aisle, with his left wrist manacled to McMunn's right wrist. Captain Hoehn sat opposite them, facing the back of the train. All went well until No. 41 pulled into Alliance for a fifteen-minute stop at about 2:00 a.m. Several minutes before its arrival, another westbound passenger train out of Pittsburgh on the Pittsburgh, Fort Wayne & Chicago line stopped in Alliance, and from three to five men alighted from it and boarded C & P No. 41. Three of them walked into the ladies' car behind the smoker, and one of them entered the smoker. Baggagemaster John Kinney, traveling back to Cleveland, saw the man in the smoker make some kind of signal to McMunn and then exit the car, making further hand motions to McMunn through the window. Kinney immediately went to the station lunchroom and notified Captain Hoehn that there were "suspicious" persons about. Hoehn returned to the smoker, and No. 41 left Alliance minutes later bound for Ravenna.

The assault came just before the train left Ravenna, and everything happened in a matter of seconds. The three men in the ladies' car got to their feet, each took a pull from a whiskey bottle, and they entered the smoking car. Marching up to McMunn and his captors, they pulled out revolvers and put a gun in Harry McMunn's hand, and one of them hit Detective Hulligan in the head with what appeared to be a rolled-up newspaper.

It wasn't a newspaper. It was a seven-pound, six-ounce iron coupling pin, filched from the Baltimore & Ohio Railroad and wrapped in a day-old edition of the *Cincinnati Enquirer.* Even as it crashed into Hulligan's skull, Captain Hoehn found himself looking at the barrels of several pistols leveled at his head.

Henry Hoehn was a brave man. He was already getting out of his seat and drawing his revolver when he heard Hulligan's first scream of pain. Hoehn was shot in the shoulder by one of his assailants but was already getting off his first rounds when he, like Hulligan, was struck in the head with a coupling pin. At this point the lights in the car went out, methodically smashed to pieces by one of the assailants. Down went Hoehn, firing wildly, as the car erupted in a melee of gunfire and the screams of wounded, frightened men. Another slug ploughed into Hoehn's thigh, but he kept shooting until knocked unconscious by another blow to the head.

It was a night of terrible sounds and sights for the witnesses. One of them was Rev. Carl Weiss of the Harbor Street Independent Protestant Church on Cleveland's West Side. He had just awakened in the smoker at the Ravenna station when he saw some men rush into the car with "newspapers" in their hands. As he got to his feet, a gunman approached him and said, "If you move hand or foot I'll kill you." Rev. Weiss immediately got down between two seats and tried to shield himself from the indiscriminate gunfire (estimated at fifteen to twenty rounds) now exploding in the darkened car. *The Plain Dealer* would henceforth unkindly refer to him as "Rev. 'Under-the-Seat' Weiss" and disparage his clerical presence in the smoker, but it is hard to see what else Weiss could have done, other than get himself killed. He later claimed that one of the ruffians hit him in the face.

Conductor Louis Ohliger was a braver man. Hearing the commotion in the smoker, he leaped onto its rear platform, where a pistol was put to his head. Brushing it aside, he tried to enter the car, whereupon the gunman fired at him but missed. Ohliger then fled to

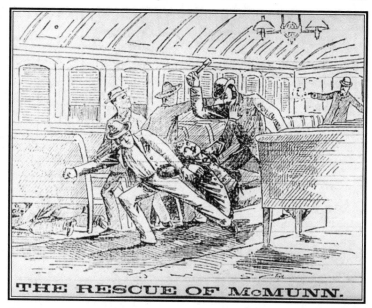

The rescue of McMunn. *Cleveland Press,* October 15, 1887.

the Ravenna waiting room, where he borrowed a pistol, which, unhappily, did not work.

It probably wouldn't have made a difference. The tragedy required but a few minutes' bloody work. One member of the assault team kept passengers and crew at bay, standing on the platform outside the smoker, "shooting each way," and screaming "Stand back or I'll kill somebody! Now hurry up and get your man out, as my shots are almost gone. I can't stay any longer. Bring out your man!" The platform shooter was later identified as Blinky Morgan.

Inside the car, in the dark, three or four men finished their work on Hoehn and Hulligan. Shot three times, his head beaten to a bloody pulp with coupling pins, Hoehn lay unconscious in a pool of his own gore. Hulligan, beaten even more severely and handicapped by being manacled to McMunn, fared even worse. Despite his terrible wounds, he continued to struggle, and was continuously beaten with coupling pins even as he and McMunn—still handcuffed together— were dragged through the darkened car to the platform outside. There, the key to the cuffs was removed from Hulligan's bloody body, and Harry McMunn and his rescuers fled down the C & P tracks into the darkness of the February night.

Blinky and his cohorts almost got away with it. Despite a hue and

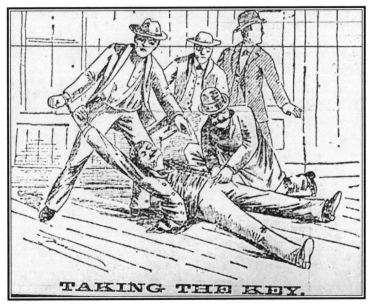

Taking the key. *Cleveland Press*, October 14, 1887.

cry that soon enveloped five states, nothing was heard of the guilty parties for almost five months. Despite numerous "sightings" of the fugitives in Hudson, Atwater, Macedonia, Wellsville, Greenville, Garrettsville, Cyclone, Brooklyn, Kent, Talmadge, Kensington, and elsewhere, the rousting of every itinerant hobo in the state of Ohio, and not a few false arrests, not a single legitimate clue was turned up by Cleveland's Finest or any other police force. It didn't help, of course, that sketches of the suspects, circulated widely throughout the Midwest, ultimately bore little resemblance to the actual culprits. Captain Hoehn would later claim that his descriptions of his assailants, made from a hospital bed, were inexplicably altered, but the fact remains that hundreds of people wasted thousands of hours searching for the wrong men over the next few months. The earth seemed to have swallowed them up. Public confidence in police sleuthing was not increased by widespread speculation that Hoehn and Hulligan's assailants had possessed inside knowledge of their movements on the fatal night. Such suspicions were unequivocally spelled out on February 10 by the *Cleveland Press*, which quoted a Cleveland police official as saying "It does look mighty funny, and it seems as if this gang had confederates in various police departments."

Meanwhile, Cleveland officials and journalists fanned public terror and vigilante fervor. Mayor Brenton D. Babcock urged police to get tough with miscreants: "Give them the scarlet hue that they may be easily recognized and captured. Make the temperature like that they will possibly eventually be consigned to. Starve them out."

Not to be outdone, *The Plain Dealer* trumpeted a do-it-yourself vigilante ethic for the Cleveland citizen:

> The burglar once in the house is a possible murderer. Prepare for his coming and prevent his becoming such by shooting him down in self-protection. The law justifies it. Don't wait for the possibility of the police detecting and arresting the robber and may-be murderer. The chances are too great. Settle him at once.

The *Cleveland Leader* echoed these sentiments to the last word:

> Meanwhile, honest citizens should remember that the man who kills a burglar in his house, or while attempting to enter it by force at night, does society good service . . . Let the police and the courts and all good citizens unite to the best of their ability in crushing out burglary by fear, by imprisonment, or, if need be, by death.

Cleveland police, increasingly humiliated by their lackluster performance in the affair, petulantly complained that media exposure of police methods and intentions was giving criminals an unfair advantage. As *The Plain Dealer* explained it:

> The mayor is of the opinion that a detailed account of the movements of the officers might serve as a warning to the robbers, who undoubtedly have confederates in the city, and so defeat the ends of justice. "I don't think it's quite fair," said Captain of Detectives McHannan, "to let the robbers know everything we are doing. If we had an account of their movements now, there would be more justice to it."

Cleveland newspaper readers might have been less than impressed by such bitter remarks had they known—as was revealed by the *Cleveland Press* seven months later—that Police Superintendant Jacob Schmitt had received a tip-off about the transfer of the stolen furs to Bedford as early as Saturday afternoon, January 30.

Schmitt's failure to follow up on this information would eventually cause the *Press* to demand his resignation—with no effect—on October 19, 1887.

Meanwhile, the mess from Ravenna had to be cleaned up. Captain Hoehn gradually recovered from two terrible scalp injuries and three bullet wounds. Within weeks, he was put on paid leave and soon commenced his own multistate search for his assailants. Things did not go as well with Hulligan. The forty-one-year-old detective had multiple skull fractures, one on the left side running all the way from front to back. His physicians were amazed that he survived his journey from Ravenna to Cleveland, much less that he battled for life until 9:32 a.m., Tuesday, Feburary 8. He died, leaving a wife and five children between the ages of eleven and twenty. The major Cleveland newspapers all joined in raising a fund for the support of his family, and a house and trust fund were eventually presented to the grateful Hulligan family.

The hunt for Hulligan's killers ground on. The summer months of 1887 dragged by, while enthusiastic police forces continued to arrest dozens of innocent civilians throughout the Midwest as suspects in the Ravenna crime. And the Cleveland police continued to harass all occupants and visitors at 168 Hamilton—Nellie Lowry's house of ill repute—while the reward fund for Hulligan's killers swelled past $15,000.

The big break finally came on June 27, when Police Superintendant Schmitt received a telegram from Deputy Sheriff J. E. Denton of Alpena, Michigan. The news was that Denton had three of the men wanted in the Hulligan murder in custody: Blinky Morgan, Pat Hanley, and Billy Harrington. Detective Hoehn was dispatched to Alpena, and the great denouement of the Blinky Morgan saga was under way.

It was a fascinating wrinkle, even in a tale as outré as this. Some weeks previously, Sheriff Charles C. Lynch of Alpena had been approached by a citizen suspicious of four men staying at the house of Mrs. F. D. Williams. (It was subsequently learned that she was yet another one of Nellie Lowry's erring sisters.) Discreet inquiries soon revealed that one of the men had a bad eye and had been variously introduced by Mrs. Williams to her Alpena neighbors as both her brother-in-law and her cousin. Sheriff Lynch's suspicions were focused even more sharply on the house when Mrs. Williams's four-year-old son was overheard bragging about his "Uncle Blinky Morgan." Lynch put the Williams house under twenty-four-hour surveillance, contacted Cleveland police, and awaited further events.

Blinky Morgan's capture. *Cleveland Press*, October 16, 1887.

These events came thick and fast on June 27. Blinky and his cohorts had been in Alpena for some weeks, exciting suspicion on account of their crude behavior and unwillingness to be out of each others' sight. On the afternoon of the 27th, they even paraded around the center of Alpena, "drinking pretty freely and acting very boisterous." Sheriff Lynch decided to move in after sunset.

They caught Blinky sitting in a chair when Sheriff Lynch and his deputies walked into the Williams house. Blinky later told reporters that he surrendered peacefully because there were children in the room. In fact, as soon as he saw Lynch, Blinky went for the gun in his right pocket as Lynch lunged for Blinky's throat. As they both toppled to the floor, Blinky shot right through his pocket, wounding Lynch in the thigh. Blinky managed to get off two more shots before Deputy Sheriff James O'Connor wrestled the gun away and Blinky said, "I give up." Two of Blinky's Alpena entourage, James Robinson and John Coughlin, were simultaneously but peacefully arrested as they attempted to board *The City of Mackinaw,* a boat on Lake Michigan.

The news hit Cleveland like a bombshell. "You're shoutin' I do!" exclaimed Superintendant Schmitt when reporters asked him if he believed the initial report of Blinky's capture. Unfortunately, it soon developed that Cleveland officials' identification of Blinky's two cohorts as Pat Hanley and Billy Harrington was wrong. The error was soon rectified and forgotten when Captain Hoehn arrived in Alpena to identify all three captured men as among his Ravenna attackers. Hoehn had searched all over the United States for Hulligan's killers for almost half a year, and it was with great satisfaction that he confronted Blinky in the Alpena lockup on June 28, as the next day's *Press* recounted:

> Hoehn: Blinky, they have you rather in hard luck.
> Blinky: Yes, they have the lines drawn rather tight just now.

Taken back to Cleveland under heavy guard, the three prisoners were eventually transferred to the Ravenna jail to await trial. Fears that the three men might either be lynched by irate citizens or rescued by other gang members proved unfounded. Meanwhile, Blinky killed the tedious summer hours by granting highly imaginative interviews to curious reporters and smoking innumerable cigars, which he cadged from his visitors. He appeared unruffled but refused to allow his picture to be taken until Sheriff Sawyer bribed him with a dinner catered by a local restaurant. Meanwhile, back in Michigan, Sheriff Charles Lynch died of complications from his leg wound in a Detroit hospital on August 17, leaving a wife and child.

Blinky's trial opened on October 10, 1887, in the Portage County Courthouse in Ravenna. Heading the prosecution for Portage County was E. W. Maxson, assisted by John McSweeney, Judge John C. Hutchins, and Isaac Siddall. For the defense was Samuel Eddy of Cleveland, assisted by James H. Nichols and E. G. Johnson. As Blinky, Robinson, and Coughlin all insisted on separate trials, the prosecution decided to try Blinky, the apparent ringleader, first before Judge J. R. Johnston.

Had there not been overwhelming local prejudice against the accused, it might have been tough to convict Blinky. Although he was wanted in a number of places for various crimes and prison escapes, he had not been publicly identified as a Ravenna culprit or connected with the fur robbery until apprehended in Alpena. He, like Robinson and Coughlin, did not resemble the pictures circulated of the Ravenna rescuers, and the latter two had been consistently misidentified as Hanley and Harrington until they were brought to Cleveland. But Blinky had a record as long as his arm and was daily brought to the courthouse through Ravenna mobs that screamed

BLINKY ARRIVES AT CLEVELAND.

Blinky arrives in Cleveland. *Cleveland Press*, October 17, 1887.

"The murderers ought to be burned at the stake!" and "Hang them!" As defense attorney Johnson later commented, "If St. Peter and St. Paul had been there and testified in Blinky's behalf he still would have been guilty."

Sam Eddy was probably the best defense lawyer in Ohio, and he hammered hard at the more tenuous links in the prosecution's case. Because Harry McMunn was the vital link between Blinky, the fur robbery, and the Ravenna atrocity, Eddy tried hard to keep testimony about the fur robbery and McMunn out of the record, but Judge Johnston ruled otherwise—allowing an 1882 photograph to stand in for the missing McMunn—and the jury, empaneled on October 15, heard a parade of witnesses portray McMunn as both squarely at the center of the fur robbery and intimately acquainted with Blinky Morgan. As ever, the nonplussed Blinky tried to make a good impression on his "twelve good men and true":

> "Blinky" Morgan appeared in court, togged in the latest style. His hair was beautifully combed and plastered over his alabaster brow. His "nigh" and "off" eyes glared through his spectacles. His low cut vest rendered perceptible his immaculate shirt front and a snowy stand-up collar encircled his neck.

Although the evidence linking Blinky to the Benedict & Ruedy job and Harry McMunn was shaky, the prosecution had little trouble placing Blinky in Bedford on January 30 and in Ravenna on February 4. C & P Conductor Louis Meyers testified he had seen three men, one of them Blinky Morgan and another Harry McMunn, get on Train No. 42 at Bedford the night the furs were shipped to Allegheny City on the same train. Conductor Lawrence Schuster of the Pittsburgh, Fort Wayne & Chicago Railroad swore he had seen Blinky and two other men on the smoking car that arrived in Alliance at 2:00 a.m. on February 4. Brakeman R. R. Todd of the same train followed Schuster on the stand and testified that he adjusted a seat for Blinky and that he thought it odd at the time that the three passengers should be taking the Pittsburgh, Fort Wayne train to Alliance, as most passengers took the more direct C & P route.

That terrible morning in Ravenna was recalled by Joseph Rauck of Bellevue, who saw Blinky and two other men board the No. 41 C & P train at Alliance and later saw Blinky enter the smoker about three miles from Ravenna. Rauck subsequently heard scuffling and a shot, but was warned away from the smoker door by a man who threatened to blow his brains out.

John G. Watts of Bristol, Indiana, testified that he was sitting a few seats in back of Hulligan, Hoehn, and McMunn when three men entered the No. 28 smoker. He identified Morgan as the man who fired the first shot at Hoehn and also remembered Blinky as the one who first hit Hoehn with a coupling pin. When pressed by defense attorney Eddy as to why he was so sure there had been a man guarding the smoker door during the struggle, he blurted out, "Because I wanted to get out pretty bad, and I took a general survey of the whole ground."

Perhaps the two most intriguing witnesses against Blinky were Nellie Campbell and Maud Smith. They were together on the ladies' car during that fateful journey to Ravenna, and Nellie's testimony vividly recalled the middle-aged gent—Blinky Morgan—who had kindly offered to get her a glass of water when she awoke from a sound sleep en route from Alliance to Ravenna. Samuel Eddy's cross-examination of both women was brutally skillful. He quickly established in the jury's mind that Campbell and Smith were prostitutes and that their memories of the critical night might have been impaired by excessive drink:

> Eddy: You are in the habit of getting intoxicated?
> Campbell: Sometimes.

Eddy: Haven't the officers told you that if you didn't testify
they would arrest you every opportunity they have?
Campbell: No sir, they never told me anything of the kind.

Maud Smith backed up Campbell's testimony in every detail, but
not before Eddy forced her to admit that her snooze on Train No. 41
had been preceded by "three or four glasses of beer . . . maybe more."
But when all was said and done, the prosecution had stitched a firm
tapestry of testimony that placed Blinky Morgan on the trains from
Bedford to Allegheny City, and from Pittsburgh to Alliance, and in
the fatal smoking car at the Ravenna station. And Nellie Lowry probably did Blinky no good when she shocked the courtroom audience
on October 21 by suddenly and loudly kissing him on the lips.

The most crucial element in sending Blinky Morgan to the drop
was Captain Hoehn's testimony. His memories of Blinky during
those terrible moments in the smoker were detailed and physical: he
remembered grabbing the moustache of the "oldish" man who hit
him with a coupling pin, and he further recalled Blinky biting his finger and shouting "Goddamit, he is getting the best of me!" He
remembered that it was Blinky who shot him in the hip, and he also
recalled seeing Blinky on a Pittsburgh street the day before their violent encounter.

The most bizarre aspect of Blinky's defense was that it was no
defense at all. Not a single witness, much less Blinky himself, took
the stand to swear that Blinky had been anywhere other than charged
on the nights of January 29 and February 4. Many witnesses took the
stand to swear that both John Coughlin and James Robinson had
been, respectively, in Elyria, Ohio, and Allegheny City, Pennsylvania, on February 4—but no one came forward to aver that Blinky had
not been on the Ravenna platform, shooting in both directions and
shouting "Bring out your man!"

Eddy's cross-examination of Carl Grimm, a prosecution rebuttal
witness, was a minor disaster. Grimm testified that Thomas Story
had met with Harry McMunn at Grimm's Woodland Avenue tavern
on the afternoon of January 29 to arrange for the transit of the stolen
furs to Bedford. Eddy's questioning elicited the unwelcome information that Story had been seen with Nellie Lowry in Grimm's tavern on numerous occasions prior to the fur robbery. And when Eddy
asked with pointed sarcasm why Grimm seemed so well acquainted
with the Cleveland police, Grimm retorted, "Why Chief Schmitt
used to come to my place almost every night. He used to come and
drink beer."

After the last rebuttal witness appeared on Friday, October 29, Samuel Eddy stunned the court, and the mostly female spectators, by resting the case without final arguments from either side. Judge Johnston's charge to the jury properly focused on "reasonable doubt" and the element of "malice" necessary for a first-degree murder conviction, and the jury went out at 9:40 a.m. on Tuesday, November 2.

After only two ballots, they returned with a verdict of guilty in the first-degree murder charge exactly eighty-three minutes later, at 11:03. The vote was eleven to one for first-degree murder on the first ballot and twelve to zero on the second. According to *The Plain Dealer*, Blinky took the decision manfully: "Not a muscle moved, not a feature changed, but his piercing eyes flashed fire for an instant, while those of the jurymen were suffused with tears."

Informed opinion had it that the crucially persuasive evidence of "premeditated malice" was the appearance in the courtroom of one of the bloodstained coupling pins, an exhibit Samuel Eddy had fiercely but unsuccessfully fought to keep from the jury's eyes.

Eddy filed an appeal immediately, citing "irregularities" in the trial and misconduct by the prosecution and its witnesses. Blinky returned to the Ravenna courtroom on November 23 at 4:00 p.m. to hear Judge Johnston reject his appeal and sentence him to the Ohio Penitentiary, ". . . where he shall be safely kept until the sixteenth day of March, 1888, and on that day before sunrise he shall be hanged by the neck until dead."

Ever the stoic, Blinky was said not to twitch a muscle while he received Johnston's fatal sentence. The next day, he was taken to the Ohio State Penitentiary in Columbus, where a special fifteen-foot-high cage had been built to isolate him from the other penitentiary prisoners and any potential rescuers. No one was allowed to touch or speak to him, and he was compelled to lie on a cot at all times, watched by a guard who pulled an alarm every fifteen minutes. But Blinky enjoyed his last railway journey with characteristic hauteur, as recounted in the next day's *Plain Dealer*:

> Hundreds of men, women and children flocked about the car, which stopped for some time at the [Akron] station. Boys and men clambered about the cars to get a look at the great criminal, who smiled and bowed like some uninterested guest and was as happy as a lord going to a Thanksgiving dinner.

John Coughlin and James Robinson fared better than expected or probably deserved. Samuel Eddy had planted potent seeds of doubt about their presence in Ravenna during Blinky's trial, in contrast to his total failure to plead an alibi for Blinky. Although Coughlin and Robinson were both convicted of first-degree murder at their subsequent trials, there was widespread feeling among the press and public that both cases involved reasonable doubt. On December 31, Judge J. R. Johnston overturned Coughlin's December 2 conviction and granted him a new trial. On April 11, 1888, the circuit court in Ravenna "nolled" all charges against Coughlin, arguing that even a second conviction would likely be overturned on appeal. Robinson fared likewise: on April 10, 1888, the circuit court in Ravenna overturned his December 18 conviction and all charges were eventually nolled on August 6. Robinson's ultimately persuasive alibi hinged on the multiple testimonies of some quite unsavory characters that he had been present at an Allegheny City masked ball on the morning of February 4. Coughlin's even less credible story that he was at his sister's Elyria hotel that day was supported by the sworn but dubious testimony of his relatives, and what seems to have been his forged name on the hotel register.

Blinky was not so fortunate. Samuel Eddy's appeal stressed Judge Johnston's alleged error in allowing testimony about the fur robbery and Blinky's connection to Harry McMunn into the trial record. But on April 10, 1888, the Ravenna court turned down Blinky's appeal and resentenced him to hang on June 1. The Ohio Supreme Court rejected Blinky's final error petition on May 2, a decision Blinky blamed on the "roastings" accorded him in Ohio newspapers. On May 29, Ohio governor Joseph B. Foraker granted Blinky a sixty-day stay of execution while his application for commutation of his sentence to life imprisonment was considered.

Surprisingly, frantic last-minute efforts were made to save Blinky from the hangman. On July 30, a petition supporting Blinky's commutation plea, signed by several hundred Columbus businessmen, was presented to Governor Foraker by ex-Columbus mayor C. C. Walcutt. It was in vain: the next day at 5:00 p.m., Governor Foraker dismissed the petition with a sentence that summarized the weakness of Blinky's case: "Gentlemen, you ask me to assume that Morgan was elsewhere when the outrageous murder occurred, when you do not even offer the man's affidavit to show that such was the case."

A final meeting between Blinky and Foraker on the afternoon of August 1 ended abruptly when Blinky, pressed by Foraker for a credible alibi, became argumentative and insinuated that Foraker was not a gentleman.

A more lurid, albeit equally ineffectual, crusade to save Blinky was mounted by detective John T. Norris. Norris's publicized theory was that Blinky's real accomplices in the Ravenna attack were Pat Hanley, William Harrington, and William Powell. In the Norris version, Blinky was not involved directly in the fatal assault but was nevertheless shot three times in the smoking car melee. Allegedly, Blinky had eventually had two of the slugs removed at a New York hospital, while Hanley and Harrington fled to Europe with the profits from the sale of the stolen furs—profits they refused to share with their confederates. It was a preposterous story, and Blinky's autopsy failed to disclose any evidence of the bullet wounds alleged by Norris.

Blinky Morgan passed his final day on earth calmly. On August 2, he refused to see the prison chaplain and took an hour's nap in the afternoon. He wrote a few letters, told a few jokes, and handed out tokens of his esteem: painted buckeyes with the legend "Cleveland and Thurman, 1888." At 10:30 p.m. Warden Coffin told him his time was short and that if he wished to make a last statement he'd better hurry. Blinky's final testament, posthumously released, reasserted his claims of total innocence and averred that he would not reveal his real name for the sake of a brother who had six children. He thanked Warden Coffin for his kindness, willed his body to Nellie Lowry, and ended with a bitter protest against his fate: "I have read of men being murdered for their money, but I am judicially, or rather injudicially, murdered for the State's money and to satisfy the claim for a victim."

Blinky's last testament also obliquely referred to the supposed alibi that he never used in court. According to Samuel Eddy, who apparently discussed this romantic fiction with reporters with a straight face, Blinky actually had been in Philadelphia on the morning that William Hulligan was murdered. The rub was that Blinky was consorting with women from Philadelphia high society at the time, and it was to spare their reputations that Blinky walked with silent courage to the scaffold at 1:00 a.m. on August 3.

The forty-odd spectators who watched Blinky Morgan hang were a selected few whittled down from over 1,000 applicants. Pronounced dead at 1:41, Blinky was said to look "natural"—except for a very bright red ring around his neck. Nellie Lowry was given custody of his body, and it is recorded both that she wept and that the "most mawkish sentimentality" prevailed throughout Columbus over Blinky's demise. Not bad for a career ruffian who had killed at least four men during a thoroughly misspent life.

Nellie Lowry paid Blinky's funeral expenses of $113.50, and he is believed to lie in a Columbus grave to this day. Her last letter to him breathed but the purest piety and love:

> It is with the saddest heart that I ever had that I write you today, and what can I say to comfort you? My last hope and yours, also, has failed, and we must resign ourselves to the inevitable . . . How I wish I could bear it for you, my good kind friend! . . . And though we meet no more in this world, I hope we will in the next. May God give you courage. And I hope for all your goodness in this world to the widow and orphans you will receive your reward and get the justice denied you here. Mother, children and all send their last farewell. Good-bye, oh, good-bye.

Within six months, almost all of his confederates were dead or imprisoned. One of Blinky's righthand men, Tom Scott, was shot dead in Newburgh while trying to hold up a bank to secure funds for Blinky's defense. In 1900, Harry McMunn was allegedly imprisoned in Mexico for bank robbery. Apparently, Mexican jails couldn't hold McMunn any better than American ones, as he was finally shot to death while robbing a bank in Berkeley, California, in 1905. About the same time, Charles Lowry was reported on the loose in Texas, having escaped from Ohio authorities by throwing pepper in the eyes of his guards while on a train in Westerville. By that time John Coughlin was dead, and James Robinson had succeeded in returning to a respectable, if presumably duller, life. As befits an outlaw of Blinky's stature, however, rumors of an immense buried treasure he had secreted in Lorain County circulated for decades. The absolute last word on the Morgan gang came in December 1908, with news that William Quinn, an erstwhile Morgan confederate, had been shot dead in Greenwich, Ohio, while performing a burglary. Captain Henry Hoehn eventually succeeded Jacob Schmitt as police superintendant in 1893 and served honorably in that office until 1896. He dropped dead in 1903.

The final incident in the Blinky Morgan melodrama proper belonged to Detective Jack Reeves, whose thoughts had been of his friend, poor William Hulligan, as Blinky hurtled through the drop. Pursued down a Columbus street in the wee hours after the hanging by the still-abusive and drunken saloonkeeper, James McGuire, Reeves finally turned on his tormenter, and "[C]atching McGuire by the nose between two fingers he gave him a slap that sent him reeling across the pavement."

The Mad Butcher of Big Creek

Brooklyn Village, July 22, 1936

The Big Creek area of western Cuyahoga County has always been a favorite spot for nature lovers. A quiet, relatively convenient sylvan respite from Cleveland's metropolitan hurly-burly, it was even quieter and more remote in 1936. It was an especially great place for hiking, which is why Mary Barkley of Hope Avenue was walking along a modest gully there, between the creek and the B & O railroad tracks just south of Clinton Road, early on the morning of July 22, 1936. It was a perfectly lovely day in an absolutely soothing place—which no doubt intensified Mary Barkley's horror when suddenly she stumbled upon the naked, headless, and badly decomposed corpse of a man in her path.

Cops from practically everywhere soon arrived on the scene in response to Barkley's report of a corpse—Cleveland homicide detectives, the Brooklyn Village constabulary, and diverse West Side city and suburban forces anxious to share in the action. What they found was starkly simple, if not very enlightening. The torso lay chest down, partially covered with brush and weeds, about a hundred yards from the railroad tracks. The victim had no identifying marks or wounds, had been dead for two or three months, and had probably met his death where he lay, judging from the amount of blood in the soil near the corpse's neck. Authorities soon located the head about ten feet away; it completed their picture of a fortyish male, about five foot five, 145 pounds, with markedly long brown hair (slightly balding), pointed chin, and good teeth (although he was missing an incisor and two molars). The head had been neatly severed between the third and fourth cervical vertebrae. Although the authorities could not know it yet, he would be the only Torso victim ever to turn up on the West Side of Cleveland.

Next to the head was a pile of ragged clothes that Coroner Pearse determined might have fit the dead man. These included a gray suit coat with a sleeve apparently slashed by a knife, a matching pair of trousers, a blue polo shirt, a leather belt, a white undershirt, white underwear, blue socks, black oxford shoes, and a gray cap with black stripes. The polo shirt and suit coat were quite bloodstained. There was nothing in the pockets to identify the dead man.

POLICE SEEKING THRILL SLAYERS

Fifth Headless Victim Found Indicates Homeless Pursued by Murderers

Cleveland Press headline, July 23, 1936.

Owing to the advanced state of decomposition, the police had little to go on and contented themselves largely with speculating to reporters. On the basis of the modest clothing and untrimmed hair, most lawmen presumed the victim had been a vagrant, perhaps a temporary denizen of the hobo camp in the Big Creek woods not far from the murder scene. There was a brief flash of hope that the body could be matched to a report of a missing forty-year-old WPA worker filed two months previously, but it proved ephemeral. Coroner Pearse was left simply to conclude that, like the other Torso victims, No. 6 (still only No. 5 in the official count) had lost his head to a very heavy, sharp knife—in this particular case wielded by a very skillful or knowledgeable practitioner, perhaps a surgeon.

Cleveland police were not quite so restrained. The July 23 edition of the *Press* quoted unnamed police officials as asserting that a "group of thrill killers" was responsible for the string of Torso killings. And quotable Charles Nevel went further, claiming that the presumed Torso killer was a pervert armed with a large, preternaturally sharp pocket knife. The strategy of Nevel's demonic pervert was to lure his victims to remote areas, cut off their heads . . . and *then* sexually assault them. Nevel didn't offer much supporting evidence for this hypothesis, and he still demurred at allowing Florence Polillo to join the roster of the headless.

Oddly, Eliot Ness, still making headlines in his fight against Cleveland's organized criminals and corrupt policemen, remained

FIEND BEHEADS LIVING VICTIMS

Police Believe Slayer of 5 Here Used Pocket Knife in Decapitations

Cleveland Press headline, July 24, 1936.

silent on the subject of the Torso murders. And no one commented on the fact that the condition of the latest victim indicated he was probably killed before the tattooed man met his death under a willow tree.

The last word belonged to the *Cleveland News,* which modestly allowed that the answer to the Torso puzzle might never be known: "Detectives admit that the answer to the five decapitation murder riddles may be a long time in coming—may never come, in fact." But that wasn't about to stop the same paper's writers from keeping public hysteria pitched as high as possible with headlines and copy like the following:

MADMAN OR COOL KILLER? POLICE PROBERS
GROPING FOR LEADS IN COUNTY'S FIVE HEAD-
LESS MURDERS

Is there somewhere in Cuyahoga County a madman whose strange god is the guillotine? What fantastic chemistry of the civilized mind converted him into a human butcher? Does he imagine himself a legal executioner of the French Revolution? Or a religious zealot determined to save the race from perdition with an axe? Or a modern Jack the Ripper who terrorized London many years ago? Or is he merely a cool and calculating killer who decapitated his victims with the skill of a physician?

Meanwhile, the long summer of 1936 wore on, and thousands more walked by the grisly death mask of the tattooed torso victim at the Great Lakes Exposition. What, they might have wondered, was going to happen next?

Chapter 5

DEATH OF THE MUSIC LOVERS

The 1908 Ziechmann-Bernthaler Tragedy

It is my belief, Watson, founded upon my experience, that the lowest and vilest alleys in London do not present a more dreadful record of sin than does the smiling and beautiful countryside.

—Sir Arthur Conan Doyle, *The Adventure of the Copper Beeches*

Although a lurid seven-day sensation in its day, the 1908 Ziechmann-Bernthaler double slaying is forgotten now. That's puzzling, as it had everything suitable to a first-class homicide. It had sin, it had sex (maybe), it had scandal, and, best of all, it was unsolved, leaving tantalizing questions to reverberate down the years. Who killed Carl Bernthaler and Lena Ziechmann on a pleasant spring day in 1908? What secret assignation brought the two together—unknown to their families—in an isolated patch of the Stillman woods? And what terrible secret did Lena Ziechmann take to her grave after someone put a .38-caliber bullet through her heart?

Cleveland Heights was still largely country in March 1908. Coventry Road was the eastern border of Euclid Heights, the still-growing gentry suburb atop Cedar Hill. Coventry skirted the dense Stillman woods to the east that flanked Cedar Road before leading south to the still more rural acres of undeveloped Shaker Heights. A desultory creek flowed through the Stillman woods east of Coventry, running for several hundred feet parallel to the road before it arced northwest to become Dugway Creek in Lake View Cemetery. Altogether, it was a beautiful rural vista, and a popular pedestrian venue for city-weary Clevelanders of the era, who could reach it by taking a streetcar all the way to Coventry and Mayfield and then walking south toward the remains of the old Shaker settlement. Which is, in part, why the fine spring afternoon of March 29, 1908, found Carl Bernthaler and Lena Ziechmann walking down Coventry toward the dense thickets of the Stillman woods.

Fifty-two years old, the mustachioed, taciturn Carl looked the part
of a successful musician and music teacher. He was well known,
liked, and respected in Cleveland music circles. A Cleveland resident for more than a quarter century, Carl was a gifted pianist, vio-
linist, and flautist who had played with the Cleveland Opera and
Lyceum Theater orchestras for many years. His colleagues and
friends, musicians like Frank Hruby and Louis Rich, had nothing but
good to say of him, and his musical sensitivity had been a byword
since his college days. Indeed, Carl sometimes even brought his flute
and played for the birds in the woods, saying to his bemused friends,
"When I play in the woods, the birds sing to me. They understand me
and I make them sing." True, it was said privately that Carl was disappointed his wife did not share his musical interests . . . but publicly, at least, they were a devoted couple. Carl was an enthusiastic
walker who often rambled the rural roads of Cleveland Heights and
Shaker Heights, and so he cannot have been an unexpected sight to
many of the eyewitnesses who saw him on this sunny March afternoon.

Carl's walking companion that day was Clara Ziechmann, a
thirty-one-year-old spinster who lived with her parents and taughtt
German at Mayflower. They must have made a handsome, if
unlikely, couple: Carl with his professorial-hiker look and the not-
unattractive Lena decked out in a blue hat and veil, blue skirt, a fur
coat, and stylish automobile gauntlets. You might even have mistaken them for a father and daughter. Unless, of course, you were
Carl's wife or Lena's parents.

Just what Carl and Lena were doing out on the Heights together
that day is not clear. Indeed, no one will ever know the real truth
about their relationship. Lena, the daughter of a Cleveland florist,
had known Carl for at least fifteen years; a classmate of his son Carl
Frederick at Central High School, she had taken violin lessons from
Bernthaler as a teenager. The violin proved too difficult for Lena, but
she became a skilled pianist, kept up her acquaintanceship with Carl,
and began taking flute lessons with him when she was twenty-nine.
Every Saturday she came to the Bernthaler home at 1763 East 33rd
for her hour lesson. Carl and Lena performed in several public
recitals together, and her apparent bond with the older man was their
mutual passion for music, as Mayflower principal Morton L. Dart
later testified: "Music was the consuming passion of Lena Ziechmann's life. In every conversation I ever held with her the talk
always turned to things musical and of what she hoped to accom-

Carl Bernthaler. *The Plain
Dealer,* March 31, 1908.

plish in the field. She once told me she had rather be a great pianist than anything in the world."

Anyone who knew Lena, though, could have told you that her *other* consuming passion was Carl Bernthaler. Evidently infatuated with him from her teenage years, Lena did little to conceal her love for the middle-aged musician, even from his family. She went so far as to tell Carl's son Albert, 12, that it was "nice to be in love with a man older than herself." Lena's parents knew of her infatuation and worried about it. But Mrs. Bernthaler apparently didn't. She accepted Carl's protestations of pity for the "lovesick" Lena and even went so far as to claim that her husband "hated" his infatuated flute student but kept her on out of pity.

Pity or not, Carl did not tell his wife his real plans that Sunday afternoon. Leaving home about 3:00 p.m., he told her he was going for a walk on the Heights and to see a "Mr. Munroe." Sometime later, before 4:00, he met up with Lena, and both of them boarded the Euclid Heights streetcar and took it to Mayfield and Coventry. It was obvious to conductor Charlie Moss that they were traveling together, whatever their pretense:

> At Overlook Road the car was stopped by a man and a woman who wished to get on. They were not standing together. The woman got on by the front platform and sat in the middle of the car. The man got on at the rear and stood on the platform. They did not give each other any signs of recognition. Yet I felt there was something wrong. The woman would give quick, sudden glances here and there. She looked self-conscious.

Moss also recalled that Lena got off the car first, followed by Carl. They walked up Coventry, and "both kept looking behind them." Lena, especially, seemed nervous about what they were doing, although they had been seen together walking in the same place the day before by two eyewitnesses, Charles Peters and Fred Stadicina. Just about an hour earlier Lena had told her parents she was going to a German music concert.

If Carl and Lena were trying to be furtive, they had certainly picked the wrong day and neighborhood. About 4:00 p.m. that Sunday, Fred Spissman, an old friend of Carl's, saw the two of them walking south down Coventry toward the Stillman woods. So did Patrick Ryan, who worked for Daniel Martin, a local dairy farmer in the Cedar-Coventry area. He later remembered Bernthaler poking the underbrush with Lena's parasol at the outskirts of the woods at about 4:00, and he saw the couple together again, he thought, about an hour later. Ryan was probably the last one to see either Carl or Lena alive.

Henry Dunn, a Coventry Road resident, heard five shots fired in the area after 4:30. His best memory was that he heard two shots, followed by three more about thirty seconds later. Robert Martin, who lived about a quarter mile away, also heard shots, as did Charles Smallsreed, who was walking on Coventry. No one who heard the shots, though, thought much about them. It was a rural area, and local residents were used to the sound of firearms at all hours.

Carl Bernthaler didn't come home that night. His family didn't worry until about midnight. The next morning Mrs. Bernthaler, instead of notifying the police, went walking in Shaker Heights in search of Carl. Lena, on the other hand, wasn't missed until about 10:30 on Monday morning. When Mrs. Ziechmann had returned home the previous night, she had simply assumed Lena was already asleep; she was therefore unprepared for the call that came mid-morning from the Cleveland Police to confirm the identity of her daughter's body:

Lena Ziechmann. *Cleveland Press*, March 30, 1908.

That comes of going out without telling us where! She went
off yesterday afternoon about 3:30 without saying anything.
I didn't think anything of it because she has been so secretive
lately. She has had all of her mail sent to school and carries
the key of her trunk in her pocket. She did not come in at supper time, and in the evening one of my sons and I went to the
German theater. We did not get back till 12:15 and then her
door was shut as usual. I did not try to open it. Monday morning I did not call her because it was vacation and I wanted her
to rest.

It hadn't taken long for the murders to be discovered. About 8:30
Monday morning, a landscape engineer named Temblett, who was
working on the Euclid Heights development, was told by one of his
Italian laborers that there were two bodies lying in the Stillman
woods. Temblett and a man named George Williams went to the
woods and were soon met there by Cleveland Heights marshal
Brockway.

They found Lena and Carl lying face down on the ground, about
seventy-five yards apart. Lena still had her beaded purse, which con-

Sketch of the Ziechmann-Bernthaler slayings. *Cleveland Press*, March 31, 1908.

tained streetcar tickets, $2.50 in cash, a penknife, a pencil, a handkerchief, a postcard, and part of a letter. Her tongue had been gashed when she fell forward to the ground, and there was a small trickle of blood from her mouth. There was some dirt on Lena's skirt, leading Marshal Brockway to theorize that the murderer had contemptuously flicked it over her after he killed her. Her body was otherwise unmarked—except for a slight stain where a .38-caliber slug had entered the left side of her back, passed through the sixth rib, torn away the top half of her heart, drilled through both lungs, and exited between the ribs just below her right breast. Her face, a spectator said, "pictured horror in every line. Her right hand was thrown up as if to ward off a blow."

It was much the same with Carl. His watch intact and still running, he lay on the ground as if asleep. Found in his pockets were thirty cents and a telephone bill with his name on it. He also had been shot in the back, the bullet entering his left side, puncturing the aorta and his right lung, and stopping in his right side. Lena's umbrella was still in his hand, and two boxes of candy were lying near him on the ground.

The investigation into the double murder was a muddle from the start. Much time was wasted on the ludicrous notion that one of the two had shot the other and then committed suicide. Such speculations were fueled by the anger of both families, their sorrow aggravated by the lurid newspaper treatment of the victims' enigmatic relationship. Mrs. Ziechmann's vehemence against Carl was characteristic of the embarrassed families' desire to find a scapegoat in one of the dead victims: "Oh, if [Lena] had only taken my advice. I have told her again and again not to have anything to do with this man . . . I spoke to her about him and she always said, 'I don't care for anyone.'"

Mrs. Ziechmann's fury was echoed by Mrs. Bernthaler's anger at her husband's lovelorn flute student: "I knew it. I knew it. She did it. I know she did. I might have cautioned Carl. But he was such a good man and I never mistrusted him." Mrs. Ziechmann's last statement was not *quite* true: she did admit to going through Carl's pockets sometimes in vain search of notes from Miss Ziechmann.

The murder-suicide theories soon collapsed under the weight of their own absurdity. Despite sweeps by bloodhounds and men with rakes throughout the woods and adjoining creek, no murder weapon could be found. Nor could such theories explain how either victim could have sustained a self-inflicted wound in the back. Not to mention the complete absence of powder marks on either corpse. Marshal Brockway's theory was eventually accepted by virtually everyone: someone had surprised the couple while they were sitting on a fence rail in the woods. The killer shot Carl first and then fired three missed shots at the fleeing Lena—one hit the fence rail—before a fourth bullet took her down. The mortally wounded Carl, still clutching Lena's parasol, staggered and fell about seventy-five yards from Lena.

The inquest, which commenced at 10:30 a.m. Tuesday, March 31, did not solve the Bernthaler-Ziechmann mystery. It did, however, expose a lot of lurid Ziechmann family skeletons to public view. There had been terrible secrets in Lena Ziechmann's life, and their disclosure soon suggested it was remarkable that she had not been murdered before March 1908.

The most obvious homicide candidate was Frank W. Ziechmann, Lena's father. A tyrannical patriarch of the old German school, Frank had long terrorized all three of his daughters, well into adulthood. Frank insisted that his daughters entertain male callers only at home, and he was unusually vigorous in enforcing this rule. It had gotten so bad by 1903, when Lena was twenty-six, that the three Ziechmann girls had left home to live with the Charles Brown family on East 88th Street.

Even that didn't stop Frank's paternal harassment. One night he followed Lena out on a date to Euclid Beach with a young doctor. On the way, Frank severely assaulted the doctor, who refused to press charges only because Lena begged him not to. On another occasion Frank was picked up by the police at night while spying on Lena through the windows of the Brown house. And on at least one occasion, Frank assaulted Mr. Brown himself, after the latter caught Frank lurking outside his house.

Was it even worse than that? Did Frank Ziechmann's possessive tyranny conceal even more brutal, abusive behavior? It is known that there were other confrontations with Lena's boyfriends—one of whom may have been Carl Bernthaler, surprised with Lena by an enraged Frank Ziechmann one night at an East 55th and Scovill nightspot. And there were darker shadows hovering around a perpetually scared Lena Ziechmann. One night in September 1903, while Lena was living with the Browns, someone tried to burn the place down with an incendiary mixture of oil-soaked rags and wood kindling. Both Cleveland and state officials investigated without result. Sometime later, in June 1904, a vial of nitroglycerine was discovered underneath the porch below Lena's room. And sometime after Lena returned to her parents' home in 1905, someone fired a shot through the Ziechmanns' first-floor window, missing Lena by inches. This incident was also investigated by Cleveland police without result. Small wonder that a number of Lena's friends testified at the inquest that she lived in constant fear for her life and was "despondent" in the weeks before her death. But whom did she fear, and why? And was there a more sinister, terrible meaning in the assertion of Mrs. F. W. Novis, Carl's daughter and Lena's friend, that Lena hated her father and kept her door locked for fear of him? (The word "incest" comes to mind, as it has to recent theorists of the Lizzie Borden affair.) We'll never know for sure, although it is interesting, especially with regard to Carl, that Lena's autopsy showed her to be still *virgo intacta*.

Guilty or innocent, the inquest was certainly an ordeal for Frank Ziechmann. Although he had a serviceable alibi for the murder hour, much of the inquest testimony was a litany of his bullying, cruel behavior toward his daughters. Even his blood relatives testified that he had a violent temper, and Frank Hruby, a well-known Cleveland musician, testified that Frank Ziechmann had been treated twice for mental illness in European asylums. Ziechmann had also told Hruby once that he would rather see one of his daughters dead than married to her then-fiancé. Speaking for himself at the inquest, Frank simply said, "I am not a coward, gentlemen. If I killed them, I would not be here today, I would have killed myself."

Frank's alibi stuck, and the investigation died out after only a few days. Chief Fred Kohler, speaking on behalf of the Cleveland Police, refused help, curtly saying, "We have troubles of our own." And

Cleveland Press headline, March 30, 1908.

Pinkerton detectives hired by the Ziechmann family failed to turn up any further leads. County Coroner Burke, after a week of boasting that he was "satisfied as to the identity of the murderer," sourly commented, "I think the family of Miss Ziechmann has its suspicions and knows more than has been told." At Lena's Woodland Cemetery interment, both her mother and a sister became hysterical and had to be led away.

Who killed Lena Ziechmann and Carl Bernthaler? The two most obvious suspects—Carl's wife and Lena's father—had solid alibis for the murder day and hour. The likelihood, therefore, is that Lena, in addition to her psychotically smothering father, was stalked by someone else in the months, perhaps even years before her death. For in addition to the shooting incident at the Ziechmann house—for which Frank Ziechmann had an alibi—there were two other suggestive incidents never satisfactorily explained by the inquest. The first occurred while Lena was living at the Browns' house. While riding in an open streetcar one afternoon, Lena was hit by a spent bullet, which did no harm but frightened her badly. The second happened in 1905, when Lena was living with a Mrs. Catherine Hayes and her daughter Anna on East 65th Street. One night Lena refused to come down to a party there, and Anna Hayes later testified that Lena told her there was a man outside with a gun who would shoot Lena if she came downstairs. Lena was not shot that night—but Anna swore that she herself had seen a man with a gun lurking outside.

Other than the graves of the victims, there is little trace of this double murder that horrified and hypnotized Clevelanders for a week in 1908. Lena's father died in 1920; her brothers eventually inherited

Cleveland Press headline, March 31, 1908.

the family florist concern and her last surviving sibling, F. Karl Ziechmann, died in 1978 at the age of ninety-three. The Stillman woods
are cut down and the creek covered over; they linger on only in the
names of the neighborhood streets (Meadowbrook, Stillman) and the
now-subterranean stream that still flows to its destination in Lake
Erie. But you might think of the neighborhood's darker secrets as you
drive down the "peaceful" suburban miles of Coventry Road some
fine spring day.

The Remains of the Day

Kingsbury Run, September 10, 1936

Fueled by Cleveland's newspapers, the hunt for the alleged crazed killer of Kingsbury Run continued in the days after the unpleasant surprise in Brooklyn Village. Every eccentric, weirdo, and nonconformist then living in the Cleveland area was liable to be interrogated by the police as the pressure—quite loudly from the newspapers and very quietly from Safety Director Eliot Ness—increased to find the supposed lone killer. A typical instance was the arrest of a forty-three-year-old self-styled "doctor" on August 10, 1936. When he was apprehended as he arrived to make a house call at a Wade Park Avenue home, the police found him insufficiently coherent and brought him in for intensive questioning. He was subsequently released. Meanwhile, Eliot Ness was still trying to keep a low profile in the Torso search, preferring to concentrate on rooting out crooked cops and shutting down Cleveland-area vice mills. But on September 10, 1936, Ness's detachment ended.

About noon that Thursday, Jerry Harris, a freight train–hopping vagrant from St. Louis, was taking his leave of the Forest City. Harris had rolled into Cleveland a few days before and was sitting on an abutment near the East 37th Street bridge, waiting for an approaching eastbound train to roll him out. As the train came abreast of him, he left the abutment and began running alongside it, keeping a watchful eye out for yard detectives. As Harris loped along, he almost tripped over an object—and then realized with a start that it was the upper half of an armless, headless human torso. He ran to the Socony Vacuum Oil Company's nearby tank station and told clerk Leo Fields what he had seen. Leo called the cops, who soon swarmed over the area, accompanied by hundreds of curious onlookers.

Within minutes of arrival the first police on the scene found the lower half of the torso, separated at the abdomen and with its legs cut off at the hips. Suspicion soon focused on a nearby stagnant pool located near the spot where a culvert brings Kingsbury Run above ground under the East 34th Street viaduct and adjacent to the Nickel Plate and Shaker Rapid Transit tracks. It was surmised that the two halves of the torso had issued from the culvert and that the missing

Searching the stagnant pool for Torso victim No. 7,
September 12, 1936.

human members might be found in the stagnant pool. Shreds of what looked like flesh on the sides of the pool deepened suspicions, and investigating police put out a call for firemen and marine divers.

Near the stagnant pool, detectives found the kind of clothing that was becoming customary at Torso murder scenes. Mixed with some bloodstained newspapers (dated September 8, 1936) was a torn, bloody denim shirt and a pair of bloody green underwear. Also found was a shabby gray hat, size seven and a quarter, which was subsequently traced to Loudy's Smart Shop in Bellevue, Ohio.

Examination of the incomplete body parts at the county morgue by Coroner Pearse and his assistants disclosed these additional details. The victim was a white male, between twenty-five and thirty, with brown hair and very fit. He stood about five foot ten, and weighed about 150 pounds, and had been dead for about two days. There were kernels of corn in his stomach. The general absence of blood at the murder scene suggested that the victim had been killed elsewhere and decapitated while alive. The head had been detached between the third and fourth cervical vertebrae and the trunk severed between the third and fourth lumbar vertebrae. The victim had been emasculated, and his missing head, arms, and genitalia were never found.

Initial police efforts focused on finding the missing body parts. Suspecting they might be in the stagnant pool, Safety Director Eliot Ness, on the morning of September 11, dispatched Cleveland fire units, who quickly laid planks over the pool and began fishing for human remains in the nine-foot, murky depths. Nothing was found, and soon diver John D. Stanton was repeatedly sent down to scour the bottom of the pool and twenty-five feet of the connecting culvert in search of the rest of Torso No. 7. The lack of results prompted Coroner Pearse to suggest dynamiting the pool, but city officials eventually settled for draining it, at horrific expense. More than three million gallons were pumped out the following month, but nothing was found. Miles of nearby sewers were also examined, with like result.

If Eliot Ness and the police were loathe to get too excited about the latest torso, Cleveland newspapers were not about to let them relax. "FIND 6TH HEADLESS MURDER VICTIM" screamed the *Cleveland News,* scant hours after the disgusting find at East 37th Street, followed within minutes by the *Cleveland Press*'s more geographically precise slant, "SIXTH HACKED BODY FOUND IN KINGSBURY RUN." The next day's headlines increased the pressure on Cleveland politicians and police, the *News* leading with "HUNT CLEW TO MAD KILLER'S VICTIM," and the *Press* kicking off with "FEAR HANGS OVER KINGSBURY RUN WHERE BUTCHER LEAVES HIS DEAD" and ending with the peremptory editorial demand of "STOP THIS SLAUGHTER."

The heat was on. The *Cleveland News* soon offered a thousand-dollar reward for the arrest and conviction of the supposed Torso Butcher, a measure quickly echoed by Cleveland councilman Joseph R. Artl, who asked Cleveland City Council to pony up a like amount for the same purpose.

The search for the presumed maniac was not without its lighter side, although it was probably not appreciated at the time. On September 12, it was announced that homicide detectives Ralph Kennedy and Leo Duffin had arrested a thirty-seven-year-old Mexican found high on drugs and wandering in a daze around the Torso search locale. The suspect was thrown into a cell and clandestinely monitored, in hopes that his drug-induced ravings might divulge details of the Torso killings. And great moments in "reefer madness" were soon recorded in the pages of metropolitan newspapers. As the

POLICE ACT ON ORDER OF NESS

Move Into Kingsbury Run, Laboratory of
Maniac Butcher, Bring in and Question All Residents in Valley

FEARFUL HOBOES AVOID GuLCH

Pool Dragged Again for Head and Hands of
Knife Fiend's Sixth Victim; Hat
May Be Clew

Cleveland Press headline, September 12, 1936.

September 13 *Plain Dealer* soberly revealed: "Michael J. Collegeman, head of the federal narcotics bureau here, expressed his opinion that the slayer was addicted to narcotics, probably marijuana,
which, he said, inspires its users with an unreasoning desire to kill."
Lest Clevelanders doubt the gravity of the homicidal marijuana menace, Collegeman disclosed to the *Press* that "there is a plentiful supply of this deadly weed in Cleveland."

Cleveland authorities could no longer treat the torso unpleasantness as business as usual. On September 14, Eliot Ness found it judi-
cious to say, "I want to see this psycho caught. I'm going to do all I
can to aid in the investigation." That same day Coroner Pearse, with
the support of Ness, called for a summit meeting of Torso experts, or
a "Torso clinic" as the newspapers irreverently termed the gathering.
Held in the ballistics laboratory of the police station at Payne Avenue
and East 21st Street at 8:00 p.m. on September 15, the conference
generated assumptions that would govern thinking about the Torso
murders for years—indeed to this day. Attendees included Safety
Director Ness, Cleveland State Hospital superintendent Guy
Williams, common pleas court psychiatrist Dr. Royal Grossman,
anatomists T. Wingate Todd and W. M. Krogman of Western Reserve
University, Inspector Joseph Sweeney, Sergeant James Hogan, Police
Chief George Matowitz, County Prosecutor Frank Cullitan, Police

Prosecutor Perry Frey, and Police Surgeon George O'Malley. (There were a total of thirty-four present.) After hours spent discussing and viewing slides of the Torso victims, the conferees agreed on a "synthetic portrait" of the mysterious murderer:

1. The Torso killer was a lone maniac. He had killed all of the presumed victims, except for the Lady of the Lake.

2. The Torso killer had some knowledge of anatomy and surgical technique. He was probably a butcher or hunter rather than a surgeon; this conclusion went against prior police intimations that the killer was likely to be a doctor, medical student, or hospital orderly.

3. The Torso killer lived near the Kingsbury Run/Roaring Third Precinct region. He ingratiated himself with his victims for weeks or months, lulling them into a false sense of security before he struck.

4. The Torso killer maintained at least one (if not more) murder studio, where he could do his sanguinary work before taking his corpses to the Run.

5. The Torso killer was crazy but not in an obvious way. Likely to be a sexual pervert, he probably hung on to some of the heads for purposes of sexual perversion or cannibalism.

6. The Torso killer preyed on transient or marginal individuals whose absence was likely to go unnoticed. Unless their torsos were found, the odds were that no one would ever know or report they were missing.

7. The Torso killer was strong, about five foot seven and about 180 pounds. He used a very sharp knife.

8. All the male victims had been found chest down—or, as a later commentator remarked, "face down, if there had been a face."

After hours of talk and hypothesizing, Torso veteran Sergeant Hogan best summed up the evening's results: "Gentlemen, tonight we're right where we were the day the first body was found."

A half-facetious comment at the Torso clinic produced more concrete, if ultimately futile, results. According to a *Plain Dealer* report, someone suggested that the "best method of apprehending [the Torso killer] is to plant volunteer police detective decoys in the Kingsbury Run neighborhood." Detectives Peter Merylo and Martin Zalewski had been working on the Torso case for some time already,

Fear Hangs Over Kingsbury Run Where Butcher Leaves His Dead

Cleveland Press headline, September 11, 1936.

and after the discovery of Torso No. 7 they were assigned to the City Hall "Torso hot line," a publicity gimmick for soliciting Torso search tips. Tiring of this task, Zalewski and Merylo got permission from Inspector Joseph Sweeney to go underground in search of the Mad Butcher of Kingsbury Run.

Which they famously did, if to little avail. While one kept a silent watch near by, the other would sleep outdoors in the Run, hoping to attract the attentions of the Torso killer. In addition, Merylo and Zalewski set out to become knowledgeable about the human flotsam and jetsam of their work area. This they also did, and a heavy personal toll it must have taken as they got to know the resident population of their beat, pitiable but scary human refuse that *Cleveland News* reporter Peter Bellamy aptly described as "canned heat addicts, broken down rum pots, stumblebums and screwballs of all kinds, and degenerates whose repertoires cover the gamut of human perversions." Merylo and Zalewski virtually lived the daily life of the Torso killer's victims for two years, and it is small wonder that they eventually fell out with each other in 1938. By that time, as one veteran Torso sleuth said, "Them guys have been so close to this thing that they're beginning to suspect each other as the Torso slayer."

Not that Cleveland police lacked for other, albeit ephemeral, suspects. The marijuana-addled Mexican was soon released, only to be replaced by an elderly West Side doctor, hauled in because a neighbor found him "suspicious" and almost as quickly released by a mortified Eliot Ness. And there was the "Chicken Freak," well known to the relentless detectives Zalewski and Merylo. A massive man, alleged by local prostitutes to be capable of orgasm only in the presence of a chicken decapitation, the chicken enthusiast was finally run to earth by the two detectives after a civic-minded prostitute supplied a license plate number. The Chicken Freak readily confessed to intercourse with chickens but was dismissed as a viable suspect when he demonstrated a palpable horror of human bloodshed.

The authorities ran down the few remaining clues as to the identity of Torso No. 7, knowing there was little to go on in the absence

Cleveland Press illustration, September 12, 1936.

of fingerprints or a head. The gray hat was traced to Piqua, Ohio—and to a woman who said she had given it to a hobo who matched the presumed description constructed from the unknown torso. A theory that the victim was Patrick Casey, a missing railroad section hand, proved invalid. Dogged police researchers dragged up the intriguing case of a 1929 decapitation murder at East 40th and Kingsbury Run, when a so-called "voodoo doctor" had been arrested after his dog was found "worrying" a human head, and a compatible corpse was found in his house. Nothing came of this search, nor of a similar query about an axe murderer who had escaped from Cleveland State Hospital in 1931. It almost came as comic relief when it was revealed on September 16 that a woman's skeleton found buried in an East Cleveland vacant lot was just a gruesome family heirloom. Reports of mysterious comings and goings near the stagnant pool on

September 9 merely reinforced the likelihood that the body parts of Torso No. 7 had been dumped there sometime in the twenty-four hours before Jerry Harris happened along.

Before inevitably dying down, police scrutiny and public curiosity suddenly shifted to New Castle, Pennsylvania. On September 16, Cleveland police journeyed there to confer with local authorities about a headless torso found in a boxcar on July 1. The technique used in severing the head of the male victim was similar to the Cleveland Torso killings, and it reminded some in New Castle of the nearby "Murder Dump" swamp of the 1920s. Six headless torsos or torsoless heads had been unearthed there in the mid-1920s, and Cleveland police now wondered whether the New Castle casualties were linked to the Torso slayings. Back in Cleveland, police continued to arrest anyone with a knife, or anyone who was in the least way strange. And so the hunt went on.

Chapter 6

BAD DAY AT NEWBURGH

The 1872 Northern Ohio
Insane Asylum Fire

Although seemingly a minor fire, the 1872 conflagration at the insane asylum in Newburgh Township presents, as Sherlock Holmes would say, "exceptional features of interest." It was not one of Greater Cleveland's classic fires—that is, a blaze of heroic proportions eventually brought under control by brave firemen. Indeed, it was a typically premodern fire: it simply burned out of control until it consumed everything within its path. But a curious oddity about the inferno was that there may not have been many "insane" persons among the 488 Newburgh inmates who endured the fiery perils of that tragic day.

Mental illness was not a well-understood diagnosis in the nineteenth century. Indeed, "insane" was a clumsy, blanket categorization used by both physicians and social reformers to label—and, more unfortunately, treat—an astonishing variety of mental and physical conditions. We may never know the number of tragedies either caused or concealed by such ignorance, but there is much evidence that the practice then was to lump together and institutionalize truly insane persons—some of demonic criminality—with congenital idiots, deaf-mutes, the aged senile population, and various abused, indigent, or merely eccentric persons of both sexes.

A perusal of the Ohio secretary of state's 1856 "Report to the Governor" on the status of Ohio's "insane" population is quite instructive in this regard. Many of the patients listed in this fascinating census of woe were undoubtedly suffering from mental illness or disabling congenital conditions such as mental retardation. But there are enough exceptions among the case histories, especially with regard to women, to make one wonder how many merely unhappy or just plain victimized persons were incarcerated at the Newburgh asylum when it went up in flames.

Who knows what personal tragedy lay behind the summary information on Isabella Creswell, 61. The state reported that her insanity had been caused by "obstruse study"—a significant phrase in an era when higher education was widely thought to be inimical to the female sex. What of Mary Collins of Hamilton County, 37, reported to suffer from chronic mania—caused by "nostalgia"—for seven years? What more dramatic misfortune and cruelty befell Barbara Beck, a nineteen-year-old domestic servant reported to be suffering from "monomania" caused by "seduction"? What of Elizabeth Swisler, 40, of Crawford County, suffering from insanity caused by "difficulty with husband"? We can laugh uncomfortably now at the insanity diagnoses of John Chandler and half a dozen others, of both sexes, who had apparently taken the most certain nineteenth-century route to the asylum: "masturbation," or in the case of poor Adelaid Countryman of Ashtabula, "masturbation of parents." But what of Elizabeth Pittenger, demented from "love"; Loretta Plymton, deranged for twenty years by "disappointment"; Sarah Brower, 27, "abuse by husband"; Christiania Geistevite, "turn of life"; Lydia Rhodes, "smoking and snuff"; or poor Mary M. Purd, 65, "bad disposition"? There were many awful and unknown roads to the nineteenth-century "crazy house," and it is well to preface the story of the Newburgh asylum fire with a pang of sympathy for the diversely tortured souls who called it home. And it could have been worse: well into the nineteenth century, mental asylum officials, especially in England, often charged an admission fee to those who wished to gawk at the afflicted.

Originally built in 1855 on land donated by the Garfield family, the Northern Ohio Lunatic Asylum in Newburgh was the second of six regional asylums set up by the state of Ohio during the 1850s. Serving a twenty-county Northeast Ohio district, the asylum housed perhaps 600 inmates in September 1872, roughly half of them male. It was more overcrowded than usual, as it temporarily housed fifteen patients from the Columbus asylum, which had recently suffered a serious fire. Sheltering afflicted persons who had formerly been held in almshouses and even jails, the Newburgh facility strove hard to provide a "homelike" atmosphere for its residents. "Homelike," of course, was a relative term, as the hospital still depended, when necessary, on involuntary seclusion, cuffs, straps, and straitjackets to control its population.

In 1872 the facility was composed of a four-story central building with three newly built side wings, plus a central brick wing at the rear separated from the main structure by eleven feet. The building, including the wings, measured 830 feet across the front and was largely fireproof, except for the actual center section, which featured

Northern Ohio Insane Asylum, ca. 1890s.

a rotunda with a windowed cupola on top, exactly 114 feet from ground level.

September 25, 1872, Newburgh residents would later recall, was a pleasant early fall day. Pleasant, that is, until about 1:15 p.m. It was at that moment that the fire apparently started. Laborers working on the roof of the central building would later claim that sparks from the rear asylum building set the central roof afire. It is far more likely, however, that the sparks came from small soldering furnaces on the center roof that the roofers were using to heat zinc for repairs there. Aside from their obvious motive for denying responsibility, their version was called into question by the later testimony of many witnesses that the wind was blowing toward the rear building, rather than from it . . . On the other hand the asylum staff *had* been burning a half dozen baskets of highly flammable wood shavings to "burn out" soot in the chimney . . .

Whatever the source, the central building went up fast. And although it contained more than enough water to put out the fire, all 8,000 gallons were stored in four giant water tanks atop the fourth floor of the center rotunda. After the hungry flames burned down through the roof, they attacked the wooden timbers and trusses that supported the water tanks.

One can hardly imagine the chaos that ensued as awareness of the disaster dawned on staff and inmates. Because the worst of the danger was confined to the central building, virtually all of the patients and staff escaped unhurt, if badly frightened, into the nearby village of Newburgh and the surrounding countryside. Local residents quickly formed lines to help the staff corral its charges in a nearby garden and a local church. Many of the inmates, however, escaped their keepers and roamed throughout the area, terrifying local residents and, quite often, themselves. It would be days before they were all rounded up and accounted for. And it was a miracle many of them didn't die in the building they called home. As the next day's *Cleveland Herald* reported:

> Many resolutely refused to leave their cells, concealing themselves in closets or under their beds, and neither persuasion or threats were of any avail. In many instances it was found necessary to pull them out of their hiding places by main force. In several cases such stout resistance was made that the strength of two or three men was required to overcome a single patient . . . The female patients were even more difficult to manage than the males. More susceptible to excitement and alarm, many of them ran hither and thither in frantic terror. . . .

Joseph Turney, a trustee of Newburgh Township saw the asylum in flames from his house in the village. Sending a man to telegraph to Cleveland for fire and police aid, he and dozens of other area residents rushed to the scene of the disaster. They found little to do when they got there. Although there was a water tower containing 1,000 barrels in the rear building, it was not brought into play against the flames that afternoon. Nor were a series of hydrants ringing the asylum, supplied by a nearby creek.

Meanwhile, the fire telegram sped to Cleveland, but help was further delayed for precious minutes until Fire Chief Hill could be found. Finally, Assistant Engineer Bennett ordered an engine out to Newburgh on his own authority, soon followed by two more engines and a hose cart some minutes later. Cleveland police superintendent Schmidt also ordered Captain McMahon, Sergeant Hoehn, and a squad of fifteen patrolmen to go to Newburgh and help maintain public order. The cops were needed: local residents, especially a gang of boys, were already making off with asylum furniture and supplies. Accompanying the police were hundreds of curious Clevelanders anxious to see the spectacle of the asylum burning down.

By the time the first Cleveland fire unit got to Newburgh and began to pour a stream of water on the fire, it was almost over. It had burned quickly through the center of the building, bringing the four water tanks crashing through four floors of stairways to the ground below at about 2:00 p.m.

Most of the fire's six fatalities occurred when the water tanks collapsed. Benjamin Burgess was one of the first victims found underneath them. Away from home to buy cattle that autumn afternoon, he had entered the central building to help evacuate patients and retrieve furniture. His arms and legs were badly burned, but his face and moustache remained intact, allowing friends to identify his corpse. Still on his body were four or five hundred dollars for his cattle-buying errand. The flesh simply peeled off his scalded body in strips when he was found.

Also found in the burned rubble under the water tanks were the bodies of Isaac Hearn, William Edwards, Alfred Brown, and Edward Morgan. Hearn and Brown lived for two days in excruciating pain, badly scalded by thousands of gallons of hot water that had come down in the collapse of the rotunda. Brown, only fourteen years old, had been one of the heroes of the afternoon until he was trapped and scalded by the collapsing tanks. Harry Schrieber, a local barber, was also scalded terribly, burned over almost his entire body.

Perhaps the most horrible death was met by Miss Mary Walker. Fifty years old, a seamstress at the asylum and "a very estimable lady," she was trapped on the third floor of the central building when the falling water tanks carried away the stairs. She stood at the edge of the rotunda for some minutes, while rescuers "beseeched" her to jump to a mattress below. Joseph Turney, Constable Dipley, and a Mr. Sherman tried to get to her but were driven back by the flames. Mary could not leap to safety. Her foot hopelessly caught in burning debris, she slowly burned to death in sight of her anguished rescuers below, "enduring the agony of her position with a fortitude deserving of a better fate." Her body was virtually consumed by the flames. Turney and Dipley, who stayed with her until her clothing caught on fire, barely escaped with their lives. Mary Walker's aged mother died of shock within ten minutes of hearing of her daughter's horrible death.

The afternoon and evening of the fire were replete with the sights and sounds of the trauma wrought on the suddenly homeless Newburgh inmates. The next day's *Plain Dealer* chronicled their pathos:

> [Some of the more disturbed patients] crouched down in the
> bottom of wagon boxes with a timidity shown by small ani-
> mals when deprived of liberty and subjected to cruelty by the

hand of man. A few walked the grounds with lordly mien, surveying the destructive element in feverish anxiety . . . Among the articles saved by patients and to which they seemed attached were bibles, fiddles and bird cages. Some of them said they were glad the crazy house had burned down. One of them said to the doctor, "I guess I'll go home, doctor, there is no use in me staying here now." The "President" (a well known inmate), said he would take possession of the vacant lot and put Gov. Noyes in the State Prison. Another swore terribly and flourished a club in close proximity to a gentleman from the *Plain Dealer* office who was suddenly attacked with an irresistible desire to visit another part of the ground.

The Newburgh Asylum board of trustees met the day after the fire and began to plan reconstruction of the asylum. Although the central building area had burned right down to the stone walls—the heat was so intense that the red-hot radiators scorched holes in the ground floor—the extreme right and left wings were in good condition and required only new roofs. The rear building, containing the kitchen, laundry, and other utility rooms, was undamaged. And although the total loss was about $500,000, none of which was covered by insurance, the asylum was quickly rebuilt as a treatment center for whatever nineteenth-century Ohioans were pleased to define as mental illness.

Another tragic fire struck the asylum on October 12, 1887. That fire, beginning in the drying room of the laundry, suddenly erupted into the asylum chapel, where most of the patients were gathered for the weekly dance. Before the ensuing panic subsided, seven women succumbed to the flames, two burned beyond recognition. The asylum was rebuilt and its operations went on.

By 1900 the asylum had treated more than 10,000 patients. It eventually became the Cleveland State Hospital, and its patient population peaked at about 3,000 in the mid-twentieth century. Gradually phased out after the 1960s, Cleveland State Hospital was converted to a facility for the mentally retarded in 1975. The original main building, scene of the two disastrous fires, was finally demolished for good in 1977.

Beulah Park Redux

North Collinwood, February 23, 1937

Back in the 1930s, the area between Euclid Beach Park and the wastewater treatment plant at East 140th Street, north of Lakeshore Boulevard, was largely a summer resort area. During the tough Cleveland winters many of the cottages and bungalows dotting the short streets that dead-end at Lake Erie were boarded up until summer brought the return of those seeking the pleasures of lakeside living. It wasn't surprising, therefore, that Robert Smith, 55, was a lonely figure as he walked along the Lake Erie shore by Beulah Park on the cold afternoon of February 23. A resident of nearby Brown Street, Smith had come down to the beach to check on his sailboat stored there, and was now gathering driftwood for his stove. Turning toward the wintry waves, he saw a white object bobbing just a few feet offshore. Could it be a dog? a sheep's carcass? he wondered. Smith took a closer look—and then scrambled home to call the police.

Lieutenant William Sargent was the first lawman on the scene, soon followed by Sergeant James Hogan. Sargent and Hogan waded into the cold surf and dragged out the upper half of a white, armless, headless, female torso. Wrapping it in a blanket, Hogan sped it to the county morgue on Lakeside.

It was the first Torso victim for new coroner Samuel R. Gerber, a physician who had unexpectedly beaten Arthur J. Pearse in the previous November election. Gerber had a taste for forensic work, and he plunged into the Torso investigation with gusto and an appetite for both controversy and conflict. Before the Torso killings petered out, they would help make him famous and cement his tenure as county coroner until his resignation in 1986.

Torso No. 8 was discovered at the same location where Torso No. 1—the Lady of the Lake—was found. It was the nude, partial body of a white female in her mid-twenties, between five foot four and five foot eight, 100–110 pounds, slender, small-boned, fair-complexioned, and with light brown hair. The victim had given birth at least once, and had no drugs or alcohol in her system. She had been in the water about two days, and had been murdered perhaps one or two days before being put in the lake. The torso had been neatly severed

Police Search Lake Shore for New Torso Murder Clews

Cleveland Press, February 24, 1937.

at the first lumbar vertebra, the condition of the lungs indicated a city dweller, and the presence of sand and weeds suggested that the body had rested on the ground during dismemberment. Coagulated blood indicated that decapitation had not been the cause of death.

Torso No. 8 was controversial among public officials from the start. Sergeant Hogan and Inspector Joseph Sweeney refused to allow her into the Torso canon, as they had with Torso No. 1, the other female found on the Beulah Park beach. Sweeney remarked, "the dissection was not marked with the same skill displayed in the others." But Gerber insisted, in a five-page report submitted to Safety Director Eliot Ness on March 1, that the knife work on all of the victims, except for the first Lady of the Lake, was likely the work of one killer. Gerber went further: the killer was right-handed and "highly intelligent in recognizing the anatomical landmarks as they were approached. . ." In other words, Gerber concluded, it was some-one with a medical background: a physician, medical student, nurse, or orderly. Gerber further argued that the killing of both sexes indi-cated that the killer was not a sexual pervert but rather someone who committed the murders while on alcoholic binges or drug sprees. Dr. Reuben Strauss, county morgue pathologist, went even further. He asserted that the Kingsbury Run killer had also murdered the Lady of the Lake. Alternatively, Assistant Safety Director Robert W. Chamberlin suggested there might be *two* torso killers, and that both Beulah Park torsos were the work of someone other than the Mad Butcher of the Run. But Detective Orly May probably summed up

The Cleveland Press   HOME

ISSUE NO. 19647 — TWO SECTIONS—SECTION ONE · CLEVELAND, WEDNESDAY, FEBRUARY 24, 1937   PRICE THREE CENTS

BABY FARM IS TORSO DEATH CLEW

Cleveland Press headline, February 24, 1937.

the common-sense fatalism of most Cleveland policemen with his comment: "He gives us one regularly every five months."

The police pursued their scant clues with the lack of success that had become the hallmark of Torso sleuthing. Two women in the missing persons files, Ann Ziebert of East Cleveland and Flavia Pillot of Canton, Ohio, were painstakingly sought—until Ziebert walked into Central Station and Pillot turned up elsewhere. A report by Euclid Beach assistant manager Frank Frederick that he had seen two men in a boat offshore Beulah Park on Saturday, February 20, came to nothing when the men were found to be two teenaged boys trying out a new canoe.

Meanwhile, the newspapers were having their usual fun. Torso days were here again at the *News*, whose February 23 headline first blared the return of the Butcher: "FIND NEW TORSO KILLER VICTIM: Fear Kingsbury Fiend is Amuck Again as Lake Yields Body." The next afternoon's *Press* suggested a novel wrinkle appropriate to a female victim with its headline: "BABY FARM IS TORSO DEATH CLEW." The police, it seems, had received tips that there was a "baby farm" (a clandestine home for unwed mothers) in the North Collinwood region. Thinking, perhaps, that it doubled as an abortion mill—and that Lake Lady No. 2 was an accidental victim of an "illegal operation" performed there—Cleveland detectives swarmed the neighborhood looking for clues and talking to neighbors. No baby farm/abortion mill was ever found.

Nor did anything come of heroic efforts by detectives Peter Merylo, Martin Zalewski, and others to comb mephitic miles of neighborhood sewer systems. On the theory that the torso might have come from one of the nearby storm-sewer outlets—one 50 east and the other 200 feet west of the torso site—the decision was made to go into the sewers. The burly Zalewski made it only to the third manhole south of the Lake, but some of the other searchers eventually traipsed underground as far east as East 171st Street in a vain, frozen search for the missing parts of Torso No. 8.

A hotter clue surfaced on February 24, when two trails of blood were discovered leading away from a large bloodstain on the sidewalk in front of 14724 Lake Shore Boulevard. One trail led west, crossed the street to Dalwood Drive, and then vanished. The other led east and crossed to Overlook Park Drive. The latter trail continued down to a path between the houses at 302 and 304 and then disappeared into a field running north to the lake. Detective Merylo was quick to theorize that two men had taken torso parts out of a car on the south side of Lake Shore Boulevard—hence the large stain at 14724—and then split up to dump their grisly cargo at separate locations. The likely time for this scenario was 2:00 a.m., February 23, the very hour a Dalwood resident reported that her dog had been barking for no apparent reason. Merylo's theory collapsed two days later, when a paperboy came forward to report that he had seen an automobile hit a dog at 14724 Lakeshore Boulevard several days earlier. The injured dog was eventually found at a nearby gas station; it belonged to an employee there, Homer Hopcraft. A report that Brady Fleming of Beulah Park had found a human collarbone on the beach the previous September was not even deemed worthy of serious investigation.

And that was that. Eliot Ness went back to keeping a low profile in the Torso phenomenon, and there was suspicion on Coroner Gerber's part—according to Steven Nickel's *Torso: The Story of Eliot Ness and the Search for a Psychopathic Killer*—that Ness put pressure on Cleveland newspapers to downplay both the latest killing and the conclusions of Gerber's five-page report. So the police continued to hunt down cranks and roust suspicious characters, and Zalewski and Merylo kept up their stints as human bait in Kingsbury Run. United States postal authorities did their bit by turning over a list of "Cleveland residents suspected of unbalanced sexual tendencies" to Cleveland police.

On May 5, the missing lower half of Torso No. 8 surfaced. Howard Yochum, an employee at the Wayne Hotel, was testing a "swan boat" that was to be used at the Great Lakes Exposition later in the year. Near the foot of East 30th Street at Lake Erie he saw something suspicious and called the police. The Coast Guard came and fished out what proved to be a perfectly matched lower torso for No. 8. The legs were missing and, like the arms and head, were never found.

Chapter 7

A FIEND WALKS IN CLEVELAND

The 1930 Death of Janet Blood

Who remembers Janet Blood? Perhaps a few aging policemen and detectives whose memories go as far back as the early 1930s. And maybe some West Side women, of a certain age, who can recall their mothers' warning as they left the house, "Walk in the middle of the street, dear—and remember what happened to Janet Blood." But Janet Blood is a forgotten name to most Clevelanders, and that's a shame. It's true that dozens of Clevelanders have been murdered every year of this century with little note nor long remembrance. But there was a particular poignancy to the death of this bright, attractive teenage girl—the last calamity for the doomed Blood family of Cleveland's West Side. Janet Blood's pitiful death touched the heart of Cleveland. It also deserves to be remembered as a murder that provoked one of the most intense police manhunts in Cleveland history.

From the legend of the Sabine women to yesterday's headlines about Nicole Brown Simpson, women have ever been vulnerable to male violence, whether meted out by family members or randomly perpetrated by criminals, and women in Cleveland in 1930 were no exception. Cleveland itself was large and cosmopolitan, a grown-up city with all the social dislocations and stresses that aggravate levels of crime and violence. Like the rest of the country, it was slipping into the bottomless economic pit of the Great Depression—although no one had yet put that name to it—and statistics for financially motivated crime were beginning to reflect it. But there was something more, something worse, at work in Cleveland. A fiend was loose on Cleveland's streets, an unconscionable gunman who preyed on women viciously and at random. This is the story of how he stalked and slew Janet Blood.

It was about 7:30 on the bitterly cold, wintry evening of January 3, 1930, when Janet Blood walked out the door of her home at 1308 West 108th Street. She was on her way to the Edward Decker home at 10220 Clifton Boulevard. Whether it was to baby-sit or to pay a social call is now forgotten, but she must have walked briskly down Clifton to her destination. Traffic was still heavy on Clifton that Friday-night rush hour, and Janet clutched her fur coat to her sides as she strode through the cutting wind. Under her arm was a book, her intended reading for the evening, Eugene O'Neill's *Strange Interlude*. Janet Blood didn't know it, but she was about to meet "The Fiend"—as Cleveland's newspapers dubbed him—and he would take her life.

No fiend of either the human or supernatural kind could have picked a more innocent or undeserving victim than Janet Blood. Sixteen years old, she was a senior at West High School and deservedly popular with all who knew her—a bright, vivacious, caring young woman. A star of her graduating class, she was also an active member of the Old Stone Church, which she attended with her father, and she worked hard in the Christian Endeavor Society.

There was more to Janet Blood, too, than one would have guessed from her pleasant demeanor and good-natured disposition. Even at her young age, she had already been marked by tragedies that might have defeated or scarred a girl of lesser character. Two years before, her mother had died, leaving Janet alone with her father, William Blood, in the upper half of a modest duplex on West 108th. Then, in the summer of 1929, the Taylor department store in downtown Cleveland, where William worked as a credit manager, reorganized his division and let him go. William Blood was a good, decent man, but he eventually crumbled under fate's blows and suffered a nervous breakdown in November 1929. For weeks he lay helpless and shattered in his bedroom, while his loving daughter Janet dropped out of school to nurse him back to health with an energy and courage far beyond her years.

But as 1930 came, it looked as though the Blood family fortunes were about to change for the better. William Blood was recovering at last, and Janet was about to graduate from West High in February, an event delayed by her father's breakdown. No one could have guessed that the Bloods' story would end in tragedy.

It is likely that Janet looked carefully around as she walked east on the south side of Clifton Boulevard. True, the street was preoccupied with traffic, and she wasn't the only pedestrian on the well-lit sidewalks in the area. But Janet was a careful, somewhat timid soul. Louise Booth of West 105th Street, Janet's friend, would later recall that Janet always insisted Louise accompany her partway back to her house when she returned from study sessions at the Booth house. Only when they arrived at Clifton would Janet take leave of Louise,

Janet Blood.

always saying, "I'm all right now."

It happened very quickly. As Janet stepped onto the southwest corner of West 106th and Clifton, a man came up behind her and pinned her arms to her sides. He said, "Don't scream kid, if you know what's good for you. Give me everything you've got and you'll be O.K." Janet, who couldn't see her assailant, replied, "But I haven't got anything." "No?" said the man. "All right then, I'll take your coat." He released Janet's arms, and, as she turned around, began pulling the coat off her. As she stared at him he said, "That's right. Take a good look at me. Then you'll know me again." Without another word, he pulled out a nickel-plated .32-caliber revolver and shot Janet once just beneath her heart.

Even as Janet fell to the sidewalk, the gunman was off and running on West 106th Street, headed south. Mrs. Isabelle Alexander, 68, of 1305 West 106th had just left her house to go to a neighbor's when the gunman crashed into her, hitting her shoulder and nearly knocking her flat in the street. He ran on without a word or a pause. Police who later followed his footprints lost the trail in the snow where it reached the heavy pedestrian traffic on Baltic Avenue.

Meanwhile, Janet's plight had aroused the neighborhood. Hearing the shot, a man opened the door of a nearby house just as Morris

Nathan of Lakewood was driving by, eastward bound on Clifton. Nathan, who may also have heard the shot, saw Janet lying on the pavement, stopped his car, and went to the wounded girl. She moaned, "Oh, take me to a hospital. I've been robbed and shot." Nathan got her into his car and drove to St. John's Hospital. Near where she had fallen, he found her purse in the snow; it was missing six dollars, which the gunman had apparently taken, leaving her coat.

There wasn't much the doctors at St. John's Hospital could do for poor Janet Blood. The .32-caliber slug had entered just below the heart, penetrating the stomach wall in two places and cracking the seventh rib before coming to a stop in her left lung. Because of the location of her wound and her weakened condition, an operation was unthinkable, so her physicians did what they could to keep her comfortable and stable.

Janet Blood spent the next two weeks in excruciating agony, both physical and mental. Although painkillers helped lessen some of the intense pain in her side, nothing could be done to alleviate her emotional torment, as she faded in and out of delirium, repeatedly reliving her nightmare at West 106th and Clifton. Sometimes she called for her dead mother, crying, "Mother, mother, I can't come to you. I can't leave daddy. I must take care of him." Other times, she called for her boyfriend, Louis Schneider of Lakewood, who was eventually allowed to come to her bedside. But most of the time Janet relived her ordeal, again and again screaming the words of her assailant before he shot her: "Give me your money. Gee, you're a pretty little kid, aren't you?"

Janet Blood was still conscious when she arrived at St. John's Hospital, and she was able to give a clear description of her attacker to Cleveland Police detective Frank Story and Captain Andrew Hagan. He was a small man, she said, about five foot five, 135 pounds, aged twenty-five to twenty-eight, with dark eyes, a dark complexion, and a long, hooked nose. He was wearing a gray cap and a dark gray tweed suit or overcoat.

Janet's description confirmed the worst fears of Cleveland policemen. They had suspected for some time that there was a particularly brutal male suspect preying on Cleveland women, sometimes with guns, sometimes not—but always with ferocious force. Evidence from incidents going back to the fall of 1929 now crystallized at last in the realization that what police had hitherto referred to as a "masher gunman" or "East End masher" was in all probability a single male predator who had decided to make war without quarter on Cleveland women.

The bullet that killed Janet Blood.

The incidents had begun on October 22, when Mrs. Florence Alvin, 39, of 8320 Vineyard Avenue had a raincoat thrown over her head near Warner Road and was robbed. Less than a month later, Miss Hilda Kilmer, 22, of East 100th Street was knocked down by a male attacker at 9905 Pratt Avenue. Only three days later, Miss Esther Atkinson of 4140 East 111th Street was attacked in the front yard of her home. On November 20, Miss Helen Own, 22, of 10005 Harvard Avenue beat off an assailant at her home. Two weeks later, on December 3, Mrs. Mary Urban, 21, of 9823 Anderson Avenue, was knocked down in the street. Three days later a woman was assaulted in the rear of a St. Clair Avenue apartment. And on December 17, Miss Naomi Devore, 20, of 8821 Marshall Avenue, was badly beaten with a railcar coupling pin several blocks from her home before her screams frightened her attacker away. The very next day brought another assault, on Miss Rose David of 2889 Ambler Avenue, who courageously fought off the assailant who attempted to drag her into a vacant lot near her home. Badly beaten and semiconscious, she managed to crawl home.

Things took an ominous turn only two days later. Mrs. Beatrice Gallagher, 23, a maid at the home of R. H. Perdue of 1856 East 87th Street, was shot by an unknown gunman as she was returning to the house from a streetcar. She was fired upon as she was unlocking the back door, by an unseen figure in the shadows. She was taken to Huron Road Hospital in critical condition, with four bullets inside her. Three days later, Mary Pshock, 20, alighted from a streetcar on East 55th in the evening. As she was walking by Utica Avenue, she was accosted by a man who asked her to go for a walk. When she refused and told him her husband was coming, he pulled out a gun and shot her in the back.

Two hours after Janet Blood was shot, Mrs. Mae Simpson, 18, of 1862 East 93rd, became the next victim. While on her way to the grocery store at about 9:30 p.m., she was accosted by a man who said, "Hello, kid. How much money have you got on you?" When she started to resist, he pulled a gun on her and dragged her off to a nearby garage. The last thing he said, as he left her, was "You're not the first one tonight."

The attacks on Janet Blood and Mae Simpson were the last straw for Cleveland safety officials. There was a disturbing similarity to the descriptions given by many of the female victims—especially the "hooked nose" of their attacker—and the newspapers were putting the heat on a department that seemed to have lost control of Cleveland's streets. On the morning of January 4, Cleveland safety director Edwin D. Barry announced an unprecedented campaign to catch the "Fiend" or "mad gunman."

Barging into Police Chief Jacob Graul's office, Barry berated him loudly for laxity in the Fiend investigation and announced that Inspector George Matowitz would now be in charge of the department's manhunt. All leaves of absence, all days off, were canceled, and all Cleveland policemen—excluding the traffic division—were to start working twelve-hour shifts until the Fiend was caught. To Graul, Barry shouted, "We're going to get him, and get him quick, or I'll know the reason why!" Later, commenting to Cleveland reporters, Graul self-righteously opined, "It has gotten so a woman isn't safe on the streets of Cleveland after dark." And Inspector Matowitz transmitted that heat right on down the line to the patrolmen on the streets: "Send them into the dives, the reputed speakeasies and the poolrooms. Tell them to arrest anyone who looks suspicious and turn them over to the detective bureau."

If Cleveland police didn't exactly catch the purported Fiend during the following days, it wasn't for lack of effort. Within minutes of Barry's order, flying squads of police in automobile cruisers, four to a vehicle and armed with pump shotguns, were patrolling the streets in search of the hook-nosed gunman. They had explicit orders to

Southwest corner of W. 106th and Clifton Boulevard, where
Janet Blood was fatally shot, January 3, 1930.

shoot to kill if they encountered any resistance. All city rooming
houses were combed for suspicious characters, and the city jail soon
began to fill with dozens and dozens of more or less plausible suspects.

The hunt for the Fiend began with a legitimate search for a
masher-gunman, as described by many of his victims. However, as
the *Cleveland Press* put it on January 7: "Hook-nosed men, Roman-
nosed men and men with just plain big noses were again the object
of police suspicion today . . ." Pretty soon, as *The Plain Dealer*'s
Don Robertson recalled in 1956, hysteria was the order of the day on
Cleveland's mean streets: "No man could look twice at a woman.
The Fiend was everyplace. A drunk would try to pick up a woman
and would wind up in a cell being grilled like a sausage in deep fat."

In addition to arresting suspicious-looking men and flooding the
streets with cops, the Cleveland authorities also dispensed useful
advice to the female population. "Scream at the top of your voice,"
suggested Inspector Cornelius Cody. "If alone at night, walk in the
middle of the street; go to the nearest house if followed."

As in any episode of public hysteria, there were some ludicrous
incidents ensuing from mounting public fears. One suspect, captured

by Oscar A. Bloomberg, the manager of the Points Pharmacy at East 152nd and St. Clair Avenue, was just a slightly drunken pedestrian whose aimless whistling, while waiting for the traffic signal to change, was misinterpreted by an anxious woman as something more ominous. Another man, who followed Mrs. Ruth Myerson, 21, to her East 51st Street apartment was able to show convincing evidence to the police that the building custodian had called him to repair the plumbing. And a burly man who approached an automobile occupied by Mrs. Ruby Stevenson and Mrs. Ernestine Winsett received rough treatment when he mistakenly thought they were beckoning to him from their car. They were not; they were just wiping the windshield, and when the man approached, Mrs. Winsett screamed and Mrs. Stevenson kicked the poor fellow hard in the stomach. Meanwhile, Central Police Station was besieged with telephone calls from hundreds of nervous-to-terrified women.

The amplified presence of Cleveland patrolmen did little to stop the reign of terror in the streets. On the evening of January 5, Miss Betty Kmetz, 18, was walking south on East 105th Street near Ashbury Avenue. A man came up from behind, shoved a gun in her back, and said, "Where you going, sweetie?" As she turned around, he started dragging her toward an alley. She screamed, broke away, and fled to a nearby gas station as her attacker ran away. Two days later, Mary Prohaska, 18, of 1418 East 53rd Street was accosted by a man on St. Clair. "Why don't you come with me, baby?" he said. She screamed and ran all the way home; the man followed her all the way to her door before running off.

Four more attacks followed the next day. Mary Tracy, 23, of East 53rd Street was on her way to a dressmaking class at East Technical High School when a man came up behind and pinned her arms. He fled when she screamed, as did the assailant of Miss Rose Arpajian, 21, of 7749 Broadway, who accosted his victim on East 82nd Street. He came up and tried to choke her before her screams drove him away. Unluckier still was Miss Lottie Molinowsky, 21, of 6444 Broadway. She was grabbed in the fog while walking on Osage Avenue; her attacker threatened to stab her, he beat her savagely, and he stole eighty-two dollars from her purse. Her coat was slashed at the back and sleeve with his long knife, but she survived the encounter.

More significant for the investigation was the attack on Miss Hilda Matuska, 17, of 7821 Laumer Avenue as she was on her way to work at a bakery on January 8. Accosted and knocked to the ground by a young man at Grand Division Avenue and East 94th

Street, Matuska fought back like an enraged wildcat, flailing with her fists and an umbrella. Although her assailant tried silencing her by stuffing a handkerchief down her throat, she finally beat him off, and as he ran away, she screamed, "I'll know you when I see you again."

The plucky Matuska was as good as her word. She thought her assailant had looked like an old school classmate, and her suspicions soon led Cleveland policemen to the door of Ralph DeMatteo, 21, of Garfield Heights. DeMatteo soon repudiated the confession wrung from him by police interrogators, but by that time he had been identified as their attacker by three women, including Matuska. Disturbingly, however, DeMatteo did not resemble the description of the much-sought "hook-nosed" Fiend—and so the desperate search for a stalking killer went on.

Cleveland police didn't want to get burned again. They had already captured one supposedly "hot" suspect. William C. Beers had filed a missing-person report on his brother, Howard Beers, late Friday night, shortly after Janet Blood was shot. Howard, a former mental patient—seventeen years in a Pennsylvania asylum—seemed to fit the description of the Fiend, so he was picked up in Detroit on January 5 and brought back to Cleveland. Even before arriving at Central Police Station, Beers confessed to shooting both Beatrice Gallagher and Mary Pshock.

Beers's story seemed plausible. He said that on December 20 he had been standing in the backyard of a restaurant where he worked as a dishwasher and had fired some random shots from a revolver. At least one of them, he claimed, had hit a woman at the back door of a nearby house. Three days later, while standing at East 55th Street and Utica Avenue, he had fired his gun again and hit Mary Pshock. And that wasn't all: he told Cleveland police he had tried to rob a girl of her fur coat at West 106th Street and Clifton Boulevard on Friday night, January 3—and then he had shot her.

Within a day of his arrest, at least one detective was already beginning to suspect that Beers's confession was the "fiction of a wandering mind." And after Beatrice Gallagher and Mary Pshock both failed to identify him, Beers broke down and admitted he had made it all up after reading the newspapers. He was charged with insanity on January 7 and removed to the county jail for further disposition. A suspect picked up in Akron after a suicide attempt in a hotel also proved to be another Fiend "wannabe" who had brooded creatively over press accounts of Janet Blood's shooting.

Still the vicious attacks on women continued. On January 9, about

Possible murder weapons found in police dragnet for Janet
Blood's killer.

5:30 p.m., thirteen-year-old Lillian Szakacs of Beekman Avenue was
returning home from the grocery store when she was accosted by a
male stranger. He grabbed her but slipped and fell on the icy sidewalk as she squirmed away. She screamed and ran, but he caught her
again and said, "Give me a kiss, honey." She continued to scream, so
he put his hand over her mouth and started to drag her to a nearby
yard. She bit his finger and screamed anew, finally attracting the
attention of a man who was backing a car out of a drive across the
street. As the man approached, Lillian's attacker ran. There was
blood pouring out of her mouth and nose but she had managed to survive her ordeal. The police found no trace of her assailant when they
arrived on the scene.

Less than two hours later, Lillian Zehe, 21, of Luther Avenue was
attacked while walking down East 12th Street between Prospect and
Huron avenues. A man grabbed her and threw her against the wall of
a building but fled when her screams attracted a passerby. Another
attack the next day on Irene Rutosky, 19, while she was walking on
Superior Avenue near East 17th Street, was aborted when a rescuer
was attracted by her screams.

By this time, not all reports of the Fiend's activities were given
equal weight by Cleveland authorities. On January 10, Inspector

Cornelius Cody told reporters that at least one victim's story was "an absolute fake," a lie made up to conceal the loss of some money. And the day after that, Safety Director Barry gave unequivocal warning to any additional Fiend "fakers": "Throw them behind the bars and prosecute them for making false police reports."

The manhunt went doggedly on. Ralph DeMatteo was charged with the November 14 assault on Esther Atkinson and pleaded not guilty on January 11. Dozens of suspects were hustled in and out of Central Police Station, many of them unsavory but none who could be definitely linked with either the Janet Blood shooting or lesser crimes. Police were especially eager to find the gun used by the Fiend, and hopes soared when H. S. Gurney of 2016 West 98th found a rusty nickel-plated .32-caliber revolver buried in the snow next to his garage. Like many other guns that came into the hands of the police, it ultimately failed to match either the bullet in Janet Blood or those that struck any of the other Fiend victims. On January 12, Julia Zima, 22, of 5419 Magnet Avenue was attacked in her backyard. The hunt continued.

Meanwhile, life began to ebb away from Janet Blood. Although she had initially been given a fair chance for recovery, she progressively weakened as the infection in her wounded lung took its toll. Her father, William Blood, virtually never left her side after he arrived at St. John's Hospital on the night of January 3. He watched helplessly, hour by hour, day by day, as she slowly but surely sank closer and closer to death. Albert Koch, who lived in the other half of the double house at 1308 West 108th, donated a pint of blood on January 12 in a desperate effort to save Janet's life. When she showed some subsequent improvement, the entire basketball team at West High School volunteered to donate more blood if it were needed. But by January 16, Janet was too weak even for that, much less an operation to remove the bullet that continued to fester in her lung.

The beginning of the end came on Friday night, January 17. William Blood was allowed to hold his dying daughter as she lapsed in and out of consciousness. About 11:00 p.m., she called to her father and said, "Kiss me, Daddy, I'm going to heaven. I'm going to mother." She never regained consciousness. An emergency operation and a second blood transfusion the next day failed to arrest her deterioration. Saturday afternoon, Janet's chief physician, Dr. J. R. Ripton, told hospital telephone operators, who were besieged by calls from hundreds of concerned Clevelanders: "If anyone calls regarding the condition of Janet Blood you will say that she is dying." Janet fought on through Saturday afternoon and into Saturday night, but her only signs of life were occasional, delirious calls to her dead mother.

Janet Blood died on Sunday, January 19, surrounded by those who loved her: her father, his brother Joseph, and various cousins. About 7:45 a.m., Dr. Harold Miller, who had been holding her hand and counting the beats of her pulse, gently laid her hand down on the bedcover. He looked up and nodded silently to those in the room. It was over. William Blood went to pieces for a few moments, pulled himself together, and issued a statement to the public that had watched and hoped for his brave daughter to win her fight: "It is wonderful—just simply wonderful. I never knew that my little girl had so many friends. I never knew that a big city could be so generous with a man in the time of trouble."

After an autopsy to remove the fatal bullet, Janet Blood's body was taken to the Saxton-Daniels-Mastick Funeral Home at 13215 Detroit Avenue. Members of the West High senior class were excused from classes to attend Janet's funeral, and Principal David P. Simpson announced that Janet would graduate with her class, complete with a signed diploma.

The grisly shadows that had hovered over Janet Blood did not dissipate for her obsequies. On the night of January 20, Lester Wakeham, an employee of the Saxton-Daniels-Mastick Funeral Home, noticed a suspicious "hook-nosed" man lurking near the building, mumbling to himself. Several minutes later, two women attending Janet's wake noticed the same man and reported him to the police. No trace could be found of him when police arrived, but the next day Cleveland authorities received a letter signed "The Fiend," which promised further killings. They were inclined to think it was the work of a crank, but they promised an extra-large police presence at the funeral, in hopes that the killer would "return to the scene of the crime."

The funeral of Janet Blood, held at the funeral home on the afternoon of January 21, was one of the largest in West Side history. More than 2,000 persons jammed the funeral home and its grounds, with automobiles congesting streets for blocks around. Vernon D. Harris, a friend of Janet's, sang the same hymns he had sung at her mother's funeral two years earlier: "Lead, Kindly Light" and "Jesus, Savior, Pilot Me." William Blood started to go to pieces again as the casket was borne out of the room, but a five-year-old girl ran up to him, threw her arms around him, and said, "Don't cry, Mr. Blood. Please don't cry." Her named was Geraldine Close, and as William Blood dried his eyes, he kissed her and said, "It was the most beautiful

Coverage of the Janet Blood murder, including sketch of "hook-nosed Fiend." *Cleveland News*, January 20, 1930.

thing that has ever happened to me."

Janet Blood was buried beside her mother in a snow-covered plot in Lakewood Park Cemetery. Her father couldn't afford another tombstone, so Janet Blood sleeps yet in an unmarked grave. Shortly afterward, William Blood left Cleveland for good. A female Cleveland neighbor who knew him later recalled that he aged very quickly after his daughter's death, spending his last years at a home for the indigent in southern Ohio.

By the time Janet Blood died, the hunt for the Fiend had just about run out of gas. There were still attacks on Cleveland females, but they seemed random and none of the perpetrator descriptions fitted the profile of the hook-nosed Fiend. Cleveland newspapers would

continue to beat the drums for an all-out manhunt, as in the belliger-
ent front-page *Cleveland News* editorial of January 20, which hec-
tored Cleveland police with the following warning:

> GET SLAYER—OR GET OUT!:
> Find the "hook-nosed" gunman-slayer of Janet Blood, or get
> out of the service! . . . To say that the police force is too small
> to stop these attacks which have terrorized the women of the
> city is inconsistent with the reports of the number assigned to
> the "hook-nosed gunman" case. The time for excuses is past.

But the Cleveland police had already thrown in the towel. On January 17, Chief Jacob Graul ordered the 874 Cleveland police on
twelve-hour shifts to return to their eight-hour schedules. The fact
was that the city could not afford the accumulating overtime, and
more police manpower was needed for a developing garment workers' strike. Indeed, the city of Cleveland was so strapped for cash that
it finally struck a deal with all of the policemen who had worked
hundreds of hours of overtime in their search for the Fiend between
January 4 and January 17, 1930. The deal was that they would be
paid the overtime due them when they retired. And that is what happened: as each police employee retired over the next thirty years, he
was paid a lump sum for the unpaid hours earned in January 1930.
Inevitably, those who received the payment came to call it their
"Blood money."

Other Cleveland organizations tried to do a little more than round
up the usual suspects. The Cuyahoga County commissioners offered
a $1,000 reward, and local American Legion officers vowed to use
"all resources" in finding Janet Blood's killer. J. M. Saunders, the
Legion's county chairman, bellowed: "Every red-blooded citizen is
aroused over the brutal attacks and murderous assaults upon women
and girls of our city . . . Cleveland must be made safe for our wives,
sisters, mothers and daughters to live in."

Almost simultaneously, a bitter William Blood unloaded some
caustic remarks on the investigation of his daughter's murder:

> The police wasted time and did not seem particularly effi-
> cient during the time I was at my daughter's bedside. They
> continually ran back and forth from headquarters to me, ask-
> ing for clews that I might have in connection with the shoot-
> ing. I told them everything I knew in the first place and
> repeated that when they questioned me again and again. I was

not impressed by the intelligence of detectives assigned to
the case.

The beleaguered Cleveland cops finally got a break on Sunday,
January 26, thanks to the dogged work of Detective George Clark.
On Friday night, January 23, Clark had gotten a tip about a suspect
who had robbed a tire shop in December and taken some money and
a .32-caliber revolver. Clark traced the suspect through seven different addresses before he finally ran him down. Propping a painter's
ladder against a second-floor window at 8010 Wade Park Avenue,
Clark climbed up and made sure his quarry was there. He then called
in other detectives, and they arrested Edward W. Ralph, 18, asleep in
his bed at 4:00 on Sunday morning.

Soon identified by both Beatrice Gallagher and Mary Pshock as
the man who shot them, Edward Ralph confessed. He insisted on
apologizing to both victims—his contrition didn't go over very well
with either of them—but maintained that he had shot them in a state
of helpless inebriation. He initially claimed that he had thrown his
gun in Lake Erie, but dubious detectives eventually located it hidden
in a friend's kitchen. Ballistics tests would eventually identify it con-
clusively as the gun that shot Beatrice Gallagher.

But it was not the gun that shot Janet Blood, and Ralph, while
admitting to the other shootings, was adamant that he had not been
involved in her murder. He was eventually convicted of the Gallagher shooting and sent to the Mansfield Reformatory. He escaped
from there in November of 1931 and was later suspected in a rash of
attacks on women in January 1932.

The murder of Janet Blood remains unsolved to this day. Apparently, she was just a nice kid who was in the wrong place at the
wrong time—and met the wrong man. There were probably at least
two "Fiends" roaming Cleveland streets in January 1930, and one of
them, Ralph DeMatteo, was probably responsible for at least half of
the attacks in late 1929 and early 1930. But no one knows who killed
poor Janet Blood, and she remains but a remembered cautionary
byword of West Side childhoods, and a plaintive phantom in an
unmarked West Side grave.

A Rose Ain't Necessarily a Rose

Stone's Levee, June 6, 1937

The winter of 1937 passed. The Roosevelt Recession arrived, and still there was no break in the Kingsbury Run Torso killer hunt. Dozens of Cleveland policemen continued to work on the case, and detectives Merylo and Zalewski persisted in their obsessive, faithful hunt for the mysterious decapitating fiend. Peter Merylo eventually caught up with a prime suspect, the infamous "voodoo doctor," but had to let him go when no evidence could be found linking him to the Mad Butcher's supposed victims. Merylo and other Cleveland policemen were also interested in the whereabouts of a gigantic hobo said to menace the transient population of the Flats—his enormous footprints could sometimes be spotted amid the muddy debris under the many bridges there. And there was even talk in law-enforcement circles of a vampire-like predator whose favorite beverage was human blood.

Fourteen-year-old Russell Tower wasn't interested in such gruesome speculations as he dawdled on the banks of the Cuyahoga River by Stone's Levee on the morning of Saturday, June 6, 1937. Not that he didn't have a morbid streak: he was down there, after all, because he was watching a police tugboat drag the river for the body of Charles Gallagher, a sailor who had drowned in the river on June 5. As Mr. Gallagher did not put in an appearance, Russell finally decided to go home.

It was while he was passing under the eastern approaches of the Lorain-Central Bridge (later designated the Lorain-Carnegie Bridge and now known as the Hope Memorial Bridge) that Russell noticed an enticing pile of stones—and decided to kick it. One can imagine his shock when his first vigorous kick dislodged a human skull displaying a hideous, incomplete grin, thanks to the gold bridgework and dentures left in its mouth.

The Cleveland policemen summoned to Russell's find discovered not only the skull but also a rotted burlap bag containing a rich find of badly decomposed human remains. Inside the bag, wrapped in a *Plain Dealer* edition of June 1936, were ribs, hips, shoulder blades,

CLEVELAND PLAIN DEALER FINAL

CLEVELAND, MONDAY MORNING, JUNE 7, 1937

FIND SKELETON, HUNT TORSO CASE LINK

Headline from *The Plain Dealer,* June 7, 1937.

a complete set of human vertebrae, and a piece of human skin about a foot long. Near by police also found a black wig (said to be the type used in minstrel shows), a dirty wool cap, and the sleeve of a woman's dress. After examining the remains and finding no wounds except those involved in the dismemberment, Coroner Gerber announced that Russell had found the latest victim of the Kingsbury Run Torso murderer.

Further study of the incomplete corpse by Gerber and Dr. Todd Wingate of Western Reserve University refined the initial analysis. Gerber estimated from the decomposition that the victim had been dead a year, possibly from as early as April or March of 1936. Traces of lime on the skull and skin fragment suggested that the presumed murderer had tried to destroy the physical evidence of the homicide. Gerber's description of the corpse as "expertly dissected" seemed to clinch the conclusion that this was the newest victim of Cleveland's demented serial killer.

Who was Torso victim No. 9? Gerber quickly abandoned his initial guess that the victim was a male and announced that the remains seemed to be those of a black woman. A chart of her extensive dental work was circulated throughout the United States, and within mere days Cleveland detectives received word from Cincinnati that the dental records matched those of Rose Wallace, a black female of about forty years. At last, the police seemed to have an identity for the latest Torso victim, the first positive ID since Flo Polillo in January 1936.

Such certainty was not to be. Coroner Gerber insisted that this latest victim had died in April 1936. This ruled out Rose Wallace, who had not disappeared off the face of the earth until at least August 1936. Eliot Ness, who was still keeping a low profile on the Torso case, also demurred on a probable match with Rose Wallace, as did *The Plain Dealer,* which averred it was "no more than a good guess" that what was left of Rose lay in the burlap sack found by Russell Tower.

Peter Merylo and many other Cleveland policemen were convinced, however, that Rose Wallace was indeed the ninth victim. Their tireless sleuthing disclosed that Rose, a prostitute of

SEEK SUSPECT AS LINK IN TWO TORSO KILLINGS

Torso Victim?

Police Learn "One-Armed Willie" Was "Friend" of Victims Four and Nine

Detectives, in their quest for the elusive torso murderer whose mad cunning has baffled them for four years, turned again today toward a character known as "One-Armed Willie."

"One-Armed Willie" is reported to

Cleveland Press headline, April 11, 1938.

"ephemeral loyalties and peculiar friends" (Peter Bellamy's apt description), had disappeared on the night of August 21, 1936. Leaving a bar at East 19th Street and Scovill Avenue with a man named Bob, Wallace had been spotted later the same evening in an automobile with three white men. Presumably these men knew what had happened to her—if only they could be found.

The police eventually discovered other interesting facts about Rose Wallace. A habitue of the more decayed fleshpots of the Roaring Third, Wallace had hung around some of the same dives and locations of ill repute as Flo Polillo. Not only that, but one of Wallace's boyfriends had been the unfortunate Polillo's acquaintance, "One-Armed Willie." And the sleeve of that woman's dress, according to one police informant, looked a lot like the frock Wallace was last seen wearing.

And that was, once again, the seeming end of another bloody trail. Suggestive clues, tantalizing coincidences, and bizarre circumstances led to . . . if not quite nothing, then little more than the additional accumulation of more unwholesome characters with disgusting lifestyles, and a repetitive and numbing inventory of body parts. Still, though, the desperate search went on. Merylo and Zalewski continued to offer themselves as Butcher Bait on the hills of Kingsbury Run, Eliot Ness kept his nose publicly out of the unsolved mess, and Cleveland's newspapers continued to hone the legend of the Forest City's own Jack the Ripper. The last word on Torso No. 9 was the announcement on June 8 that Cleveland policemen were about to shift twenty thousand pounds of sand near the Stone's Levee site in an intensive hunt for evidence about the elusive Torso killer. And, most interesting of all, Rose Wallace was never seen alive again on this earth.

Chapter 8

A FATAL BOTTLE
OF BEER

The J. J. Phillips Mystery of 1907

It's a familiar narrative to connoisseurs of Cleveland crime. A long holiday weekend. A prominent Cleveland family about whom unseemly rumors are beginning to swirl. A brutal murder in the middle of the night, committed within scant feet of an innocent sleeping child. Suspicious hours that pass before a call for help is made. The cry for aid at last put through—but to a nearby neighbor, not the police. The signs of an apparent burglary—too apparent, say the police. Sensationalistic newspaper headlines that convict the accused before trial and drag a family through the gutter of public gossip. And an ensuing mystery that remains ultimately unsolved to this day.

The 1954 Sheppard murder? No. This tragic story concerns the equally puzzling death of businessman J. J. Phillips on the morning of September 2, 1907. Never solved, it became a grueling ordeal for his accused wife, a frustrating marathon for law-enforcement authorities, a feast for the four Cleveland daily newspapers, and a multifaceted puzzle that makes little sense no matter what explanation is selected.

The saga began officially on the stormy morning of September 2, 1907 at 4:00 a.m., when Marshal James H. Stamberger of the East Cleveland police picked up the receiver of his ringing telephone. The call came from the J. J. Phillips residence at 50 Mount Union and it bore grim news. Dr. Ellis B. Rhodes, a neighbor of Phillips's, was on the line, and he told Stamberger that Phillips had been shot and lay gravely wounded in his upstairs bedroom.

Stamberger got to the Phillips house within minutes. There he found the dying man; his wife, Charlotte Phillips; Dr. Charles Richardson, a neighbor and osteopath; the Phillipses' ten-year-old adopted daughter, Ethel; and Dr. Rhodes, whom Dr. Richardson had called after examining the badly wounded man. Although wracked by fits of coughing and spitting up blood, Phillips was able to talk, and it was quite a tale he unfolded to Chief Stamberger.

The dying man's story was that he had awakened in his second-floor bedroom at about 1:15 a.m. and, feeling thirsty, had gone down to the kitchen to get a bottle of beer. Groping his way back up the stairs, he lit a match on the landing. At the instant he lit the match, there was the flash of a pistol and Phillips felt a stinging sensation at the back of his neck. Falling against the door on the landing that communicated to the kitchen, he cried "Oh, My God!" and fainted.

No one could say later how long Phillips was unconscious. His wife Charlotte said she was awakened by his cry but didn't leave her room—Mr. and Mrs. Phillips had separate bedrooms—for some minutes. When she did, she found J. J. trying to climb the upper flight of stairs to his bedroom. With the help of Ethel, the adopted daughter, Charlotte got her husband to the bathroom, where she looked at his wound. He had been shot in the back of the neck and was bleeding freely—yet he made light of it, saying that he wasn't hurt badly and begging Charlotte not to call the police or doctors. When she told him she was going to telephone, he forbade her, saying that the burglars who had shot him were still downstairs and would kill her and Ethel, too. He asked for whiskey, and when informed there was none in the house, settled for alcohol and water. Almost three hours went by.

What happened during those three hours would be the subject of cynical supposition and puzzled inquiry for the next several months. Charlotte Phillips would steadfastly insist that her husband told her there were burglars on the lower floor, and she swore to the police that she could hear them ransacking the rooms below. She initially said that she remained mute, but later claimed that she went to several windows and screamed for help. And she eventually produced three different explanations for why she waited almost three hours to call Stamberger: 1) she "forgot"; 2) she didn't think he had a telephone; and 3) she tried repeatedly but a terrible thunder and lightning storm had put all the lines out of order.

Ethel Phillips backed up her mother's story with minor variances. Her memory was that she was awakened at 12:30 a.m. by a door slamming downstairs. She got out of her bed, unlocked her door, and went into the upstairs hall. She saw her father coming up the stairs to the landing, saw him strike a match, and then saw the flash of the pistol. Her memory was that the kitchen door he was leaning against was closed—Charlotte insisted it was open—and that her mother opened the front door of the house and shouted for help immediately after getting her husband to his room. None of them—Phillips, his wife, or Ethel—had seen who had fired at Phillips on the stairs. But

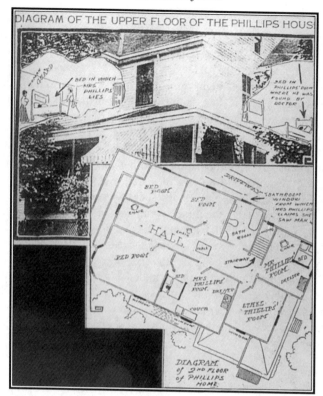

Diagram of second floor of Phillips house. *Cleveland Press*, September 7, 1907.

both Ethel and Charlotte claimed they had looked out the bathroom window and seen a man standing underneath a tree outside the house and near the streetlight. He was short, squat, dressed in dark clothes, and apparently standing guard for the burglars who yet roamed the Phillipses' first floor.

J. J. Phillips died at 5:59 a.m. Charlotte had called Dr. Richardson just before 4:00 a.m., and he had called Dr. Rhodes when he realized the seriousness of Phillips's wound. Which Phillips himself apparently did not: he walked around for several hours after he was shot, deprecating the gravity of his injury and insisting that his wife was far more in need of medical attention than he was. Rhodes and Richardson eventually became so concerned as to call in surgeon C. A. Hammond. But it was too late: Phillips's lungs began to fill up with blood, and he succumbed to loss of blood and lung failure from damage to the nerves that controlled his diaphragm. He died while the doctors were out gathering instruments for his surgery. His last words before losing consciousness were "I'm all right. I don't want any fuss made over this."

Chief Stamberger thought something smelled fishy from the start. He was puzzled by the three-hour lapse between the shooting and the call to the police, and he was even more mystified by the supposed burglary scenario. Before he died, Phillips himself told Stamberger that he had been shot by burglars—Mrs. Phillips said she could hear them downstairs—and both Ethel and her mother claimed to have seen one standing outside. Yet the circumstantial evidence in the house suggested no burglary at all. There was no evidence of forced entrance or exit. True, the dining room was in disarray, with buffet drawers pulled out, tables overturned, and silverware scattered on the floor. But the other rooms of the house were undisturbed, and virtually nothing was missing except six solid-silver spoons, which Ethel soon found neatly wrapped under a bush outside the house. Chief Stamberger knew of few instances in which burglars shot without provocation at a man going upstairs, much less hung around the house for several hours after they had shot a man. It didn't make any sense.

Nor, to James Stamberger's mind, did the evidence of the shooting. Although Phillips had a messy wound that had bled freely in his room and on his bedclothes, there were no traces of blood on the stairs, except for one patch on the wall that might have been made by a wounded man stumbling by. And the gun that killed J. J. Phillips could not be found at all.

Most suspicious of all, Stamberger felt, was the behavior of Charlotte Phillips, behavior which would aggravate his suspicions mightily throughout the coming days. She seemed reluctant to give straight answers to his questions and appeared almost paranoid at the prospect of her daughter being interrogated privately about the fatal night's events. Worse yet, she tried to forestall his questions by consulting her lawyer on the telephone and talking of her "rights," notions not quite so common in 1907 as they would become later in the century.

Meanwhile, the death of J. J. Phillips sent shock waves through the Cleveland financial community. Regarded as a respectable coal merchant and capitalist by his neighbors and many business connections, Phillips had had a net worth rated at almost half a million dollars only the previous year. Now, within mere hours of his death, he was exposed and publicly vilified as an unscrupulous, brazen specu-

John J. Phillips. *Cleve-land Press*, Sept. 23, 1907.

Mrs. Charlotte Phillips. *Cleveland Press*, Sept. 4, 1907.

lator and financial double-dealer who had dissipated his fortune, and probably the fortunes of his wife and many others who had trusted him, in so-called "bucket shops"—security dealers of ill repute and suicidally speculative character. Indeed, operating under aliases and through third parties, Phillips had come to be known to savvy speculators as the "Bucket Shop King of Northern Ohio." Rumors quickly spread that the assets of Phillips's estate would not cover even a twentieth of the liabilities. Such gossip about Phillips's presumed financial speculations was heightened by word that he had very recently taken out a number of very large life-insurance policies. It looked like a scandalous ending to the J. J. Phillips story, reminiscent of the poem "Richard Cory" or the disgraceful death of Mr. Merdle in Charles Dickens's *Little Dorrit*.

Stamberger didn't believe Charlotte Phillips's version of J. J.'s death for a minute; his initial theory was that Phillips had committed suicide. The burglary was obviously faked, and who could have done that but Phillips or his wife? And what possible motive could they have had to make his death look like murder? . . . except the knowledge that suicide would probably nullify any hopes of insurance money. So, Stamberger reasoned, Phillips had shot himself and, with or without his wife's complicity, had made it look like murder. This, too, was the Cleveland media's initial take, typified by the *Cleveland Leader*'s September 3 headline: "J. J. PHILLIPS IS A SUICIDE; Death Sought When Failure Was Imminent."

There were some difficulties with the theory. A major stumbling block was the testimony and demeanor of Ethel Phillips. She made a terrific witness at the inquest, which opened Tuesday morning, September 3, and except for minor inconsistences, such as the position of the kitchen door and whether and when Charlotte screamed for help, she could not be shaken from her straightforward and ingratiating testimony. Ethel *swore* she had seen her father shot on the landing, she *swore* she had heard burglars below, and she *swore* she had seen a short, squat, suspicious-looking man standing outside the Phillips house for several hours after the shooting. A man, she now insisted, who looked a lot like Charles Herzberg, a half-witted, illiterate chauffeur formerly employed and subsequently fired by J. J. Phillips.

J. J.'s siblings and in-laws were adamant that he had been murdered. His brother, Clyde Phillips, brushed the idea of suicide aside with contempt: "he never killed himself." J. J. Thomas, a brother-in-law, insisted, "he had no motive for suicide; on the contrary he had prospects that would have made him independently rich within a few days." W. D. Gray, a friend of Phillips's who had talked to him at 9:00 the night before his murder, remembered, "He was never more cheerful."

Meanwhile, the inquest ground forward. Stamberger appeared and told of the surreal goings-on at the Phillips's house on the murder morning. He mentioned that Charlotte Phillips had told him of an angry, anonymous voice on the telephone three years before, a voice that had threatened, "Phillips cannot walk the streets and with my money, for I will have his life blood." The inquest shut down after two days, as deputy coroner Houck ruled the death a murder— but not the kind of murder Phillips or his wife had claimed: "It was murder. There was no suicide. Neither were there burglars."

The circumstantial evidence was overwhelming to Houck. With no powder burns on Phillips's neck, it seemed clear that the shot came from behind. The initial theory that the shot had been fired through the mouth was also disproved by an autopsy, conducted by Dr. Rhodes and Dr. Oscar T. Schultz of the Western Reserve Medical College, which found that "[t]he bone of the neck was broken and splintered, while the bullet came cleanly out of the skin of the roof of the mouth. There were no powder burns on the neck . . . there were none on the tongue."

The financial implications of Phillips's death continued to snowball. Although there were still those who loudly trumpeted Phillips's business probity and financial acumen, they were drowned out by a chorus declaiming that smart money men and wise bankers had known for several years that J. J. Phillips was headed toward ruin. A

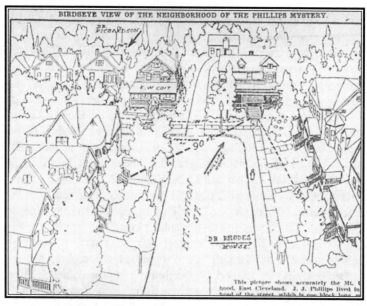

Diagram of Phillips house locale. *The Plain Dealer*, Sept. 5, 1907

smart man when it came to coal—Phillips invariably made money at the retail, wholesale, and investment levels—he had become a victim of his own speculative frenzy, a mania that had made him a pariah to his more savvy financial fellows in the months before his death. Now these naysayers came out of the woodwork to tell of his string of a dozen or more bucket shops in Ohio, New York, and Pennsylvania; his crazed speculations in worthless securities; and his increasingly dishonored checks. There was even a rumor that his financial machinations had compromised the fortunes of the Glenville Banking and Trust Company, a rumor his first wife's father, E. J. Evans, a director of the bank, was quick to squelch with pious assurances that his bank was sound and uninvolved in the collapse of Phillips's fortunes.

The personal and financial disasters falling upon the Phillips home did not spare the widow from defamation. It was gossiped in the newspaper columns that Charlotte's first husband, Isaac Andrews, had successfully escaped from their discordant marriage by killing himself with an overdose of laudanum. Some of her neighbors related that she had broken her normal reticence in recent weeks to complain of her husband's drinking and his incomprehensible telephone conversations. Others remarked unkindly that Charlotte had been in a state of nervous breakdown for some time and that her talent for avoiding unpleasantness by chronic "fainting proclivities" had been the wonder of her acquaintances since girlhood. The reliability of newspaper comment on Charlotte Phillips can be acutely discerned from revelations published simultaneously by the *Cleveland News* and *Cleveland Press* on September 6. Interviewing Mary Force, a Finnish servant girl briefly employed by the Phillips family, the *News* divulged that she had worked in a tense, unhappy home. Said Mary: "Mrs. Phillips was a very unpleasant woman. She seemed to be mad at something all the time. I never heard a kind word spoken between her and Mr. Phillips all the time I was there." The same day's *Press* provided this contrasting comment from the same source: "There was no family jar of any kind and nothing to indicate that there was any family unhappiness."

As the shadow of the law lengthened, the bereaved widow took refuge in one of the fainting fits in which she was reputed to have specialized since childhood. By the time the inquest ended on Tuesday, it was clear Stamberger was going to arrest Charlotte as the only likely suspect, and she went into a marked decline the next morning. Her decline, indeed, was so accelerated that she was unable to attend her husband's funeral, which took place on Wednesday afternoon in the Phillips house for a private audience of friends and family. Phillips's body was then hauled off to Lake View Cemetery, where it still lies today. It was rumored, again unkindly, that Charlotte's impenetrable stupor was aided by a deliberately ingested and very powerful drug.

Stamberger and the county prosecutor's office justified the warrant for Charlotte Phillips's arrest on a number of grounds. Charlotte had the key to the puzzle of J. J. Phillips's murder, and arresting her would both force her to talk and prevent her from killing herself, a likely possibility, given her nervous temperament. Stamberger's summary of the incriminating evidence was also compelling, if circumstantial: The burglary story didn't make sense; the bullet that killed Phillips was fired by someone standing level with him—and Mrs. Phillips was the perfect height for firing the fatal shot; Mrs. Phillips said her husband fell on the landing, yet there was no blood there; Phillips himself could not have fired the bullet, especially as there were no powder marks on his neck; the "stolen" spoons could easily have been thrown out of an upstairs window; three hours or more went by before even a doctor, much less the police, was called; Ethel Phillips, however charming, seemed to be concealing something; and, finally, Charlotte's reaction to her husband's death was "consternation, not grief," and she had not cooperated at all with the police. Assistant Prosecutor Mooney put it this way:

> This office is firmly convinced that Mrs. Phillips killed her husband. . . . I think she killed Phillips in a fit of anger, suddenly with premeditation [sic]. I think she killed him that way. I think that neither of them had any idea he would die and that he forgave her outburst and they made plans to shield her, and that when he came to die he still forgave her and did not say a word to alter those plans.

Exactly what Mooney meant by the contradictory phrase "suddenly with premeditation [sic]" is unknown, but it is indisputable that on September 4 Chief Stamberger had an affadavit sworn charging Charlotte Phillips with second-degree murder. He sped off to the Phillips residence soon afterward.

Unfortunately for Stamberger, the rumor of her impending arrest had already reached Charlotte. Stamberger arrived in a high-speed Stearns racer—thoughtfully provided by F. B. Stearns himself—only to have his dashing plan of spiriting Charlotte off to the county jail go awry. She was in a deep swoon by the time he got to her bedroom, which he tested to his own satisfaction by passing lighted matches over her tightly shut eyes. He then departed, leaving a female detective on guard outside her bedroom and two patrolmen on watch outside. Arriving back at Cuyahoga County sheriff McGorry's quarters, Stamberger fell asleep, having been on the case and completely without sleep since 4:00 a.m. Monday morning, September 2.

The next few days settled down into a test of wills between Marshal Stamberger and Charlotte Phillips. Each day he would arrive at the Phillips house to serve his warrant, and each day her relatives and doctors would assure him that she was much too ill to be disturbed with a murder charge. By now Mrs. Phillips also had significant aid from lawyer and former judge W. B. Neff. He managed to stave off the arrest for a few more days, even after Stamberger enlisted the aid of Doctor J. S. Tierney, whose examination of Charlotte produced the not unexpected conclusion that she was shamming unconsciousness to avoid her court appearance.

While he waited for Charlotte to recover, Stamberger pushed forward his investigations. Repeated searches of the Phillips house, from cellar coal bins to the cobwebbed garret, failed to turn up the murder gun, producing only a rusty old .22 pistol that hadn't been fired in years. Study of the bullet extracted from Phillips's cheek disclosed that it was a .32-caliber regulation Winchester bullet weighing eighty-five grains and powered by a black powder cartridge, not a smokeless one. There was hope of a breakthrough on Friday, September 6, when a partially burned bundle of bloody linens and newspapers was found in the Phillips furnace. But subsequent chemical analysis and the testimony of relevant individuals soon proved that the linens were from Phillips's deathbed and that the newspapers had been spread underneath the body during the autopsy performed in the Phillips house. Stamberger, increasingly wroth with Charlotte Phillips, let it be known that she had "tried to stare him out of countenance" and that her unpleasant eyes compared unfavorably with notorious swindler Cassie Chadwick's.

Charlotte Phillips finally faced the judicial music on Monday, September 9. By that date, as *The Plain Dealer* reported,

> [t]he belief that she has been shamming is officially accepted . . . that Mrs. Phillips has been feigning unconsciousness is thoroughly believed now by the officials. When she is examined they say she shuts her eyes very tight, which tips off the fact that she knows what she is doing.

A preliminary hearing to set bail took place on Sunday at the East Cleveland town hall. Assistant County Prosecutor William H. McGannon (who thirteen years later would figure in his own lurid murder mystery) took the lead for the state, demanding a $10,000 bail for Charlotte, and intimating that the prosecution had evidence that she had threatened her husband's life and that their relations were notoriously sour. McGannon and Judge Neff sparred for some time, until a weary Justice William Brown of East Cleveland split the difference at $7,500. Neff was joined in his spirited defense labors by attorneys Edson B. Bauder and C. W. Dille.

Charlotte's long-delayed arraignment came off with suitable drama at about noon on September 9. Carried to an invalid carriage on a stretcher from her home, she arrived at the East Cleveland town hall arrayed entirely in black: black crepe gown, a black hat trimmed with black flowers, a black veil, and a black-bordered handkerchief. (As soon as she left her house Sheriff McGorry and his men searched her bedroom from top to bottom, looking for the elusive murder weapon.) The bond was brought out to her in her carriage, helpful arms raised her to sign it, and she was driven back home. Judge Neff particularly distinguished himself as her legal champion on the occa-

Ethel Phillips at the final inquest hearing. *Cleveland Press*, November 11, 1907.

sion, roaring "The wildest prosecutor in the throes of delirium tremens never could reasonably hope to convince twelve honest men . . ."

Meanwhile, odd pieces of information pertaining to the case cropped up. Three persons sitting on a porch at 37 Mount Union Street on the murder night, about 125 feet away from the Phillips house, claimed they had heard a woman scream twice from that direction about 12:30 a.m. (That agrees with the time testified to by Ethel Phillips, not with the 1:15 hour insisted upon by Charlotte.) The timing of the screams was quite definite, as one of the witnesses had caught a scheduled streetcar back to Cleveland at the end of Mount Union, at Euclid Avenue, about 12:50 a.m.

Night watchman Todd of the Clarence Building, where Phillips had his offices, surfaced with his own odd story on September 10. It seems one night several weeks prior to Phillips's murder, Todd had been summoned by one of Phillips's clerks to the office at 9:30 p.m. There, the astonished clerk pointed at an open safe with its drawers askew on the floor. Nothing of value seemed to be missing, and when Phillips was informed of the incident he told the clerk and watchman never to mention the matter again. More rumors of threats against

Phillips's life were also bruited about. W. H. H. Gorham, a friend of Phillips, told of seeing him a few days before his death. While walking on Euclid they were accosted by four men, one of whom threatened to kill Phillips over a money dispute. C. C. Lones, an attorney who represented Phillips, claimed that Phillips several times insisted to him that he would probably meet a violent death over business matters. Phillips's employee, Norval C. Logee, also recalled a letter received three weeks before Phillips's demise that predicted a violent end for him. And James J. Dunn, Jr., Phillips's private secretary, related threats made against Phillips by the fired and missing chauffeur, Charlie Herzberg.

The legal mess occasioned by Phillips's death became more and more complicated, baffling all parties concerned. The administrators of his estate—he died intestate—found great difficulty in identifying either his assets or liabilities. More of the latter were accumulating every day, and it was eventually disclosed that a number of lawsuits against Phillips had been under way at the time of his death. Only the Thursday before his death, a Cleveland court had attached his office fixtures, and the county prosecutor had been on the verge of indicting him for violation of an antitrust statute.

The scandal of the Phillips mystery even enveloped little ten-year-old Ethel, who continued to charm all with her winning smile, straw hat with white ribbon, and brown eyes and hair. Though she was initially identified as the daughter of Mrs. Phillips's deceased brother, it came out that she had been adopted out of the Protestant Orphan Asylum in 1905 by Mr. and Mrs. Phillips. The asylum director would say no more than that Ethel was not actually related by blood to either of her adoptive parents and that her biological mother was desperately trying to find her. Meanwhile, Stamberger left town to run down Charlie Herzberg, the missing Phillips chauffeur, and in his absence had his underlings drag the neighborhood sewers for the missing death weapon.

Charlotte Phillips continued her extended, prostrate decline, and her arraignment hearing was pushed forward by successive delays into November. Her case was much aided in late September by two revelations strengthening the theory that Phillips had killed himself.

The first disclosure came from two employees of the Traveler's Insurance Company. Their story was that Phillips had frantically tried to buy more life insurance in the weeks just before his death. More pointedly, he had repeatedly asked agents Arthur J. Frith and Burr Scott about the suicide and murder clauses of the policies. This aligned perfectly with the thinking of those who believed Phillips

J. J. Phillips and James Dunn, Jr., struggle for the gun. *Cleveland Press*, Sept. 23, 1907.

killed himself only after setting it up to look like murder. As one unnamed acquaintance figured it: "J. J. was a cunning, crafty man. He littered up his house and carried out the spoons to make the burglary story look good."

More sensational disclosures were squeezed out of Phillips's private secretary, James J. Dunn, Jr., by the relentless Marshal Stamberger in late September. Dunn confessed that Phillips had tried to kill himself in his own office on the afternoon of August 27, only one week before his death. Seeing a pistol in his hand, the muscular Dunn had put the less athletic Phillips in an arm lock, and they had struggled desperately for the gun, according to Dunn's exciting, persuasive recollection:

> Phillips: "Let go! Let go or I'll kill you first!"
> Dunn: "Drop the gun!"
> Phillips: "I'll kill you first!"
> Dunn: "Drop the gun!"

The gun went off in the struggle but neither man was hurt; Dunn claimed that the bullet ricocheted off the wall but that he found it on the floor and threw it away. The careless Dunn also claimed he wrapped the gun, a pearl-handled revolver, in paper and threw it off the southeast end of the Superior Viaduct on his way home from work that same day. Dunn also confessed his belief that Phillips had been drinking heavily for some time and was using drugs, too, the latter to treat insomnia. "I heard he was a morphine fiend," said the now not-so-private secretary. Two days of dragging the Cuyahoga River failed to produce the alleged revolver of Dunn's melodramatic story. When the county inquest reopened on September 25, Dunn amplified his portrait of an unhappy Phillips. He said Phillips had claimed he would leave his wife if she didn't stop nagging him, and Dunn allowed he had heard rumors that Phillips was sleeping in his garage to avoid her. In additional sworn testimony he related that Phillips told him he was "tired of life," and that Dunn had often fished him out of drinking binges at local hotels—the Hollenden, Gillsy, Euclid, Colonial, and Norman—at Mrs. Phillips's anguished request.

Charlotte Phillips's ultimate day in court finally came on Monday, November 11. Ethel Phillips repeated her inquest testimony, admitting under questioning that she hadn't heard either J. J. or Charlotte say anything about "burglars" until about 3:45 a.m., at least two hours after Phillips was found shot. Dr. Richardson testified next, repeating his memory of Phillips's seeming unconcern at his wound and his tale of the burglar who shot him on the stairs. He added that Phillips had made him leave the room twice so he could talk privately with his wife.

Clyde Phillips testified at the end of the first day and his story was a bombshell. Clyde had upheld the facade of his brother as a happy family man for two months, but that sham now dissolved in Clyde Phillips's portrait of a man terrorized by his termagant wife. He said his brother John had for months lived in constant fear of Charlotte. About a month before the murder, Clyde and his wife had paid a visit to the house on Mount Union. Only Mrs. Phillips was there, but they soon heard J. J.'s car pull into the barn out back. When J. J. didn't come into the house, Clyde forced his way into the locked barn to find his brother fast asleep in his car. When he woke him up, J. J. told Clyde he was terrified of Charlotte: "Last night she threatened and attempted to brain me with a beer bottle and I will not stay in the same house with her alone. She means to kill me and I do not intend to let her."

After thirty minutes of persuasion, he entered the house, only to encounter Charlotte, whereupon he hurriedly left. It was the last time Clyde saw his brother alive.

Stamberger appeared next. His testimony was essentially the same as ever, although he elaborated on how he had sternly instructed Mrs. Phillips to leave the evidence untouched—and returned a few hours later to find the "burglarized" dining room restored to perfect order and all the bloody linens put to laundry. In testifying about the improbability of burglary, Stamberger laid particular emphasis on the character of the first floor as he first found it at 4:00 a.m., September 2:

> An examination of all the doors and windows down stairs which I made soon after I first arrived showed them to be all securely locked. The kitchen door was open. The key of this door lay on the floor about eight inches away from it on the inside. The door itself led to a porch which was enclosed with an intact wire fly screen. In this screen was a door which was bolted on the inside. No one could have escaped from any part of the downstairs.

Dr. Ellis B. Rhodes reiterated his previous inquest testimony on November 12. He mentioned the odd fact that Phillips told him he had been looking in the telephone book when he was shot. And he described Mrs. Phillips's hysterical disbelief when he told her that her husband was dead: "Don't tell me he is dead; no, he isn't dead; he can't be dead!"

Justice Brown handed down his decision on Tuesday after hearing the concluding pleas of Judge Neff and County Prosecutor Sylvester McMahon. Judge Neff's plea was a two-pronged defense which, while somewhat contradictory, focused on gaps in the evidence. Arguing that there was no proof Phillips was in his house between 9:00 p.m. and 1:00 a.m. on the murder night, Neff suggested that he was killed elsewhere—probably as the result of an illicit liaison—and either staggered or was brought home by third parties, one of whom apparently left a feminine handkerchief—which Stamberger's men had recently discovered on the back porch. And for those who leaned toward the suicide theory, Neff stressed the possibility that Phillips could have shot himself in bed, using a towel to prevent powder burns. This was the theory that Deputy Coroner Harry McNeil had espoused from the beginning, and Neff pushed it hard. He ended his peroration with an attack on the third-degree methods he claimed the police had used on his fragile, grieving client: "Never in my life have I seen such coarse and brutal means used in an attempt to collect evidence."

McMahon's response caught everyone off base, especially Neff, who objected to various parts of his plea until he belatedly realized where McMahon was headed. McMahon started out by saying there was no evidence of a burglary and that Phillips and his wife had conspired to defeat the law. Nonetheless, he concluded: "I don't believe there is any legal evidence to hold Mrs. Phillips. The time to solve the mystery was the morning of the death. My duty is also to the woman. I do not think there is any evidence to hold her to the grand jury."

Almost the instant McMahon stopped speaking, Justice William Brown dismissed the charge of second-degree murder against Charlotte Phillips. She thanked Brown quietly and left, telling insistent reporters, "I have nothing to say." Several days later Charlotte placed the following notice in area newspapers: "Mrs. J. J. Phillips wishes to express her deep gratitude to her many friends, acquaintances and people through[out] the country for their sympathy, loyalty and devotion during her recent bereavement and affliction."

The next day, Celia Congalton of Steubenville, Ethel Phillips's natural mother, announced plans to sue for custody. She claimed that Ethel had been adopted without her permission; orphanage officials replied that she had completely surrendered her legal rights to the child. It was rumored Ethel might be heiress to an enormous fortune from an out-of-state relative.

The Phillips tragedy eventually passed from the pages of the daily newspapers and was forgotten but for an occasional journalistic retrospective. Mrs. Phillips sold the spacious, ten-room house in 1908; she probably couldn't afford it, and it had acquired neighborhood repute as a "Jonah" house that invariably jinxed its inhabitants. (Two previous owners had endured unhappy experiences, including a well-publicized divorce.)

The legal consequences endured a bit longer. The Glenville Banking & Trust Company went under in December of 1907, and examination of its books revealed that Director E. J. Evans—Phillips's former father-in-law—had aggravated the bank's financial troubles by secretly funding the worthless notes of his former son-in-law to the tune of at least $100,000. Things got uglier two months later, when Charlotte Phillips was forced to sue the Provident Insurance & Trust Company for the proceeds of one of J. J.'s life insurance policies. It seems that Evans had persuaded a distraught Charlotte to sign the insurance policy over to the Glenville Bank on September 9. Evans in turn had taken the policy to a Glenville Bank directors' meeting and flourished it as a guarantee that its proceeds would indemnify the bank against any losses on Phillips's financial paper. It was a sordid proceeding that slogged through the courts until Mrs. Phillips won her lawsuit five years later.

Who killed J. J. Phillips within the shadow of John D. Rockefeller's summer home (which as Forest Hills Park still abuts the former Phillips property today)? Well, it sure wasn't burglars. The allegedly fake burglaries set up for the 1919 Dan Kaber murder and the 1954 Marilyn Sheppard slaying were choreographed masterpieces compared to the genteel mess that someone cooked up in the Phillips dining room on the morning of September 2, 1907. The "burglars" took nothing, and they certainly would not have hung around a middle-class residential street after killing someone in the middle of the night. No experienced law enforcement person believed it at the time, and it is hard to imagine that even Charlotte Phillips believed it. Not that she cared a whit about the credibility of her story. As she indifferently commented to a *Press* reporter: "That's up to the police to figure out the theory. They have the facts. Let them come to a decision."

Did J. J. Phillips commit suicide? There is a strong probability that he did. Deputy Coroner McNeil's theory was that Phillips shot himself in bed, confessed to his wife that he had botched the job, and then helped her stage-manage a cover-up with his remaining strength. This theory doesn't explain what happened to the murder gun, but it at least explains why there was little blood on the stairs and why Charlotte seemed rather vague about the time sequence.

It is possible, of course, that Charlotte Phillips shot her husband. But she certainly doesn't seem the type: it would have been difficult for such an obviously passive-aggressive and chronic hysteric to follow through so stolidly and so persistently with such a bold, contrived scheme. This hypothesis would also assume that Phillips gallantly, not to say suicidally, covered up for a woman with whom by all accounts he was not getting along.

The stumbling block for all of these theories is the presence of Ethel Phillips in the house on the death night. It is hard to believe that this preternaturally self-possessed little girl was lying about everything she said she saw on the murder night. The conflicts with her mother's testimony were inconsequential, and it is in fact possible that almost everything she said she witnessed was the truth, not something she was coached to say or made to believe through suggestion.

Which leaves us with Neff's explanation, which is just improbable enough to be true. In this scenario, Phillips comes home shot and manages to crawl up the stairs to the landing and scream. He tells his wife and Ethel that a burglar shot him, and they take his assertions at face value as they assist him to his room. Perhaps Charlotte knows or suspects better, but she has innumerable reasons for not saying otherwise, and Ethel will accept whatever interpretation her parents will agree on as long as it doesn't stray too far from what she has actually seen. The man outside under the tree, as Neff intimated, is explained as one of the persons who accompanied the wounded financier home.

There are minor alternate versions for all of these theories. Perhaps Phillips conspired with his wife—before or after the fact—to make his suicide look like a murder. Maybe he faked the burglary evidence in the dining room; perhaps she did; maybe they did it together. Whatever happened, it seems inescapable that both of them were lying through their teeth as death closed in on J. J. Phillips. From what mixture of motives, it may never be known.

There was one final reverberation from the Phillips case, and you may make of it what you will. Among the many lawsuits churned up by the byzantine business affairs of the deceased J. J. Phillips was an action by the First National Bank of Bealsville, Pennsylvania. They filed suit in 1908, alleging that E. J. Evans, acting in his capacity as an administrator of the Phillips estate, had sold property of the East Ohio Coal Company at a suspiciously low price to the Rice Coal Company. Interrogated under oath, Evans's lawyer, Frank Ginn, admitted that the Rice Coal Company was owned by Ginn's law partner, William Lowe Rice. The same William Lowe Rice was mysteriously murdered two years later on August 5, 1910, while walking home to his mansion on Euclid Heights Boulevard in Cleveland Heights Village. Coincidence?

Torso No. 10:
The Legend Grows

West Third Street Bridge, July 6, 1937

Decapitated torsos weren't the only warnings of violence in Cleveland in 1937. Down in the Flats and all the way through the Youngstown Valley, bloody history was being made as organized labor clashed with industrial conglomerates in what would become famous as the "Little Steel Strike" of 1937. After the breakdown in late May of talks between C.I.O. organizers and producers including Republic Steel, Youngstown Sheet and Tube, and Inland Steel, union officials called their men out on strike. Cleveland mayor Harold Burton bought some time with his shrewd decision to shut down Republic's St. Clair Avenue airfield—from which it planned to airlift strikebreakers to outlying plants—but by early July the situation was moving toward violence. With determined union spokesmen claiming an effective strike, and adamant Republic officials tempting wavering workers to cross picket lines, there was bound to be trouble, and on July 3 Cuyahoga County sheriff Martin O'Donnell and Mayor Burton begged Ohio governor Martin Davey to send in the Ohio National Guard to prevent bloodshed when the mills opened. By July 6, the day Republic reopened its plants, Ohio national guardsmen armed with rifles and machine guns dotted the industrial acres of the Flats.

Private Edgar M. Steinbrecher of the 147th Infantry Regiment, O.N.G., had probably never expected to be where he was on the morning of Tuesday, July 6, patrolling the West Third Street bridge over the Cuyahoga River near the Upson Bolt and Nut division of Republic Steel. He certainly couldn't have imagined that he would walk over the bridge at 5:30 that morning, look down, and see . . . something—something that looked like a department-store mannequin or a corset dummy floating in the water underneath the bridge. As he watched the object, it was overturned; and then Private Steinbrecher realized it was not a corset dummy after all. It was part of a human being. Steinbrecher ran to tell the bridge tender, John Haggerty, and two of his fellow guardsmen, privates John Smith and Charles Demminen. They must have fished around in the river for some time, as it was 9:55 a.m. before they got in touch with Captain Martin Ratterman, of their regiment, who called the police.

By the time Cleveland police arrived at the scene, Steinbrecher and the others had fished out an impressive collection of body parts. Their initial find—the lower half of a male torso—was soon joined by two halves of a left leg, separated neatly at the knee. Soon after that, a burlap Purina chicken-feed bag was hauled out of the muddy river. Inside, wrapped in some pages of a June 22 Cleveland newspaper, was an upper torso, half which matched Steinbrecher's first catch of the day perfectly. The police soon spotted the right thigh wedged in some bridge pilings, and a Coast Guard boat crew ferreted out an upper left arm and part of a lung about 250 feet west of the bridge.

After all the body parts were carted off to the county morgue and reassembled, Coroner Gerber announced that it was the work of the same fiend responsible for the previous Torso killings. Sergeant Hogan was even more emphatic:

> There is no doubt that this is another of the series of torso murders. The body was dismembered in the same manner; the parts of the body were found near the place where the last discovery of a victim was made; the disposal of the parts checks with the previous cases.

Gerber reiterated his usual comments about the "expert" nature of the murderer's technique, although there were some novel wrinkles that should have made him more cautious in his comments. There was some evidence of rather crude hacking where one of the arms had been severed, and part of one lung had been carelessly sliced away. More unusual still, this victim had been completely disemboweled, and the heart had been torn out. Death, apparently, had occurred by decapitation.

All the missing parts except for the head eventually turned up in the river—the forearms and hands on July 7, the upper right arm on July 10, and the lower right leg and foot on July 14—but Gerber already knew enough on July 7 to hazard some public guesses about the victim. He appeared to be a white male, between twenty-five and thirty-five years old, 180 to 190 pounds, and about six feet tall, with a head of coarse brown hair. He was powerfully built, well nourished, well groomed, and in excellent condition, except for a mildly arthritic spine. There was a scar on his right thumb and a cross-shaped mark of unknown origin on his left calf. Gerber theorized

10TH VICTIM OF TORSO SLAYER FOUND IN RIVER

Dismembered Trunk, Legs and Arms Spur Hunt for Missing Head

Cleveland Press headline, July 6, 1937.

that he had probably been killed late Saturday or Sunday and that his body parts had been in the water about forty-eight hours.

Without a head there was little hope of identifying the latest victim. Despite a good soaking in the Cuyahoga River, the hands yielded good fingerprints, but they could not be matched to any on file with local police, Columbus authorities, or the FBI. Deputy Inspector David L. Cowles employed a newfangled ultraviolet light in a painstaking but fruitless effort to pick up latent prints on the Purina bag and the newspapers found inside it. But the bag was at least three years old and untraceable. Nor could anything be made of a silk stocking found in the bag or two hairs found in the stocking: a long black-and-white strand (probably belonging to a dog) and a short blond one, definitely human.

With the body furnishing few clues, Cleveland police turned to conjecture about the location of their grisly find. As there had been very heavy rains in the days preceding the torso discovery, it was thought that the body parts had been washed from their original resting place on dry land into the river, possibly from the Kingsbury Run area upriver. It was also more than likely that their sudden appearance on the morning of July 6 was due to a passing boat, whose prop had churned up the remains.

The usual suspects brought themselves to police attention with their usual subtlety and the usual results. On the evening of July 6, a drunken man in a cafe near Hamilton Avenue and East 9th Street

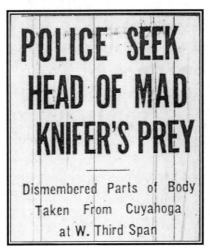

Cleveland Press headline, July 6, 1937.

began boasting to some female customers there that he knew "all about" the Torso murders and was "good at cutting people up." One of the frightened women called Coroner Gerber, and Cleveland police soon had the braggart in custody. He turned out to be a former ambulance driver with no likely involvement whatsoever in the case. A similar suspect surfaced six weeks later when a former dissecting assistant at a Cleveland hospital was picked up after drunkenly boasting about his prowess with a dissecting knife. The man insisted to police that he had been discharged from his hospital job because physicians there were "jealous" of his dissecting ability, but the truth was that he had been fired for stealing formaldehyde and surgical tools. His wife told Cleveland detectives that he was a "confirmed liar" and that he simply "imagines all those things." The testimony of a bridge tender at the West 3rd Street span that an ill-shaven, burly, middle-aged man had thrown a bundle into the river there on Friday night, July 2, also came to nothing.

Cleveland police authorities may have been disappointed by the lack of clues in the latest torso murder, but the paucity of facts disappoint Cleveland reporters. It was clear to them now that the Torso killer was the answer to a newspaperman's prayer, and their coverage was increasingly an outright *celebration* of the seeming emergence of a world-class homicidal maniac in Cleveland. Befitting its role as the least sober organ in Cleveland's journalistic pantheon, the *Press* led the way with a one–two journalistic punch that ran on July 9 and July 10, 1937. Omar Ranney set the stage with his review of police efforts in the Friday edition:

> This is the inside story of the greatest manhunt in the history of Cleveland, a search that has been going on since Sept. 5, 1934, when the first of the 10 torso murder victims was found. The story of what Cleveland police and detectives have been doing to trace the mad butcher in those 34 months rivals any crime detection thriller.

Ranney went on to enumerate the endless variety of clues, cranks, crackpots, and dead ends that had led Cleveland cops on a wild goose chase for almost three years. The efforts chronicled included the following: a file of over 500 letters and telegrams crammed with useless "tips"; 300 suspects interrogated and inventoried; thirteen detectives assigned full-time duty on the Torso hunt; numerous excavations of suspected torso laboratories; frequent raids for suspects in hobo camps; tramps through miles of smelly sewers in search of body parts and other evidence; endless house-to-house searches in neighborhoods where the victims were found; countless hours spent on tugboats cruising the Cuyahoga River and Lake Erie shores in search of evidence; the draining of every pool that might contain a body or evidence; and the canvassing of dozens of laundries and dry-cleaning shops in search of the laundry marks on Torso victims' clothes. For all that, as Ranney admitted in closing, the Cleveland police were still "without a definite clew."

But Ranney had merely set the stage for Ira Welborn, who did the Torso Fiend proud in the next day's paper, signaling his legend-building intentions with the opening headline:

> *Who Is This Mad Killer? Ranks Among History's Fiends*
> Ten times in Cleveland a mad headsman has killed—and 10 times he dissected with consummate skill the body of his victim . . . What is he like, this ghoul who delights in cutting up the bodies of men and women, leaving legs and arms and heads and torsos to be found by small boys, bridge watch-men, chance passersby?

Welborn, of course, had no idea what the Torso Fiend was really like—but that didn't stop him from speculating that he might well be like, say, any one of a catalog of chilling, cold-blooded murderers whose descriptions he proceeded to reel off for the delectation of

Cleveland Press headline, July 10, 1937.

Press readers. Was the Torso Fiend like Fritz Haarman of Hanover, Germany, who lured several dozen young boys into his room, where he turned them into chopped meat and sold them as sausages? Was he like Dr. Harvey Crippen, mild-mannered and henpecked husband, who poisoned his wife in 1910 and buried her under a floor? Was he like Henri Desire Landru, the modern French Bluebeard, who made love to 283 women, became engaged to 13 of them, and murdered at least 10 for their money? Reporter Welborn couldn't quite decide which one of these murderers the unknown Torso Fiend was really like—but he sure had fun presenting his gallery of history's most bloodthirsty killers, whose roll call was accompanied by wonderfully creepy illustrations. In any case, Welborn's ultimate conclusion, rendered in his last sentence, was nothing more or less than the truth: "Police do not know."

And the hunt continued.

Chapter 9

MEDINA'S NOT-SO-MERRY WIDOW

Martha Wise's Deadly Crying Game, 1925

It is well that the meek shall inherit this earth, because a lot of them sure get kicked around here initially. Most never get a chance to kick back. Sometimes, though, they do, and their revenge, taken to occasional extremes, constitutes a fascinating, if discordant, element in what Thomas Gray so justly termed the "short and simple annals of the poor." Martha Wise's vengeance on the world that mistreated and malformed her is just such a tale, and is likely to breed disquieting chills of horror and guilty gratification in even the most jaded breast.

It was not so very long ago, and hardly far away. But it might as well have been, for Medina County in 1925 was a world far distant from the bustle of big-city Cleveland, twenty-three miles removed from its largely rural fastness. And Hardscrabble, a hamlet of modest farms in the center of Medina's Liverpool Township, was probably as far away from the Forest City's metropolitan sophistication as you could get. Newspaper accounts of the Wise tragedy invariably characterized Hardscrabble as "mud-bound" or "muddy," as assuredly it must have been—especially in a rainy spring season—thanks to its largely unpaved roads. But the same accounts hinted at something darker and more uncivilized lurking in Hardscrabble: an almost feral population of neolithic life forms oozing out of the "forsaken mud and slime crossroads where the black death of the Dark Ages comes. . ." So was modest Hardscrabble viewed by Cleveland's Roaring-Twenties sophisticates when the curtain rose in late 1924 on the series of deeds that would bring notoriety to miserable, misbegotten Martha Wise.

Even by Hardscrabble standards, Martha Wise had lived an unfortunate life. Forty-two years old in 1924, she had been born Martha Hasel to a family of unpretentious farming folk, Wilhelm and Sophie Gienke Hasel, in 1884. From the beginning, Martha was slow, sickly, markedly morbid, and vulnerable to the contempt and bullying of those around her, especially her family. It would later be said that her youthful mental and emotional precariousness worsened noticeably after a dog bit her, but other evidence suggests her psychological and physical fragility stemmed from chronic, undiagnosed epilepsy and a severe adolescent bout with spinal meningitis. The latter ordeal, townsfolk remembered, left Martha with a "cluttered brain." Suffice it to say that Martha Wise came of age at the turn of the century as a hysteric with a notorious enjoyment of funerals—especially the weeping—and a full-fledged hypochondriac.

Given the limited entertainment available in 1920s Hardscrabble, Martha's appetite for funerals seems a likely and innocent enough diversion, from the perspective of the 1990s. As Walter Morrow, a *Cleveland Press* writer of the 1930s, explained, the emotional delights of funeral obsequies opened up a hitherto blocked channel of release in Martha's unhappy, difficult, and stunted life:

> There was music and there were flowers. The children were clean and dressed in their best. And from nowhere, almost, there appeared the usual association of bearded ladies who hover about the homes where death has visited to offer consolation and solace. Martha became a regular attendant at funerals, She came to love them. Dressed in her weeds she attended all within reach, her sobs and lamentations rising above the smothered tide of keening by the bereaved women. Weeping became sheer joy to her.

Morrow, no doubt a hopeless romantic, liked to think that Martha first discovered the pleasures of public grief at her husband Albert's 1923 funeral—an event occasioned by Martha's poisoning him with arsenic—but the fact is that Martha was already notorious by 1924 as one who had not missed an area funeral for twenty years.

She was equally well known by that date for a galloping case of hypochondria and its concomitant need for medical attention and sympathy. There is ample evidence that Martha Wise had an unfortunate medical history, but her legitimate physiological complaints were not enough for her as she grew to middle age in "American Gothic" Medina. Dr. Henry John Abele of Lakewood would eventually admit at Martha's trial for first-degree murder that he had been treating her for a variety of "imaginary ailments" since 1898, when Martha was fourteen. On one occasion she had come to him with a "sore" arm. Upon removing the medical dressing she had contrived, Dr. Abele discovered an arm obviously "bruised" with Easter-egg dyes. On another occasion, she came to his office with severe blistering on her arm, clearly caused by the turpentine she had deliberately rubbed into it.

Martha left school at the age of fourteen. Such an abbreviated education was not uncommon for a farm girl of her time and place, but there were additional reasons for Martha to forsake her lessons. As her teacher, Mrs. Elma Reisenger, remembered, Martha was clearly mentally retarded even as a child; as Reisenger put it, "She couldn't learn. She was queer and erratic. She was not a normal child." Her education ending with the fifth grade, Martha spent some years working as a kitchen girl in various Medina homes. Then, at twenty-four, she met Albert Wise—and her life took a turn for the even worse.

Albert Wise's family had come into the Rocky River valley where Hardscrabble lay sometime in the early twentieth century. Why he married Martha Wise is not known, but we know that the subsequent fifteen years of marriage produced five children, and a decade and a half of misery and joyless toil for Martha Wise. For Albert Wise, even by the unsentimental standards of a rough-hewn farming community, was a hard case. He set the tone for their union at the outset by refusing to buy Martha a wedding ring, and she soon became his thankless drudge and victim. Beating her frequently, Albert made her toil like a common field hand on their 100-acre Hardscrabble farm as day followed day in year after endless year of backbreaking labor. The morning after her first child was born, he sent her out to work in the fields. She became notorious—to her tearful shame—as the only woman in Medina who had to slop the hogs. George Hammond, who worked briefly for Albert Wise as a farmhand, later testified at Martha's trial that he left after three days because the work demanded was too heavy. Small wonder that Martha Wise took increasing comfort in funerals and in complaining to doctors.

And, apparently, in fantasies of revenge. No one knows exactly when or why the worm turned, but it probably revolved decisively in 1923. For it was in that year that Martha apparently poisoned Albert Wise, a murder never proven—the official cause was an "infected arm"—and not even suspected for some years, and an act that must have suggested a way out of further difficulties and heartaches. It must have seemed to unhappy Martha Wise, with her circumscribed existence, that her Hardscrabble world of tribulation and tears was opening up at last.

As Lady Macbeth found in like circumstances, her triumph was not to be. For in 1923, the same year she disposed of Albert Wise,

Martha started really going off the rails. Hitherto known as "queer" and abnormal, she raised community eyebrows yet further with increasingly bizarre behavior. She took to roaming the Medina countryside after dark, appearing unexpectedly and sometimes foaming at the mouth, rolling her eyes, or even barking like a dog, symptoms indicative of both her probable epilepsy and a mind giving way under an unprecedented strain. To her family of siblings and in-laws, she admitted having frequent hallucinations, including visitations by angels and white doves. What she didn't tell her relatives was that she had also taken to burning down the barns of her Medina neighbors and stealing their jewelry and farm implements. At least ten mysterious fires would eventually be linked to Martha's activities, and she herself eventually confessed as much:

> Some of the fires I started at night. Some of them I started in the daytime after the devil had told me at night to do it. I was afraid to go out at night—I always saw him when I did and he always told me something new to do. I didn't think about the fires killing anybody at first, but later I knew they might—that's when I started out to set them at night, so I could surprise people. I never stayed at the fires—no. I slipped away to a hiding place and watched them blaze and crackle and burn.

Love, as poets and popular songs remind us, oft takes us by surprise, and so it apparently astonished Martha Wise that same year after her husband died. We shall never know the truth about any of her alleged liaisons; she was rumored to have at least three different "sweethearts" and ultimately confessed one amour in particularly intimate detail to avid reporters. What we do know, though, is that Martha, at least, believed one of her swains seriously wished to marry her. It must have seemed like an unlooked-for happy ending at last for the Widow Wise, socially forlorn and with a brood of four young children to raise (one had died as an infant). As a later commentator put it, she was at last within reach of a "protector and love she had not known when her first husband was living and work, work, work was her song of love."

It was not to be. Upon catching wind of Martha's nuptial hopes, her family, especially mother Sophie and uncle Fred Gienke, put the collective family foot down. They had not been amused by Martha's carryings-on and erratic behavior since Albert Wise's demise, and they were dead set against her choice of a second mate. The man in

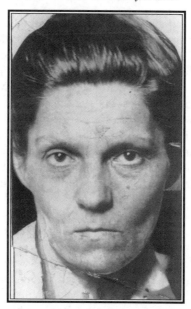

Martha Wise, 1925.

question, Walter Johns—who for the historical record ever after denied being more than Martha's platonic friend—was reputedly of a different religious creed. The Gienke-Hasel clan, moreover, was quite upset about the gossip that swirled about Martha's head in the close-knit Hardscrabble community. Much of that gossip, reputedly, had its source in the women of the Ladies of Aid Zion Lutheran Church in nearby Valley City, which organization had for some months furnished the Widow Wise with the bread of charity in the form of vegetables and clothing. Rumor was that the victuals of this ecclesiastical charity were being shared by Martha's unworthy male friends, and the ensuing discomfort of the Ladies of Aid had reached the sensitive ears of Sophie Hasel, who forbade Martha to marry. Actually, she did more than forbid it: She threatened to cut Martha out of her will and publicly disown her in the bargain.

It can only be imagined what such a threat must have meant to an individual so marginal as Martha, in a community so close and con-servative as Hardscrabble. Already publicly reviled and teased as a moron, made a figure of fun for her epileptic symptoms, and scorned as an object of public charity, Martha Wise was now threatened with what was—in the black hole of Hardscrabble—social death. She wept, she ranted, she raved, and finally, apparently, she gave in.

But the "postman always rings twice," and those who kill once will likely kill again. The Gienkes and the Hasels didn't fear that truism because they did not realize that Albert Wise's death had been an unnatural one. But Martha knew it, and an already proven path out of her difficulties led her now to the pharmacy of Medina druggist W. H. Weber on November 24, 1924. There she purchased two ounces of arsenic, which she signed for with her own name, as required by law, in the poison register. She told Weber she needed it to kill rats. Several days later, she went to her mother's house, a double dwelling that Sophie shared with Martha's brother Fred Hasel, for Thanksgiving dinner. Sometime during her visit on this family holiday, Martha contrived to put a potent pinch of arsenic into the water bucket in Sophie Hasel's kitchen. Several days later, she repeated the dose at a stronger level, having replenished her supplies at Weber's store to the tune of another ounce.

The results weren't long in coming. There were minor stomach complaints for those who attended Thanksgiving dinner at the Hasel residence. And then, in early December, Sophie Hasel came down with terrible abdominal pains and weakness in her legs. She didn't linger long: after several days of nonstop agony, she succumbed on December 13 to what her doctors were pleased to describe as "influenza and inflammation of the stomach." On her deathbed, Sophie Hasel called her daughter Emma to her side and tearfully begged Emma, with her final words, to look after her troubled sister: "See that Martha is taken care of; she needs your help."

Martha didn't need as much help as Sophie thought. Everyone would later remember how Martha carried on at Sophie's funeral, sobbing and shrieking in paroxysms of grief: "My dear mother, who was so good to me; why didn't God take me and leave mother? How are we ever going to get along without her? She suffered awful. I want them to sing 'All the Way My Savior Leads Me,' it was her favorite hymn." And then, at a gathering at the Hasel house after Sophie's funeral, two days after her death, Martha's brother Fred, his wife, his son Edwin, and two other relatives, Paul and Henry Hasel, became violently ill after drinking coffee and water.

As with Sophie's death, no questions were raised about this untoward event at the time. And why should they have been? As the county prosecutor, Joseph Seymour, would later characterize the situation, there was at the time no reason to think anyone had it out for the Hasel or Gienke families: "There is no apparent motive for the crime. The family is highly respected in their community. There are no known enemies. There was no domestic trouble. No one is under suspicion . . ."

It is unknown what tortured sequence or rationale in the mind of Martha Wise led to her next lethal acts. There was speculation—after the fact—that she thought her uncle, Fred Gienke (Sophie Hasel's brother), suspected her hand in his sister's sudden death. Hardscrabble gossip would later depict Fred Gienke approaching Martha after her mother's funeral, picking her up, shaking her violently, and telling her to mend her ways.

We can be certain that Martha Wise didn't mend her ways, and we can be equally sure that giving up pinching arsenic into her relatives' water supply was not one of her 1925 New Year's Resolutions. For that is exactly what she did during a New Year's Day dinner at Fred Gienke's house. It must have been an impressive quantity, for Fred Gienke, his wife Lillian, daughter Marie, 26, and sons Fred, Jr., 24, Rudolph, 17, and Walter, 8, as well as Fred Hasel and his son Edwin, became violently ill within twenty minutes of eating the festive dinner of pork stew, washed down with water and coffee. It was reported in later press accounts that a Mrs. Martha Wise had also experienced gastric discomfort, but no mention was made of her four children, who also attended the happy New Year's Day family reunion. No doubt—as Lester Wise, 14, Martha's eldest child, remembered—this was because of Martha's repeated maternal advice to her offspring: "Mother told us never to drink the water when we went to the Gienkes."

Arsenic poisoning is not a nice way to die. Lillian Gienke writhed in agony for three days, wracked by the tortures characteristic of heavy-metal poisoning—stomach pains and stiffening in the leg muscles—before expiring in a house full of family almost as sick unto death as she. She died on January 4 and soon joined her sister-in-law Sophie in the Gienke-Hasel plot in nearby Myrtle Hill Cemetery.

The dramatic results of Martha's activities had not gone completely unremarked by the authorities. The physician who attended Lillian Gienke in her death throes notified Medina County coroner E. L. Crum and County Health Commissioner H. H. Biggs about his suspicions. He was subsequently informed that there was nothing to investigate.

If Martha Wise had ceased her homicidal activities at this point, she probably would have gotten away with murder. Sophie Hasel and Lillian Gienke were dead, but her other victims were recovering.

But Martha just couldn't stop herself, and the Gienke family physician's suspicions became further inflamed by a new series of attacks on January 16. These were even more virulent than the others, and soon Fred Gienke, Sr., and his children Rudolph, Marie, Herman, and Richard, plus Lillian's sister, Rose, were felled with the mysterious symptoms that had brought death to Sophie and Lillian. By February, Rudolph and Marie were in Elyria Hospital, soon to be joined by Fred, Sr. In the meantime, a Cleveland nurse, Rose Kohli, had become ill after making coffee at the Gienke house but soon recovered. Fred, Sr., died on February 8, 1925, in Elyria Hospital after days of excruciating agony. The listed cause of death was "inflammation of the stomach."

The second wave of Gienke poisonings had at last sufficiently aroused the police powers of Medina County. Health Commissioner Biggs ran tests on the victims of the late January poisonings—but these turned up negative. A subsequent test on the contents of Fred Gienke, Sr.'s stomach was not completed due to the illness of Elyria city chemist E. G. Curtis. But Elyria Hospital doctors were convinced something was terribly amiss with patients Rudolph and Marie Gienke, and doctors W. H. Hull and A. G. Appleby insisted that they be thoroughly tested. By February 12, Medina county prosecutor Joseph A. Seymour had the results—and they showed a lot of unexplained arsenic in the bodies of Rudolph and Marie Gienke.

The newspapers later reported that Prosecutor Seymour subsequently conducted a "secret" investigation into the source of the Hardscrabble poisonings. It must have been very secret, indeed, for little word of it leaked out to the wider world until March 13, when the story suddenly burst into lurid tabloid bloom on the pages of *The Plain Dealer,* the *Press,* and the *News.* It soon became an obsession with all three papers, and remains to this day a terrific period piece in the annals of sensationalistic journalism.

It was a story that had everything for urban Clevelanders hungry for lurid thrills. It had an exotic locale: remote Hardscrabble peopled by beings caricatured by disdainful urban journalists as ignorant, sweaty rubes inhabiting a region unimaginably remote and primitive to a city dweller. As a *Plain Dealer* reporter with a penchant for the picturesque put it: "This is a rubber boot country. An almost impossible mud road—Methodist road on a surveyor's map—leads to the house . . ."

It had gothic, inexplicable violence, too. Backwards and forwards, with repeated relish, Cleveland's three newspapers recited the list of victims—three dead and fourteen sick (including Martha)—

TWO DEAD IN ARSENIC PLOT

Cleveland Press headline,
March 13, 1925.

and wondered when next an unknown, demonic poisoner would strike. Or as Dick Williams of the *Press* put it, in words that would not have pleased any local chamber of commerce: "The ghost of a series of wanton murders, apparently directed at the extermination of a peace-loving and industrious family, today arose from the mud and slime of Hardscrabble to add its ghostly name to Ohio's record of crime."

And it had mystery. Whence, why, and by what unknown hand had these homicides come? Virtually every possible theory—and some impossible ones—came into play in the minds and column inches of fevered journalists. The original assumption that the New Year's Day mass sickness at the Gienke-Hasel homestead had been due to ptomaine poisoning was shunted aside with a flourish as the *Press* trumpeted the hue and cry of "Super-Killer Hunted in Medina-Co." (". . . a super-murderer who kills for the mere joy of killing"). Not everyone agreed. Rival newspapers discussed the possibility that the arsenic could have originated in chemical sprays used on Hardscrabble apple trees, carbide gas used for cooking purposes in the Gienke kitchen, or even, somehow, in the metal finish of the Gienke coffeepot. And the *News*, either to mock *Press* speculation or with impressive prescience, simply stated that a "moron" was being sought as the probable poisoner.

By March 14, the investigation was in high gear and moving closer to the trial that would make Martha Wise's name a feared byword in Northeast Ohio. Martha Wise's signature had already been found by the police in druggist Weber's register, and there was evidence that her signature for a subsequent arsenic purchase had been badly scribbled in a clumsy attempt to disguise her identity. The authorities, led by Seymour and Medina County sheriff Fred Roshon, were already suspicious of Martha. She was just the kind of local eccentric to fall under a cloud of suspicion at such a time—in medieval times she probably would have long since been burned as a witch—and it was clear that she had enjoyed sufficient access to the Gienke-Hasel house and—more significantly—to the Gienke-Hasel food supplies.

Suspicions about Martha intensified over the weekend of March 14–15. Richard and Fred Gienke had nourished some doubts about Martha since the beginning of their family troubles, and Richard voiced his growing suspicions in an interview published in the March 16 *Press:*

> This woman [identified as a "woman crazed by hallucinations"] threatened to get us. We heard about that, but didn't pay attention to it . . . After mother and dad died we began to wonder about the poison, but didn't think of the threats. But when the rest of us kept getting sick, we remembered them.

And just to ensure that the cops didn't miss the point, some kind soul sent a letter, postmarked Valley City, to Prosecutor Seymour that read: "I just want to make a suggestion. See if you can find out if there was any ill feeling between Martha Wise and Lilly Gienke. She claims to have been sick, too, but that may be a lie."

On Wednesday, March 18, the body of Lillian Gienke was exhumed from its grave in the Myrtle Hill Cemetery. The stomach was removed and sent to Elyria for a postmortem, which was conducted by Coroner Crum and doctors A. H. Woods and H. P. Robinson. Elyria city chemist E. G. Curtis's final report would show enough poison to kill three persons; the stomach and intestines were thoroughly saturated with arsenic, which had almost totally destroyed the major tissues of the bowels. Plans to exhume the corpses of Sophie Hasel and Fred Gienke, Sr., were considered but eventually dropped.

Meanwhile, the net was closing in on hapless Martha. On Monday and Tuesday, March 16–17, Cleveland newspaper accounts of the poison investigation included coy references to the dragnet for an "unknown woman" and a "mysterious poisoner." But Martha was no longer mysterious to Medina County sheriff Fred Roshon, who motored up to Fairview Park Hospital on Cleveland's West Side on Wednesday. Martha Wise had also come to Fairview Park that afternoon to have an arm infection treated, and it was in the hospital waiting room that Roshon arrested Martha and asked her leave to take her back to Medina for questioning.

Martha agreed to come with disarming cooperativeness, despite the fact that Roshon had not brought a subpoena and had no legal power to compel her return. *Cleveland Press* writer Dick Williams was allowed to accompany Martha and Roshon on the ride back, and to Williams Martha expressed seemingly heartfelt sympathy and shock for her recent victims:

> My heart bleeds for them. It must have been a monster that would kill them, and my poor, innocent old mother, why did they kill her? It was terrible. I sometimes think they were poisoned by accident. Because I can't imagine anyone being so terrible.

With compelling evidence of Martha's guilt already in hand, Sheriff Roshon could easily imagine someone in particular being so terrible, and upon their return to Medina, he and Martha repaired to Prosecutor Joseph Seymour's office for an official interrogation. Also present at Martha's questioning were Coroner E. L. Crum, Roshon's wife, Ethel, and stenographer Nell McCarrier.

As Dick Williams later re-created the scene (he may have been allowed to be present by the cooperative Sheriff Roshon), Martha stonewalled her questioners for two hours with repeated cries of "No, no, no! I didn't, I didn't, I didn't!" She eventually cracked, however, owing to the sympathetic manner of Ethel Roshon, who invoked Mother Nature's aid in eliciting Martha's confession. It had been raining all afternoon, as Dick Williams melodramatically recounted:

> "Listen to that rain," said Mrs. Roshon. "Do you know what it is saying, Martha? It is saying, 'You did it, you did it.' It is the voice of God, telling you to tell the truth."
>
> Widow Wise half rose from her chair. "I didn't, I didn't, I didn't," she screamed out as the raindrops chanted Mrs. Roshon's words: "You did it, you did it, you did it." Widow Wise's face blanched.
>
> "Listen to it, Martha," said Mrs. Roshon. "See how it says 'You did it, you did it, you did it.'"
>
> "Oh, my God," the harassed woman cried, "maybe I did."
>
> "No, not maybe," said Mrs. Roshon, "not maybe, Martha. It says, 'You did it.'"
>
> Widow Wise listened. "Oh, God, yes, I did it," she shouted. "The devil told me to."

Martha's official confession followed, and she never altered its details afterwards. As she remembered it, she had gotten the first dose of arsenic from druggist Weber in late November. Although she told Weber she was going to "pound it into meat and put it into the cellar to catch rats," she instead put "just a pinch" in her mother's water bucket on Thanksgiving Day and continued doing so until Sophie Hasel was dead. Her second round of killing began New Year's Day, when she came to the Gienkes' for milk (Fred Gienke had been letting her use his cow ever since her own had gone dry) and began dosing the Gienkes' kitchen water bucket.

All in all, Martha's confession was a straightforward piece of work, although it was stronger on mechanics than motivation. All she could say as to her purpose was: "I don't know why I did it. I just couldn't help it. The devil was in me . . . Something seemed to make me do it. I lost my mind. My mind wasn't right . . . it has been working on me since last summer."

While thus plainly admitting her horrifying deeds, Martha could not disguise her relief at discharging the terrible burden of fear and guilt that had weighed on her mind for months:

> After I did it, it bothered me and worried me. I worried about it all the time. I feel better now . . . I feel better since I have told you all about it . . . It is the Lord's will that I should be punished and I know I must be.

That same night, Martha further elaborated on her fatal decision-making process to *Press* reporter Alene Sumner:

> The Devil made me do it. He came to me in my kitchen when I baked my bread and he said, "Do it!" He came to me when I walked the fields in the cold days and nights and said, "Do it!" Everywhere I turned I saw him grinning and pointing and talking. I couldn't eat. I couldn't sleep. I could only talk and listen to the devil. Then I did it!

Needless to say, Martha Wise was a cynical city editor's dream. The same *Cleveland Press* story which disclosed Martha's guilt trumpeted a compelling, if woefully distorted, portrait of the pitiful Martha and her methods with the screaming headline: "WIDOW CONFESSES SHE POISONED THREE THRU CRAZE FOR FUNERALS." And Dick Williams's accompanying text delivered

Cleveland Press headline, March 19, 1925.

the goods promised by the label of a woman gone berserk for sheer lust of public grief:

> People didn't die often enough in Hardscrabble to satisfy Widow Wise's morbid appetite. So Widow Wise made her own funerals. She killed her mother, her aunt and her uncle, and almost wiped out their families. Widow Wise walked miles to attend a funeral. She had not missed a funeral in 20 years in her home town.

Meanwhile, following her confession and incarceration in the Medina jail, Prosecutor Seymour had Martha examined by doctors and began preparing for Medina's first capital poison case in thirty-five years.

If Seymour had enjoyed his druthers, Martha would simply have endured a lunacy hearing and been committed to Lima State Hospital for life as an insane person. But public opinion, greatly inflamed by media coverage, demanded a murder trial, and the psychiatric testimony of the physicians who examined Martha excluded any alternative. Doctors H. H. Drysdale and Joseph S. Tierney both interviewed Martha and judged her fit to stand trial on a charge of first-degree murder. As Tierney put it: "She is of an inferior constitution and mental grade, but she is not insane, nor was she insane prior to or at the time of her acts. If she killed to attend funerals, it

Cleveland News, March 14, 1925.

wouldn't make her insane. It would only show a greater degree of moral turpitude."

Tierney concluded his examination with the informal observation that Martha was "the most wretched bit of humanity I have ever seen in a criminal action." Tierney's conjecture was that her criminal actions were the result of long-repressed emotions stemming from the many years of mistreatment suffered at the hands of her dead husband. Meanwhile, Martha languished in the Medina county jail, longing for her children and worrying about the possibility of the electric chair. She was indicted for first-degree murder on April 7, with fourteen witnesses appearing before the grand jury, and her trial was set for May.

Martha's trial opened on May 4 in the Medina County Courthouse and, as anticipated, proved to be the social event of the decade. Hundreds of spectators, mostly farmers and their wives, showed up hours before the 9:00 a.m. starting time to procure good seats. It was estimated that women outnumbered men by a ratio of forty to one. Many spectators brought their lunches with them, lest the demands of Nature cost them their coveted seats. A local undertaker had provided extra folding chairs. When Judge N. H. McClure finally gaveled the proceedings to order, there were almost two hundred people in the courtroom, with as many more standing outside. And if press accounts are to be believed, no one present was disappointed by the appearance of the "super-killer" as she was led into the courtroom by Ethel Roshon:

> Her face was drawn, her eyes downcast. There were lines about her eyes and mouth, testifying to the mental suffering thru which she has passed during the months that she has been in jail. Her hair was combed straight back from her wrinkled and yellow forehead. Her eyes were weird, dark caverns, deep-sunk behind her steel-rimmed glasses. When she was arrested her hair showed few traces of gray. Today it is thickly streaked with white . . . The woman walked like one very tired. Her shoulders sagged. Her head dropped on a sunken chest. Her clothes were clean, but ill-fitting over her gaunt form. Her hands hung listlessly at her sides, one clutching, claw-like, a small blue handkerchief.

As always, in that heyday of yellow journalism, the media did not skimp in descriptions of the accused's attire: "Mrs. Wise was simply dressed and wore no hat over her piled black hair. A tan coat covered her dress of blue and reached to her new patent leather shoes. From time to time she fingered a necklace of imitation pearls or adjusted her gold rimmed glasses."

Considering the state of Medina County public opinion, Martha Wise received a reasonably fair trial. Although in the entire venire of more than 140 persons called for possible jury duty, no one could be found who hadn't formed an opinion, eventually seven women and five men were selected after they testified they were capable of putting their opinions aside in evaluating the evidence. Martha's defense attorney, Joseph Pritchard of Cleveland, and County Prosecutor Seymour, assisted by Special Prosecutor Arthur Van Epps, then began calling their witnesses to the stand.

The trial lasted ten days and proved something of an anticlimax. Prosecutor Seymour announced at the outset that he would not seek the death penalty for Martha, so the ensuing legal contest was a mere battle to decide whether Martha was insane or not.

Joseph Pritchard did not dispute the facts in the case. He could not challenge Martha's confession because the state did not introduce it as direct evidence, although Ethel Roshon was allowed to testify about the multiple oral confessions made to her by the talkative Martha. Nor could he challenge the results of his client's actions, which were made painfully evident when a still-paralyzed Fred Gienke, Jr., limped into the courtroom, and when his sister, Marie, crippled for life, was brought from Elyria Hospital on a stretcher to give her tortured testimony in evidence. The effect of her sufferings on the jury can be imagined, as attorney Van Epps asked her what it felt like to ingest arsenic. "It nearly tore my heart out," Marie said. Martha couldn't even bear to look as another of her victims, cousin Herman Gienke, limped into the courtroom on a cane. And even as it was, the state's case against Martha was almost halfheartedly argued: the only charge legally brought against her was the murder of Lillian Gienke.

Defense attorney Pritchard had subpoenaed 139 witnesses, and 52 of them actually took the stand to paint a consistent portrait of Martha Wise as a congenital half-wit and pathetic village eccentric extraordinaire. Martha tried to keep up a steely front, but she broke down and cried when one of her former male friends testified that she had barked like a dog and foamed at the mouth. Indeed, it was obvious to all spectators that by the time her witnesses finished describing her as a murderer, arsonist, thief, hypochondriac, and moron, Martha Wise was a totally shattered woman. Attorney Pritchard's summation was a concise precis of their portrait of an almost incredibly sick and distressed woman: "Pyromania, plus kleptomania, plus epilepsy, plus spinal meningitis equals insanity." It is said that Pritchard wept aloud as he pleaded with the jury to find Martha insane.

The state's case was simple and to the point. Druggist Weber came forward to swear that Martha Wise had purchased 960 grains of arsenic from him, and Elyria city chemist Curtis testified that he found five of those grains in Lillian Gienke's corpse. And Seymour's summation rebutted the defense's picture of a bewildered idiot with an alternative portrait of a cunning killer:

> Slipping into the Gienke home when no one was watching, pinching arsenic into their water pail, returning twice to add further poison—that's not the manner in which insane people kill. She bought enough arsenic to kill every one in the Hard-

scrabble district where she lived. She came to the Gienkes
when they all were ill and told their doctor she thought their
illness was influenza. That's not the act of an insane woman.

Joseph Pritchard's most promising defense strategy eventually
blew up in his face. He was aware that Edith Hasel, the wife of
Martha's brother Fred, had lately been troubled by delusions that it
was *she*—not Martha—who had poisoned the Gienke and Hasel
families. Aware that Pritchard might put her on the stand in an effort
to portray his client as harassed by similar hallucinations, Edith
slashed her own throat with a paring knife on May 6, necessitating a
delay in the trial while the Gienke-Hasel clan made preparations for
yet another unexpected funeral. In fairness to Pritchard, though, it
should be stated that Hardscrabble gossip had it that Edith had killed
herself because of morbid guilt stemming from an old family feud
with Martha. On May 13, the state rested its case with a plea for a
guilty verdict with a recommendation of mercy. In his final words,
Prosecutor Van Epps sounded the note of awestruck pity for Martha
that was seemingly shared by everyone in the courtroom: "I, like
every man, woman and child in the courtroom have nothing but the
deepest respect for Mrs. Martha Wise. It is natural for us all to feel
sorry for her in her predicament."

But, Van Epps continued, justice warranted a response sterner
than sympathy, and it was telling that the defense had not had enough
faith in its client to allow her to take the stand. The case went to the
jury at 10:21 a.m. on May 13. The seven women (six of them house-
wives) and five men (three of them farmers) returned little over an
hour later with a verdict of guilty of murder in the first degree—with
a recommendation of mercy. The deliberations had taken only fifty-
eight minutes, and a second ballot had been taken only to confirm the
unanimity of the first. Upon hearing her fate, Martha said, "I am satisfied. They did their duty," and left the courtroom with Mrs.
Roshon. Subsequently sentenced to a life term at Marysville, she
told Judge McClure, "Thank you for your kindness."

There remained some unfinished business yet in the case. Attorney Pritchard had been badgering Prosecutor Seymour with allegations that someone had helped persuade Martha to kill her family,
and the Medina authorities now pursued that notion. Lester Wise,
Martha's eldest son, came forward to testify that he had been with
his mother in early November when he heard her talking with a man
about poisons. When the couple became aware of Lester's presence,
they told him to leave. But the matter had preyed on Lester's mind

and he finally broke down and told his uncle Paul Hasel about the conversation. The upshot was the arrest on May 16 of Walter Johns on a charge of first-degree murder.

The truth about the Wise-Johns relationship will never be known. But if hell hath no fury like a woman scorned, Martha Wise now certainly came forward to play the part of a scorned female. She was now as anxious to justify her behavior as she was to incriminate her alleged former sweetheart: "I would have carried this to the grave. I never intended to tell. But now that everybody is talking about it, I can't hold my tongue any longer. He never came to see me in the jail and at the trial he never looked at me, although he was there every day."

At the same time, Martha now was willing to let Satan off the hook: "Walter Johns told me to do it. It wasn't the devil—it was Walter Johns. They didn't want me to get married. He said to get Mother out of the way, and I did."

Confronted by a seemingly shocked Johns at the Medina jail on May 18, Martha elaborated further: "He made me do it! He put me up to it! He kept at me to do it! He told me I should get the arsenic and get rid of my mother, and then I'd be free and happy . . . I took my punishment. You scorned me. Now I tell."

Subsequently ensconced in a nearby jail cell, Johns could only repeat the same denial over and over: "She lies. I don't know anything about this."

The case against Johns collapsed almost as quickly as it had inflated. A father of five and a steady worker employed by a Cleveland firm, Johns had a good reputation and there was little evidence to support Martha's claim that he had been her lover. There was no way the state would ever take the risk of putting Martha on the stand in a criminal trial, and the testimony of Lester Wise was considered insufficient to support a convincing case.

Inevitably, Johns was finally released for lack of evidence on May 21 and returned to his family in Cleveland, no doubt a chastened man. For her part, Martha calmed down and was soon taking an almost jocular, baiting tone in her jailhouse conversations with Ethel Roshon: "It's a good thing you caught me when you did. Why didn't you catch me sooner? I'm glad you did get me and I know I have to be punished."

The two-month Medina sensation slowly dissipated. Efforts went forward to place Martha's children—Lester, 14, Everett, 11, Gertrude, 10, and Kenneth, 7—in adoptive homes. Martha's estate was pitiful, consisting only of her eighteen-acre farm and an $1,800

Cleveland News headline, May 13, 1925.

bank account. And the latter asset would have been significantly diminished by court-assessed witness fees had not Judge McClure taken pity on Martha and reversed his own ruling.

The rest of Martha's life at Marysville Reformatory was a long anticlimax, and probably happier than the years that had preceded her incarceration there. Experts predicted that Martha would be crazier than a bedbug within eighteen months of her arrival, but she confounded them by making a good adjustment to the routine of prison life. Put in charge of the chickens and ducks, she developed a real liking for the animals. She was eventually celebrated as Marysville's best laundress ever. There were some bad moments for her, as she confessed to an interviewer in 1930: "I see ghosts. Every night they come and sit on the edge of my bed in their graveclothes. They point their fingers at me."

She was still relatively calm five years later when *Cleveland News* reporter Howard Beaufait called upon her, although she wistfully confessed to him, "I want my freedom. I pray to God for it."

In a macabre miscarriage of judicial clemency and executive procedure, Martha almost got her wish—but only after she had ceased desiring it. Denied parole in 1946, 1951, and 1956, Martha finally had her first-degree murder conviction commuted to a second-degree charge by Governor Michael DiSalle on December 26, 1962. This had come about through the efforts of a Lutheran group interested in her situation, and the same group soon succeeded in securing Martha's parole, which was announced on January 30, 1962.

It was all a horrible mistake. Seemingly older than her 79 years and suffering multiple physical ills, Martha was in no shape or mood to take up whatever vestige of "normal life" would have been possible for this eternally unhappy woman, whose total assets were $570. As her children expressed no desire to take her in, the state had made arrangements to have Martha board, at a state-paid fee of eighty-five dollars per month, at a private nursing home run by a woman in Blanchester, Ohio. (It was alleged by cynical-minded parties that the state of Ohio's intention was to simply "dump" Martha Wise, owing to her rising medical expenses, but there is no solid evidence as to that charge.) The callous denouement came on February 2, when Parole Officer Helen Nicholson drove a weeping, fearful, and disoriented Martha Wise to her presumed new home. Upon their arrival, the woman who had agreed to board her came out to the car and abruptly announced the deal was off: "Oh, my God, no. She can't come into our house. I'm a food caterer. This is a very small town. People would talk. What do you think would happen to my business?"

Nicholson drove Martha to her own house, where they spent the night, and Martha returned home to Marysville for good the next day. Martha died at the age of 89 on June 28, 1971, at 4:40 p.m. and was buried at Marysville.

TORSO INTERLUDE 9

Another Lady, Another Dead End

Cuyahoga River, April–May, 1938

One of the regrettable, if inevitable, casualties of the endless and unproductive Torso killer search was acrimony among the searchers. After almost four years of mayhem and an ever-increasing catalog of body parts, Cleveland authorities had nothing to show for thousands of hours of police work and numerous statements that they would "get their man." Meanwhile, the body count continued to mount. It was just a matter of time before the Torso searchers fell out amongst themselves through sheer frustration; that time came in the spring of 1938.

Steve Morosky, a thirty-five-year-old WPA worker, was walking along the east bank of the Cuyahoga River at 2:15 on the afternoon of April 8 when he spied what looked like a dead fish caught amid rotted pilings near the foot of Superior Avenue. Upon closer inspection and some poking with a stick, Morosky realized it was something more unpleasant and called the police. They soon arrived and took custody of part of a human lower leg, neatly severed at the knee and ankle joints.

Within hours Coroner Sam Gerber announced that Morosky's modest discovery was definitely the latest work of the Kingsbury Run Torso slayer. Gerber estimated that the victim had been dead three to five days and that the leg showed little decomposition. As always, Gerber insisted that the butchering technique had been "expert," noting that the dismemberment had been done "cleanly at the joints with a sharp knife or physician's scalpel." Yet, simultaneously, Gerber admitted that "crude knife marks indicate the slayer was in a hurry." Later evidence would further undermine Gerber's presumption of a skilled carver, but the coroner already seemed ambivalent as to the finesse of the much sought-after predator. In any case, Gerber had given his critics just the opening they desired.

The first public cracks in the Torso investigation came the next morning when Eliot Ness's assistant, Robert W. Chamberlin, requested that Morosky's find be examined by pathologists at Western Reserve University. Gerber wasn't about to stand for such inter-

ference on his turf and the criticism it implied, and he publicly
riposted in a blistering statement that *The Plain Dealer* jocularly
characterized as a "slight difference of opinion":

> Director Chamberlin wanted the leg to conform to the time of
> a missing person and the facts wouldn't bear that out. I
> refused to let Chamberlin send in a person to examine the leg
> because I want someone who is absolutely impartial.

That impartial someone being Sam Gerber, the case was closed,
although Chamberlin sniffed, probably disingenuously, "I thought
Dr. Gerber wouldn't mind other experts corroborating his findings."

With only half a leg to go on, the police concentrated on more
remote forensic and circumstantial findings while they waited for
more evidence to surface. Newspaper accounts recalled the report of
Jefferson Street bridge tender James Macka, who had seen a man
throw a heavy bundle into the Cuyahoga River on the night of March
3. (Macka remembered that the man had alighted from a "stream-
lined, expensive" car.) Subsequent dragging of the river, though,
produced no heavy bundle. A report that someone had been seen
skulking in a sewer outlet adjacent to the site of the half leg came to
nothing, as did Detective Merylo's investigation of a pile of women's
clothing found on East 65th Street, near Kingsbury Run on January
17. The heap of garments had included an imitation chinchilla coat,
a black felt hat, and some rayon underwear, but its connection to the
partial leg was clearer to Merylo than to anyone else. It was widely
assumed that the leg might have been washed out of the Kingsbury
Run area by torrential rains in the days before it was found. Edward
Brusheau, a deckhand on a river dredge, claimed he had seen what
looked like a woman's head in the river early on the morning that the
leg was discovered.

On April 13 news came that the dogged eighteen-month quest of
Peter Merylo and Martin Zalewski had finally paid off. For some
time, the inseparable duo had been convinced that the key to the
Torso slayings lay with the earliest victims, especially Edward
Andrassy, Torso victim No. 2. For some months now Merylo and
Zalewski had been focusing on Andrassy's bisexual adventures, and
in early April they hit paydirt. They had retrieved some photographs
of Andrassy from his parents and were much intrigued by background details in the pictures, which showed an ornate room with
flowered wallpaper, a Japanese lantern, and a heavy vase. Could this
be the "butcher's workshop" they had so long sought? The pictures

Cave at the foot of Superior Avenue in the Flats, searched for torso bits, April 16, 1938.

were published in Cleveland newspapers, and a tip soon led them to a young man who identified the room in the photograph as a second-floor bedroom at 1734 West 28th Street. On April 13, a previous tenant of that room, fifty-six-year-old restaurant worker John Moessner, was arrested at his apartment on Fulton Road.

Moessner seemed too good to be true. A homosexual—luridly identified for readers of the *Cleveland Press* as a "small, thin, hook-nosed man with piercing dark eyes"—he admitted to knowing Andrassy and to having taken photographs of the latter in his West 28th Street room several years earlier. Better yet, in the room itself Cleveland police found a sharp butcher knife in a chest and what appeared to be bloodstains on the floor. And it must have looked like money from home when detectives Merylo and Zalewski found a photograph in Moessner's room of a young man in a naval uniform. *The man looked just like Torso victim No. 5—the Tattooed Man!*

The case against Moessner evaporated almost as quickly as it had precipitated. The bloodstains turned out not to be bloodstains at all, and it was eventually agreed that the young man in the naval uniform didn't resemble Torso victim No. 5 in the least. One can imagine, however, the horror of Clevelanders when confronted with the

SEARCH RIVER FOR PARTS OF TORSO VICTIM

Police Told Driver of Expensive Auto Hurled Bundle Into Cuyahoga

CORONER SPURNS AID

Dr. Gerber Refuses to Permit W. R. U. Experts to Check Gruesome Find

Cleveland Press, April 9, 1938.

detailed decadence unearthed by those intrepid sleuths Merylo and Zalewski—a virtual re-creation of Moessner's satanic West 28th Street flat: "The second-floor den, itself, though small, was indescribably bizarre, with its hanging Japanese lantern and walls covered with tapestry and small, exquisite Japanese water colors and French nudes."

Moessner, the seemingly harmless brother of two unmarried, elderly sisters with whom he lived a blameless existence, was subsequently booked on a charge of sodomy with a Lorain County youth.

Perhaps it was the collapse of their case against Moessner. Maybe it was just the stress of too much intimacy, aggravated by the professional tensions of a baffling, never-ending investigation. Whatever the reason, Martin Zalewski went to Inspector Charles Nevel on April 13 and told him he was "washed up," didn't want to work the Torso beat anymore, and didn't want to work with Peter Merylo. Merylo's only public comment about what must have been a fraternal tragedy for the Damon and Pythias of Torso sleuthing, was bitter: "Any recommendation he wants to make will be okay with me; maybe I'll get a partner who'll work." Zalewski would eventually return to the Torso beat and even to occasional work with Merylo,

Torso Hunting Wears on Nerves, Detectives Split

Cleveland Press, April 14, 1938.

but it was clear that the bloom was off the rose betwixt the premier Torso investigators.

As everyone had expected, the other shoe dropped, so to speak, in the investigation of Torso No. 11. Late on Monday, May 2, two bridge tenders at West Third Street, Oscar Meister and Albert Mahaffey, noticed two burlap bags floating in the Cuyahoga River. Inside the bags were most of the missing parts of the eleventh victim: the two halves of the torso, two thighs, and a left foot. Coroner Gerber's reassembly of the body parts suggested that the victim was a white female, short, thin, flat-chested, between twenty-five and thirty, five foot two, 115 to 120 pounds, with brown hair and small feet. Death, as usual, had come by decapitation. In an unusual twist, there were drugs in the system, suggesting that the victim was an addict, and examination revealed at least two cesarian births and the removal of the appendix.

The latest grisly discovery further compromised Coroner Gerber's insistence that the serial dismemberments were done by a skilled dissector. The removal of the arms of No. 11 had been very crude; there were ghastly, slashing thigh wounds (most of the previous Torso corpses were unmutilated); and the killer had broken some ribs in his haste to sever the trunk. The head, hands, arms, and lower right leg and foot of Torso victim No. 11 were never found.

The tiresome investigative work went on, although one suspects that the heart had gone out of the hunt. Eliot Ness and Sam Gerber were at loggerheads; the two best manhunters were essentially missing in action; and even omniscient Sam Gerber had nothing more to show than another incomplete inventory of body parts.

On May 9, a seventy-three-year-old Clevelander was arrested for the crime of having allegedly been seen at various times in the company of both Flo Polillo and Edward Andrassy. At the same time, Ohio National Guard planes flew over the Kingsbury Run area in an effort to discover, via aerial photography, the "secret paths" by which the Torso slayer disposed of his dead and eluded capture.

Meanwhile, Peter Merylo dropped a ten-pound ham into the Cuya-hoga River in an effort to test how long a fleshy substance might remain afloat. Attached was a metal tag, asking anyone who found it to return it to its owner.

In spite of the dissension and public clamor that the Kingsbury Run Torso slayings had occasioned over four years, even the general public was tiring of the hunt. On May 9, 1938, *Plain Dealer* reporter Philip W. Porter described the situation in terms that still ring true today:

> [The] general attitude seems to be, "Tsk, tsk. Another torso victim. Too bad, too bad." Only the newsboys and a few policemen seem to get excited. The reason is obvious—the victims for the most part have been nameless. In only three or four cases have there been identifications, and even then, the murdered people were all too obviously bums or degen-erates. Nobody knew them, except in the crumby world in which they moved. The others, unidentified, mean absolutely nothing as individuals, because the public in this day and age appears to be unmoved by crime, violence or bad faith in the abstract. It is easy to imagine the uproar that would have swept the community if, say, ten industrial leaders or ten members of the baseball team or even ten councilmen had been thus butchered.

Chapter 10

"THEY'RE KILLING THEM ON THE BRIDGE!"

The 1920 Sly-Fanner Payroll Murders

It was a "wide-open" town. If you could make one sound generalization about Cleveland in 1920, it would be this. The city was almost defenseless against the depredations and outrages of both organized and unorganized criminals. The columns of the three daily newspapers shouted it, whether it was in headlines of the Kagy-McGannon murder/perjury scandal, the brazen mayhem of the "Jiggs" Losteiner gang before its fatal rendezvous at Bedford, the almost daily revelations of police and judicial corruption stimulated by the recently enacted Volstead Act, or in the ever-increasing incidents of robbery, rape, and murder in the streets of Cleveland.

No fewer than seven Cleveland policemen were murdered between March 1919 and January 1921, and a score more were wounded by gun-toting thugs the police seemed helpless to stop. Only one criminal was killed committing a violent act. No fewer than thirty-nine major robberies took place during the last seven months of 1920—one every five days, resulting in an average of one civilian death a month. Almost all of these violent thefts, involving the loss of over $150,000, were successful, leading more and more Clevelanders to believe that the police—perhaps ineptly, perhaps cynically—had lost control of the streets and public safety. Public apathy was beginning to set in as 1921 loomed, and it must have seemed like a miracle would be required to stun Clevelanders into doing anything about their "wide-open" city.

Something did happen to wake up the citizens, but it wasn't a miracle. It was a shocking, almost unbelievably callous double homicide on the last day of 1920: the unforgettable double murder of Wilfred C. Sly and George K. Fanner on a West Side residential street.

The W. W. Sly Manufacturing Company was a more or less thriving foundry concern at Fleet and Junction avenues, not far south of where the Nickel Plate tracks ran east and west under the streets of the northern near West Side. Founded by Wilfred Sly's father in 1874, the Sly company had manufactured sand blast machinery, cupolas, tumbling barrels, and other foundry equipment for almost half a century at its West Side site. Employing between seventy and eighty men in the recessionary slack period of 1920–1921, the firm was widely known as a paternalistic concern that worked hard to take care of its employees and to listen to them. George Coleman spoke for many of his fellow employees in eulogizing Sly and Fanner just hours after their deaths:

> You couldn't find better folks to work for. When I was on the shop committee Mr. Sly and Mr. Fanner heard every complaint we had and fixed up all the troubles. A man could come into Mr. Sly's office in his overalls and talk to him about his job. He was one of the most easily approached men in Cleveland. Every man in the shop would say that.

Wilfred Sly had lived almost all of his fifty-eight years in Cleveland, growing up with his father's firm and becoming its president after the death of W. W. Sly in 1911. In his youth Wilfred had been quite an athlete, winning several state and regional high-wheel bicycle championships. In middle age he had evolved into an avid fisherman, yachtsman, and outdoorsman, spending two months of every summer fishing in the Canadian wilderness. His home on Lake Avenue in Lakewood was a fashionable showplace noted for its extensive gardens and as the site of an annual New Year's Eve masquerade ball at which Sly and his wife, Marie, liked to entertain their many friends. Wilfred Sly particularly admired vigor and courage in other men. Only the week before, he had discussed a recent Chicago payroll stickup with a friend. When told of the resistance put up by the victim against the armed robber, Sly commented enthusiastically, "[t]hat's the kind of man I admire."

George K. Fanner, 33, was the superintendant of the W. W. Sly concern. The son of the former vice president, he also lived in Lakewood, with his wife and their ten-year-old daughter, Marian. Like Wilfred Sly, George Fanner was a well-known man, well liked by both friends and employees.

In retrospect, the Sly-Fanner tragedy seems almost inevitable. As was the custom in that era before the use of commercial armored-car services became standard practice, Wilfred Sly and George Fanner personally picked up the cash payroll of several thousand dollars every week in a satchel at the First National Bank on lower Euclid

The Cleveland Press

W. C. SLY AND GEO. FANNER MURDERED BY ROBBERS

Cleveland Press headline, December 31, 1920.

Avenue. And not only did they pick it up at the same time every Friday morning, but they also always took the same route back to the factory in Sly's gray touring car. It was a dangerously predictable routine in a year of almost daily payroll robberies, and someone was bound to notice.

As the police later pieced the story together, the man who noticed it first was a young hoodlum named Louis Komer, a.k.a. "The Toledo Kid." Komer may even have been an ex-employee of the W. W. Sly company. He had been thinking for some time about what an easy heist the Sly-Fanner payroll would be when he ran into another gangster named Frank Motto in a poolroom at Superior and East Ninth Street on a late December afternoon in 1920. There was much on Frank Motto's mind that winter day, and he unburdened his troubled soul to Komer. A member of the notorious Serra Gang of automobile thieves, Motto had been arrested in November 1919 for multiple car theft. Convicted on five counts of same in December 1920, Motto was facing a long prison term, which was to begin in late January. If only he could get $1,500, he whined to Komer, he might be able to pay for a successful legal appeal. But where could he lay his hands on money like that?

Komer told him about the Sly-Fanner payroll, and the two thugs set to work recruiting gunmen and planning the heist. The plotters were soon joined by Dominic Benigno, Angelo Amato, and Dominic Lonardo, all associated with the "Mayfield Road mob" that was beginning to build its organized crime empire in Cleveland in the wake of the newly enacted Prohibition laws. By the end of December the conspirators had all the men and guns they needed, and set out to recruit a car. Which is how it happened that Dominic Benigno sidled up to his friend Ignatius "Sam" Purpera on the night of December 30 at the Dreamland Dance Hall at East 13th Street and Euclid Avenue.

Although he was over six feet tall, Sam Purpera looked like a kid, with his twitchy eyes and petulant, prominent lower lip. But looks were deceiving: at the age of sixteen, Sam Purpera was already an experienced car thief, strong-arm guy, and petty felon. Arrested the month before for car theft in Pittsburgh, Sam had jumped his $1,000 bail and returned to Cleveland. Rearrested, he was committed to the Cuyahoga County Boys' Detention Home on Franklin (now the Cuyahoga County Archives) on December 18. The next day, he slugged a guard who had unwisely opened a window next to a fire escape for ventilation, and escaped.

Several hours after talking to Benigno at the Dreamland, Purpera obtained the keys to a freshly stolen Stearns touring car from a car thief named Clarence Brown. The car had recently been stolen from Frederick Goff, the president of the Cleveland Trust Company— right out of its parking spot in front of the bank at East Ninth Street and Euclid. Such was the boldness of even small-fry felons in the wide-open Cleveland of 1920.

Sam Purpera took the Stearns to a lot at Scovill and East 35th Street. Early the next morning, New Year's Eve day, he picked it up and met Frank Motto at East Ninth Street and Orange Avenue. Motto took the wheel, drove to West 47th Street, and cased the site of the intended robbery—the West 47th wooden viaduct over the Nickel Plate railroad tracks (now the RTA Red Line). Motto then drove back downtown and parked outside the Williamson Building at Public Square, just several hundred feet from the First National Bank. There, Purpera and Motto met Benigno, driving a Jordan with Amato, Lonardo, Komer, and at least one other, never-identified gunman in it. The Jordan left first, just minutes before Sly and Fanner emerged from the bank with the $4,200 payroll. The two executives got into Sly's gray car, and Sly began the drive back to the West Side, unknowingly pursued by Motto and Purpera in the purloined Stearns.

It all happened so fast. It was about 11:00 a.m. The Jordan was already waiting on the north end of the viaduct with its engine running when Sly's car turned left from Lorain Avenue onto West 47th Street, just a few blocks away from the W. W. Sly plant. Just as Sly's car entered the viaduct, the quickly accelerating Stearns, piloted by Motto, overtook it and veered suddenly and deliberately into the side of Sly's southbound automobile. Before Sly and Fanner even knew what was happening, their automobile, pushed by the force of the larger Stearns, smashed into the wooden side of the viaduct, splintering the railing and almost hurtling the fifteen feet to the railroad tracks below.

What happened next was witnessed by about twenty men, women,

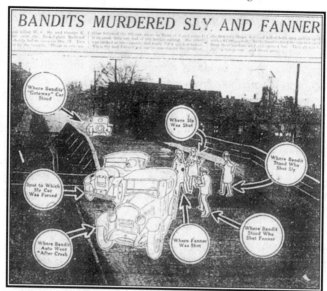

Diagram of the fatal events leading to the murder of Sly and Fanner. *Cleveland Press*, January 7, 1921.

and children of the neighborhood who were either already out on the residential street or drawn there by the increasing commotion. As Sly emerged from the smashed side of his car, he drew his gun, warily advancing on two men who had already alighted from the Stearns and were walking toward him. Maude Toohey of West 47th Street had been on the viaduct when the crash happened, and as Sly passed her she said, "You have had a narrow escape. They nearly pushed you over onto the railroad tracks."

As Sly came up to the two men, he said, "What do you mean by smashing me like this? I believe you did it on purpose. It was absolutely your fault." One of the men, Sam Purpera, dressed in a brown suit and brown cap, replied, "Why I did nothing of the kind, you old bastard!" Meanwhile, four more men had emerged from the Jordan and were walking toward the four men arguing by Sly's wrecked car.

Maybe it was the boyish smile on Sam Purpera's face. The dozen eyewitnesses who sent him to the electric chair remembered that he was smiling as he tried to calm the irate Sly, and apparently he soon succeeded in persuading him that the whole thing had been an accident. There's no other explanation possible, because Sly put his gun away, took out a pencil and paper, and began asking men and women in the growing crowd on the bridge to give their names and addresses as witnesses to the accident.

By this time, George Fanner had emerged from the wrecked car, and his attention was suddenly drawn by one of the men from the Jordan, who reached into Sly's car and drew out the payroll satchel. As George Blaich, a neighborhood resident who had just signed his name and address for Sly, watched in horror, Fanner tried to wrest the satchel away—and all six gunmen from the two cars immediately opened up a deadly fusillade of gunfire on the helpless Sly and Fanner. It was probably nervous Sam Purpera who shot first, hitting Sly in the stomach. As Sly doubled up and fell to the wooden viaduct deck, Purpera stepped up to him and shot him twice in the head, blowing half his face off. Meanwhile, George Fanner died almost instantly, falling in a hail of gunfire, one bullet entering just below his right eye and smashing into his brain. He screamed once, "Oh, my God!" and lay still. As nearby resident Irene Walker put it, influenced no doubt by the culture of the day: "Then I saw guns flash and heard bullets sing." Six revolvers blazed away as pedestrians and neighbors dived for cover and little children ran screaming down the street. Little Helen Barnes of 2100 West 47th Street ran into the house and told her mother, "They're killing them on the bridge!"

It was over almost as quickly as it started. Shouting at the crowd to "Beat it!" and firing over their heads to encourage them, five of the gunmen jumped into the Jordan, which then sped north to Lorain and turned left. Ironically, the Jordan may have been passed by a squad of Cleveland police on their way to the scene of the reported robbery. It was last seen that day at West 65th Street and Bridge Avenue. Sam Purpera, for reasons never explained, did not leave with the others in the Jordan, but fled through a backyard to the Nickel Plate tracks before vanishing from sight. Two bystanders, William Adams and Joseph Harvey, tried in vain to start the Stearns for a pursuit of the bandits.

Otto Walter, a West Side florist, refused to run, despite the threats and bullets of the killers, and was still on the blood-spattered viaduct as the getaway car disappeared in the distance. With the aid of others, he loaded Sly and Fanner into his truck and took them to Fairview Hospital, then at West 28th Street. Both men were pronounced dead on arrival, with multiple .38-caliber slugs in their bodies. Fanner's unused pistol was still in his blood-soaked pocket.

For crime-weary Clevelanders—and the newspapers that served them—the Sly-Fanner killings were the last straw. The McGannon scandal had been bad, the Losteiner reign of terror worse, and the unending incidents of armed robbery an intolerable disgrace. But *this* was different: two well-liked, peaceful men with families had been shot down on a public bridge without even being given a chance to surrender their money. Mrs. Fanner spoke for thousands of incredulous Clevelanders when she tearfully cried: "But I can't understand why they shot him. Why didn't they take the money and go? They need not have shot him down in cold blood."

Not that she was surprised by such cold-blooded boldness, Mrs. Fanner added bitterly. After the recent merciful verdict that had spared the infamous "Jiggs" Losteiner from a deserved place in the electric chair—what else could you expect from a corrupt, inept, and soft-headed system of justice?

The newspapers couldn't have agreed more, and held forth with the most scalding criticisms of a police force of incredible and suspicious incompetence. "MAKE CLEVELAND SAFE!" demanded a front-page *Cleveland Press* editorial:

> With one voice this demand goes up from the entire city. The ruthless murder of Wilfred C. Sly and George K. Fanner by payroll robbers filled all law-abiding citizens with horror and indignation. On the heels of this frightful crime came others of equal boldness, though unaccompanied by bloodshed, such as the wholesale holdups at the Cedar-av car barns, Clark's Euclid-av restaurant and the Miles theater on Friday, Saturday and Sunday Nights . . . Many causes are given for this increase in violent crime, but at the bottom of it all lies the fact that for five years past Cleveland has had a reputation of being an "easy" town . . . Gunmen and thieves flocked thither, making this city not only a field of operations, but a base from which to operate in nearby towns, as instanced by the murderous activities of the Losteiner gang.

The *Press,* echoed by the *News* and *Plain Dealer,* snarled for immediate, tough action:

> FREE CLEVELAND of its reputation in the underworld of being an "easy" town. Give Cleveland instead, a reputation of being a hard town for crooks . . . THE SUREST WAY to do this is to jail or drive out all known crooks. Let those leaving take with them the message to gunmen and thieves everywhere that Cleveland has grown "too hot."

Getting more specific, the *Press* demanded the reform of the bail bond system, less lenient sentencing of criminals, an end to suspended sentences, a tough housecleaning of the parole system, and the use of armored cars to transport large sums of money.

Meanwhile, the Cleveland Police, led by Chief Frank W. Smith—not exactly a legendary figure among Cleveland lawmen—tried to appease outraged and rather contemptuous public opinion with an intensive manhunt for the Sly-Fanner killers. While complaining that his force numbered only 821 men—only about two-thirds of its authorized strength of 1,200—Chief Smith promised an unprecedented manhunt under his personal supervision.

Although the police were given little credit for it, that manhunt soon produced results, albeit initially abortive ones. One of the eyewitnesses to the murders, George Hejna, had copied down the license plate number of the getaway car, and the police were soon able to trace the Jordan to the Bolivar Road garage of the Hotel Winton. (It took a couple of days, because the killers had deliberately bent the edge of the plate, obscuring the last numeral.) The garage was staked out by Cleveland Police detectives, who subsequently picked up three men on Sunday, January 2, as they tried in sequence to retrieve the Jordan from the garage. The police became even more excited when the garage attendant told them that the driver of the car, who had brought it to the garage at 11:43 on Friday morning, had asked the attendant to lie and say that the car had been there all morning.

Meanwhile, thanks to a tip from a Cleveland cabbie, another group of suspicious gangsters fell into the hands of the police. The cabbie had overheard some men talking about a bank heist planned for Monday, January 3, and heard them name a room at the Graystone Hotel, 2118 Prospect Avenue, as their rendezvous. A squad of detectives raided the room in the wee hours of that morning and netted three men and five pistols. Making their captives lie back down on their beds and pretend to be asleep, the police waited several more hours in the dark and caught three more as they walked through the door. That afternoon, police officials announced that they had the Sly-Fanner killers in custody.

But did they? As it turned out, the thugs arrested in the two raids included Dominic Benigno, Dominic Lonardo, and Angelo Amato. But the police couldn't make the charges against them stick, especially after none of the score or so of Sly-Fanner murder witnesses could identify any of the men in police lineups. No one could say whether it had anything to do with the report that suspicious

Sam Purpera. *Cleveland Press*, March 17, 1921.

strangers had been canvassing the West 47th Street area, knocking on doors and telling residents that something bad would happen to anyone who testified against the Sly-Fanner killers. But one by one the suspects were let go, and the investigation returned to square one. The unclaimed rewards posted by groups like the Cleveland Chamber of Commerce and the Cleveland Automobile Club soared to $11,500 and would eventually climb to a figure of $20,000.

Although they didn't know it at the time, the police had picked up a very valuable lead in their early January roundups. One of the suspects, investigation disclosed, had a close professional relationship with a young hoodlum named Sam Purpera. Suspecting that Purpera might be involved in the Sly-Fanner killings, Cleveland police obtained his mug shot from federal officials in Pittsburgh, who had photographed Sam the previous December, and circulated it to police departments throughout the United States.

After two days of high hopes, followed by two months of dead ends, word finally came from Los Angeles on March 11, 1921, that police there had arrested Sam Purpera. The story he told of his odyssey since the Sly-Fanner murders did not reflect well on either the Cleveland Police or their counterparts throughout the United States. Realizing that he was wanted after his friends were seized in the Graystone Hotel and Winton Garage raids, Purpera took a train to Boston, narrowly escaping out one door of a Cleveland restaurant when a Cleveland detective who knew him walked in another. From Boston, Purpera went to Philadelphia, Chicago, El Paso, and Juarez, Mexico, the latter destination reached with passports forged by his criminal friends in Cleveland. From Mexico, Purpera went to San Francisco, where he stole a car. While he was driving it to Los Angeles, the bearings burned out, and he took it to a garage in San Miguel. There, the garage owner, C. J. Larsen, became suspicious and informed Harry J. Raymond of the Southern California Automobile Club about the young man, who called himself George Palmer. The upshot was Palmer's arrest in Los Angeles, where he quickly admitted his real identity and confessed to taking part in the Sly-Fanner robbery. Purpera's claim, then and until the day he died, was that he had a gun but did not use it; his story was that he threw it into the Stearns and ran away.

The crowing of Cleveland lawmen at Purpera's capture almost drowned out the disquieting report that Purpera had been kept well informed about the actions and intentions of Cleveland police throughout the nine weeks of his transcontinental flight. Something was quite rotten among Cleveland's Finest, but the important thing now was to get Purpera back to Cleveland and make him talk. Which was duly accomplished. Brought back to Cleveland on a train dubbed the "Buckeye Murder Special" by County Prosecutor Edward Stanton and detectives Banks and Sterling, Purpera cooperated fully, spontaneously offering another written confession and readily furnishing the names of his erstwhile criminal confederates.

History, no doubt, did not glimpse Sam Purpera—under indictment for first-degree murder—at his best. But it must be said that he made a sorry picture throughout his moment of public notoriety. Perhaps as young as seventeen when apprehended—he may have been older, as suggested by Cleveland school records introduced at his trial—Sam was a classic example of an unexceptional slum child gone bad. Born to Sicilian immigrants who lived on Central Avenue, Sam had left school at the age of fourteen or fifteen to become a barber. Drifting into a life of petty crime and bad associates, he first came to the attention of the police as a young car thief in 1920. His mother, Mary, the only person he ever publicly demonstrated any affection for, readily excused his criminality right up to his ultimate date with the electric chair:

He was a good boy until about three years ago. Then he got sick, and has been nervous. He got into some trouble because some other boys prompted him to help them steal an automobile. But I know he wouldn't do anything as bad as this crime he is charged with. I think the police made him say he did it.

It was remarked by virtually all witnesses and reporters that Purpera was highly nervous and immature, had "shifty, blinking eyes," and little grasp at any time of the reality of his position or prospects. Rather than facing the fate that his car-stealing proclivities had brought him to, he preferred to blame his predicament on an unlucky destiny and faithless comrades in crime:

It's funny, too. Here I am about to go to the chair. And for what? I didn't get a cent of the $4,200. Some of the others got the money and beat it. I never showed for my cut. Here I was chasing all over the country to avoid arrest. But they got me. Something tells me I have been double-crossed. I am almost certain those who I thought my friends squealed.

More foolishly, Purpera also made it clear, in repeated and well-publicized statements, that he thought his tender age would spare him from the electric chair. When he arrived at Union Station at West Ninth Street on March 25, 1921, his first comment to a reporter was, "They don't give anybody under twenty-one the chair, do they?" His other public comments exhibited a mild remorse and an edifying awareness of just where and how he had lost his youthful virtue:

It was a [hell] of a thing to shoot up those two decent fellows like that. Sure, I felt sorry for them and for their families. This is the first time I ever got into trouble in Cleveland, except a little automobile job . . . Poolrooms are the places where young fellows meet bad companions and start to go wrong.

Could Professor Harold Hill have said it better?

Arraigned before Judge Alvin J. Pearson on two separate charges of murder on March 26, Purpera pled not guilty and soon secured legal representation from Attorney J. V. Zottarelli. Meanwhile, Purpera's confessions were bringing others closer to judgment.

Frank Motto, who had shrewdly turned himself in at the Mansfield Reformatory in January to serve his scheduled car-theft sentence, was brought back to Cleveland and booked for the two murder raps on March 28. Confronted by Motto, Purpera justified his behavior as payback for an alleged prior betrayal: "You ditched me. When we wrecked the pay car and got out of our machine you walked away and left me to face the men alone."

Motto, with a keener grasp of the situation than his youthful betrayer, said only this: "I have nothing to say. I am slated for the electric chair if I talk, and I am slated for it if I don't talk, so what is the use of me saying anything?"

Purpera, unfettered by such reticence, went further and identified Motto as the driver of the Stearns and the man who ended up grabbing the payroll satchel and getting it over to the Jordan. It didn't look good for either man: virtually all civic organizations were demanding the death penalty for anyone convicted in the Sly-Fanner case, and Prosecutor Edward Stanton had already announced that under the existing law all participants in the murders would face the death penalty whether they had fired the fatal bullets or not.

Nine days after Motto was formally indicted on two murder counts on April 21, Louis Komer was arrested in Detroit. Identified by fingerprints on a circular sent from Cleveland, Komer waived extradition, admitting that he was on the viaduct on the fatal day but—like Motto and Purpera—denying that he fired any shots.

The first trial, that of Frank Motto, opened on May 2, 1921, before Judge Florence Allen, four months after the murders. The county prosecutors had the additional assistance of attorney Frank Merrick, on loan from the Cleveland Automobile Club. Oddly, owing to peculiarities in the law, Governor Davis had to issue a conditional pardon to Motto for his auto-theft conviction, so that he could be tried on the murder indictment. (The pardon would be automatically revoked if Motto beat the murder rap.) Two days after the trial began, the prosecution got a boost when Louis Komer led police to a lumber pile in the Baker, Rauch and Lang yard at West 80th and Edgewater Drive. There, under an almost impenetrable pile of wood and debris, the police found two of the rusty, still-loaded revolvers used in the Sly-Fanner killings.

Unexpected developments in Motto's trial gave rise to additional flurries of excitement. Thomas Graci of East 39th Street was arrested on May 9, when police found concealed weapons on him as he attempted to enter the courtroom. Defended initially by J. V. Zottarelli and A. A. Cartwright, Motto lost the counsel of the latter

Louis Komer. *Cleveland Press*, December 15, 1921.

when Cartwright had to withdraw because of a contempt citation stemming from his connection with the highly perjured defense of Judge William H. McGannon. He was replaced by former county prosecutor Samuel Doerfler.

Motto's defense was that he was not a member of the gang and that he was not even at the crime scene. This couldn't have impressed the jury much, as five witnesses to the killings—plus the testimony of both Komer and Purpera—put him at the scene and at the wheel of the Stearns. The final arguments were dramatic and worthy of such a life-and-death case. As flashes of lightning lit up the darkened courtroom, Prosecutor Stanton drew scornful conclusions for the jury about Motto's impassive silences and occasional nervous reactions:

> Marked across his forehead now, you may read the word "guilty." Did you notice the quivering of his lips on the witness stand, his shaking in his chair? He was afraid he might utter a word that might show how he lied. If any of you were accused of murder and the person who was supposed to be implicated said, "Yes, you were there and I was with you," wouldn't you jump from your chair and say, "That is a lie, I

was never there." Frank Motto sat quiet when Purpera said that to him.

Assistant Prosecutor James T. Cassidy was even harsher, demanding the ultimate penalty in the name of the outraged living and honored dead:

> Motto would kill at the slightest provocation to avoid capture. . .Motto may cringe and cry and beg for mercy. You say to him, as I say to him now, as Mr. Sly would say if he could come into this courtroom from his cold grave: "Be just as merciful to him as he was to me." . . . Mercy! What right has Motto to claim mercy? There is no such thing as mercy for a fiend such as he.

Even before the final arguments were finished, Prosecutor Stanton announced that Purpera would be tried on the second murder count if he were acquitted of the first.

Zottarelli and Doerfler did the best they could, considering the damning testimony of the eyewitnesses. Correctly noting that none of them had initially identified Motto when shown his picture in the week after the murders, they scoffed at the prosecution's portrait of their client as the robbery mastermind and claimed Motto had left the Jordan at Public Square and gone into—you guessed it—a pool room.

The case went to the jury shortly after noon on Saturday, May 14, 1921. Six hours later, eleven men and one woman, foreman Edith Markell, brought back a verdict of first-degree murder. It had taken ten ballots, and the contest ranged from seven to five on the first ballot (death versus a life sentence) to ten to two on ballots 7, 8, and 9. Zottarelli demanded that the jury be polled and then had the dubious satisfaction of hearing them all individually pronounce his client guilty. When asked by Judge Florence Allen if he had anything to say, Motto replied, "I have not had a fair trail. I did not have all the questions asked me that I wanted either by the prosecutor or by my own lawyers."

"You have had a fair trial, Motto," said Judge Allen as she sentenced him to die in the electric chair on August 29, 1921. Allen then stepped from the bench and explained to the jury that she was willing to impose the death penalty, despite her personal repugnance for capital punishment. It was the first time in Cuyahoga County history that a female judge sentenced a criminal to death. It was also the first time a female jury foreman concurred in such a verdict. Both Mrs. Sly and Mrs. Fanner, who had attended every day of Motto's trial, publicly congratulated the prosecutors on a job well done.

Thirty-seven hours after Motto was sentenced to death, Sam Purpera's trial opened under Judge Maurice Bernon. He was ably defended by the ubiquitous William J. Corrigan (who represented Eva Kaber, Joe Gogan, and Sam Sheppard, among others) and by Zottarelli. Purpera's defense was that he had walked away from the confrontation with Sly and Fanner without firing a shot. But several witnesses put him at the scene as the man in the brown suit and cap who argued with Sly, and Edith Marklew and other witnesses testified that Purpera shot both Sly and Fanner and then fled through Mary Blaich's back yard. Despite minor inconsistencies, Corrigan couldn't shake Marklew on the stand, and Assistant Prosecutor Cassidy expertly enmeshed the easily confused Purpera in a mass of contradictions on the stand. Purpera stoutly insisted that he had done no shooting on the viaduct, but his eventual admission that he knowingly went there for a payroll robbery was enough, under the law, to put him in the electric chair. Not that William J. Corrigan didn't try to save him. His final argument for mercy was a classic sob-sister plea for a slum boy unwittingly gone wrong:

> This child—and he is a child—was not the perpetrator of the deed. He does not deserve the same punishment as Motto and the rest. They used him as a tool in this matter, and that's all he was . . . Go over the conditions of this boy's youth. You have a son, Mrs. Garrett [one of the jurors]. You have exerted every good influence over that son of yours. This boy was raised in the slums. At the age of 6, as you heard it from the stand, he went to work in a barber shop. He was raised in the gutters. He has not brains enough to realize the predicament he is in. Sending a seventeen-year-old to the chair is not going to stop crime in this city. Eradicate the slums in the congested districts and you will have eliminated the cause of crime. The boy's life is ahead of him. There is some good in him yet. Perhaps, through a life of penitence, he may yet redeem himself.

Corrigan was, as ever, quite good, and it was reported that a number of spectators sobbed throughout his moving peroration. Unfortunately for Sam, none of them was a juror; the eight men and four women deciding his fate returned a unanimous guilty verdict on May

20. It came after sixteen and a half hours and thirteen ballots. All four women had been for death from the start. Asked if he had anything to say, Purpera muttered almost inaudibly, "I am innocent."

"You are not innocent," riposted Judge Bernon, who sentenced him to die on August 29, the same day as Frank Motto's scheduled execution. William J. Corrigan immediately filed an appeal, noting that Judge Bernon had not mentioned any lesser verdict than first-degree murder (e.g. manslaughter or second-degree murder) in his charge to the jury.

Purpera's initial reaction to the verdict was not positive. He trashed his cell and was restrained from further violence with great difficulty by county deputies, shrieking volley after volley of oaths and curses. But his native optimism, or possibly mere naivete, eventually returned, and he continued, even when he became Prisoner No. 555 on death row at the Ohio Penitentiary, to express disbelief that the state would execute anyone as young as he claimed to be.

No sooner was Purpera's fate sealed than thrilling news came from Mexico of the capture of Dominic Benigno and Charles Colletti, the latter also thought to be implicated in the Sly-Fanner murders. It was quite a tale, and impressive evidence that the Cleveland police were taking the business of internal reform seriously. It had all begun some weeks before when Detective Charles Cavolo heard that Benigno had sent a letter from Guadalajara, Mexico, to friends in Cleveland. Obtaining the letter, Cavolo asked permission to go to Mexico and bring the two fugitives back.

Cleveland Police authorities were in a quandary. There was no money to finance such an expedition, and it was obvious that the fugitives might be tipped off by corrupt elements in the police, as had obviously happened before in the Sly-Fanner manhunt. A solution was found to the first problem when Fred Caley of the Cleveland Automobile Club pledged the necessary funds to apprehend Benigno and Colletti. The implacable resolve and dedication of the Auto Club throughout the history of this case was well expressed by Caley in his words to departing detectives Cavolo and George Matowitz: "We don't care what it costs. Follow them to the end of the world if necessary." And the security problem was solved by publicly transferring Cavolo to a fictitious case and transferring Matowitz to the sick list. Posing as Automobile Club agents, Cavolo and Matowitz left for Mexico City.

The ensuing journey became a legend in Cleveland police annals. Arriving in Mexico City, the two detectives conferred with the American consul and were just about to leave for Guadalajara when they bumped into Benigno and Colletti just outside the Hotel St. Regis. Seizing the fugitives, the detectives barely escaped with their prisoners and their own lives after Benigno began provoking nearby crowds in Spanish, which neither detective spoke. With the aid of Mexican police, the two lawmen finally got Benigno and Colletti into a jail and sat down to await extradition procedures. They passed the time playing checkers with their prisoners.

The next six weeks turned into a bureaucratic nightmare with no seeming end. The United States had no extradition treaty with Mexico, and President Alvaro Obregon was not anxious to accommodate Cleveland justice, all the more so as the United States refused to recognize his government. To complicate matters further, both Benigno and Colletti were falsely claiming to be Italian citizens, not Americans. Eventually, however, Obregon was prevailed upon, and an order was issued to expel the fugitives—but from Vera Cruz, rather than from the northern border to Laredo, Texas, which is what Cleveland police had hoped.

Almost another month went by, rife with rumors of assassination plots and bribery conspiracies, as tension increased for the two detectives guarding their antsy captives. Finally, just before the prisoners were scheduled to be taken aboard the Spanish liner *Monserat*—a booking that would have taken them to Spain and into yet another extradition fight—Matowitz and Cavolo somehow managed to spirit them aboard the American-flagged liner *Monterey*, bound for Cuba and New York City. It was technically a kidnapping of dubious international legality, but the intrepid detectives accomplished the deed, and, after more nerve-racking hours while the ship stopped at Tampico and Progresso, brought their long-sought prey out of Mexican territory. The *Monterey* docked in New York City on July 14, 1921, and by the next day Colletti and Benigno were in a Brooklyn jail—after one last attempt to evade punishment by demanding to be taken to Ellis Island as aliens. Colletti was soon freed, however, when prosecutors realized he could not be tied directly to the events on the West 47th Street viaduct.

Benigno put up a brave front as he was taken back to Cleveland and duly indicted on two first-degree murder charges: "I have nothing to fear. These steps are not necessary for I will be free soon. . . I cannot believe my car was used, but if so someone else used it. Why, I will even use two Cleveland detectives as alibi witnesses."

But even Benigno, the most imperturbable of the captured killers, must have realized that things didn't augur well for his case. A week after he was brought back to Cleveland, the Supreme Court refused to stay Frank Motto's execution. Even Motto's inventive eleventh-hour fabrication that a Cleveland policeman had been involved in the payroll robbery plot couldn't save him, and his execution went off as scheduled on August 29. His final hours were spent with the prison chaplain, and witnesses reported that he walked to the chair without hesitation or comment. Several hours before his execution, Mary Sly, the mother of the murdered man, died at age eighty-four, her death hastened by the tragedy of her son's murder.

Dominic Benigno almost beat the rap. He was expertly defended by P. J. Mulligan and John Babka, and the case against him was significantly weaker, despite the prosecution's insistence that he was the real "mastermind." None of the neighborhood witnesses placed him at the death scene, and his defense was that he was elsewhere while his car was used without his knowledge. But his guiltless stance was compromised by Thomas Barrows, the Hotel Winton garage attendant, who identified him as the driver who brought the Jordan in at 11:43 on the murder morning—and also as the man who asked him to lie and say it had been in the garage all morning. And Louis Komer was brought back from prison to swear Benigno was on the viaduct with him when Sly and Fanner were gunned down. Sam Purpera also showed up to testify that Benigno was driving the Jordan that fatal December morning.

It almost ended there. The jury went out on Friday, September 23, and had already balloted eleven to one for conviction when one of the jurors had a stroke while walking up the four flights of stairs in the old courthouse that same day. Judge Homer G. Powell immediately declared a mistrial.

Benigno, by his own account, liked his second trial, held before Judge Harrison M. Jewell, better than the first. After hearing several days of testimony in late October, the second jury went out at 10:29 a.m. on October 28 and returned with no verdict after twenty-five hours of debate, with the balloting at ten to two for acquittal. It was widely believed that Benigno's near acquittal resulted from the prosecution's decision not to use Purpera at the second trial.

Benigno's third and last trial, before Judge Dan B. Cull, opened on Monday, December 5, 1921. It was held under tighter security conditions, its tense mood influenced by rumors of plots to rescue Benigno using armed force. Such plots gained additional credence after Mrs. Josephine Galletti, Purpera's sister, was arrested at the Ohio State Penitentiary in November while trying to smuggle a .32-caliber revolver to her brother. Meanwhile, Purpera's family asked for police protection, claiming that Benigno's friends were threatening retaliation for Sam's testimony.

RIOT FOLLOWS BENIGNO VERDICT

Cleveland Press headline, December 14, 1921.

The enhanced courthouse security paid off on December 14. When his third jury returned with a guilty verdict, Benigno's wife lunged at Assistant Prosecutor Cassidy, screaming "I'll kill you on sight! I'll kill you on sight! I'll go to the chair with my husband. He's not guilty!" She quickly became the focal point of a surging crowd of Benigno's relatives and friends, who tried to drag Cassidy from behind a rail. After county deputies seized Mrs. Benigno, the crowd's attention shifted to trying to free her. Benigno himself remained calm and motionless, handcuffed to a deputy, as women screamed, children cried, and the angry mob cursed, shouted, kicked, and clawed while an increasing flow of deputies and policemen poured into the room. Stanton later described it as the worst riot in the history of Cleveland courts.

One month later, Louis Komer pled guilty of first-degree murder in a juryless trial and received a life sentence. Judge Thomas D. Price reluctantly agreed to the verdict, allowing that Komer's testimony was still needed for future trials of the killers still at large. But Price wasn't happy about it: "Otherwise I would have had no compunction in sending him to the electric chair. Such men are not fit to live. His intelligence makes him one of the worst criminals in Cleveland."

Sam Purpera had yet evaded the ultimate penalty. Originally scheduled to die with Motto on August 29, 1921, he was granted a stay while his appeal went forward. And, as the date of his rescheduled February 12 execution approached, elements of Cleveland's Italian community began to agitate for commutation of his sentence. Their argument, stripped of legal pretensions and sentimental pity, was that the varying sentences of the Sly-Fanner killers reflected anti-Italian prejudice. As Rev. U. C. Piscitelli of St. Rocco's Church expressed it, in a telegram to Governor Harry L. Davis on February 7:

> We hereby protest the method in electrocuting the two Italian boys, Purpera and Benigno and at the same time sparing the life of Louis Komer as the crime was committed by the three alike and [they] are of the same guilt. We are of the belief all should receive the same punishment and thereby not show favoritism on the one.

At the last minute, Purpera's stay of execution came through, but not because he was Italian. Hoping still that Angelo Amato and Dominic Lonardo might be caught—and wary of the specter of a new trial for Benigno—Assistant Prosecutor Cassidy and Judge Cull, through Purpera's lawyer, successfully petitioned the Ohio Supreme Court to stay Purpera's execution for another thirty days.

And so the cycle began again. Purpera, still clinging to the fantasy that his youth would save him, alternated between hope and despair: "It doesn't seem they would kill me—I am so young. That doesn't seem right, for I haven't killed anybody. It makes it hard for me to die. I am so young."

Ohio Supreme Court Justice R. M. Wanamaker, for one, was disgusted by the legal ploys that continually delayed Purpera's execution. Excoriating his colleagues' stay, he wrote bitterly in words that spoke for exasperated majority public opinion in Cleveland: "Purpera had a fair trial in the lower court. . . This species of lawlessness has pretty nearly run riot in Ohio. Courts ought not to give it further encouragement by reprieves on purely technical grounds . . ."

Not everyone agreed with Wanamaker's criticism, least of all the Order of the Sons of Italy, which now mounted an ambitious crusade through its thirty Ohio lodges and 150,000 members to save Purpera. Led by Dr. G. A. Barricelli of Cleveland (whose home at Cornell Road and Murray Hill today houses the Barricelli Inn), the movement took on increased momentum when Governor Davis issued a sixty-day stay on March 8, again to preserve Purpera as a possible prosecution witness.

The fight got very ugly now, as the passions of the murdered men's families clashed publicly with the fears and resentments of Ohio's Italian community. William J. Pope, brother-in-law of George K. Fanner, put the case for the victims in the columns of the March 13, 1922, *Cleveland Press*: "Only one side of the Sly-Fanner murders is being told—the side of 'young and innocent' Samuel Purpera, and why, because of alleged youth and alleged innocence, he should not die in the electric chair for his part in the double killing. . ."

Painting an anguished portrait of the devastation wrought on the Sly and Fanner families, Pope focused on the presumably misguided sentimentality of those arguing for Purpera's life:

> Those who, working to secure leniency for Purpera, are set-
> ting forth an argument that he was only 16 at the time of the
> crime are misinformed. The records taken from Brownell

Four Men Held in Sly-Fanner Murder Probe

"These four men were picked up within two days of the Sly–Fanner Murder—but released for lack of evidence." *Cleveland Press*, January 8, 1921.

> School, which Purpera attended, and which were introduced as evidence at his trial, prove that at the time of his participation in the double murder he was 19. If the people who, because of widespread propaganda, see a mere boy of 16 standing in the shadow of the death chair could but see this "young and innocent boy of 16," their opinions in the case would change sharply. Purpera, with his six-feet and one-inch of height and huge, muscular frame, gives one a very different perspective of the man they are inclined, in their feverish desire to cheat the law, to call a "mere boy."

Barricelli would not concede an inch in his March 17 *Press* reply to Pope's passionate argument. Although he accepted Purpera's implausible claim that he had thrown away his gun (it was never found) and run away from the murder scene without firing a shot (no witness supported his story), Barricelli focused most of his attention on issues of ethnic fairness involved in the four Sly-Fanner verdicts:

> Before Komer's trial . . . local Italo-Americans were speculating on the probable outcome of Purpera's trial, and the unanimous conclusion was that if Komer, the only one not Italian and the worst of the gang, be shown leniency, Purpera, the boy guilty of having only procured an automobile and not of murder, had to be protected because we cannot tolerate a justice with two sets of weights for her scale. Had all been sen-

tenced to the chair, we would have submitted ourselves even to the electrocution of the boy, however implicated in the hideous crime that called for the severest punishment of all.

There is still force in Barricelli's fairness argument, eighty years on, although it must be said that he brushed aside the copious eyewitness testimony of Purpera's brutal gunplay quite peremptorily.

Purpera's luck finally ran out on May 6, 1922, when the Cincinnati Appellate Court refused Dominic Benigno a new trial. After that, the state of Ohio no longer had any motive in keeping Sam Purpera alive, which it demonstrated with unseemly haste in the wake of the appellate decision. Although Governor Davis had already granted another sixty-day stay to Purpera in anticipation of Benigno winning his appeal for a new trial, the contrary decision allowed Davis to legally withdraw it, as it had not been signed. The Order of the Sons of Italy threw in the towel the next day, and Zottarelli's final legal manuever, an appeal to U. S. Supreme Court Justice William R. Day, was turned down on May 8.

Louis Seltzer, then a young *Press* reporter, covered Purpera's execution on May 9, 1922. Talking with Seltzer in the hours before his death, Purpera, white and shaking, gave him one last message to convey. "Tell Mrs. Fanner," he murmured, "that I am sorry."

"Why only Mrs. Fanner?" asked Seltzer.

"No—just tell Mrs. Fanner—Mrs. Fanner. . ." is all that Purpera would say.

Ordering chicken and spaghetti for his last meal, Purpera ate "heartily" and smoked large, black cigars incessantly in the last hours before his death. His skull was shaved by the prison barber so that the electrodes would work. "I hope they don't burn my face," Purpera said. "My mother is old."

Warden P. E. Thomas and the guards came for Purpera about 1:00 a.m. on May 9. As he passed Benigno's cell, Dominic arose and shook his hand and they said good-bye. They strapped Sam in and turned on the juice at 1:07. A minute later the whirring of the generators ceased, and Dr. W. A. Whitman, the prison physician, pronounced Sam Purpera dead. His body was taken back to Cleveland and buried in Calvary Cemetery.

Dominic Benigno died a month later. Toward the end, he made no further attempts to delay the process and seemed to accept his fate with resigned impassivity. Perhaps he had already had enough of prison life, as he commented:

I want to be free or I want to be executed. I don't want to spend years and years here, being punished for something I didn't do—maybe spend my whole life here . . . I'm glad to die and be away from all this. After all, tomorrow at this time I won't have any worries and I know I am innocent.

Twenty-five witnesses watched as 1,700 volts went through Dominic Benigno early on the morning of June 14, 1922. William J. Pope, Fanner's brother-in-law, was there to watch him die.

Although police and prosecutors hoped for more arrests, the Sly-Fanner excitement subsided for awhile. There was a brief spate of headlines in October 1928, when Dominic Lonardo was discovered in San Francisco, living under the identity of "Joseph Piazza," a successful commission merchant. Cleveland detective Cornelius Cody was sent out to arrange extradition, but the suit to bring Lonardo back from California for trial failed when witnesses to his presence on the West 47th Street viaduct retracted their statements. Thus, Dominic Lonardo became the only identified Sly-Fanner killer to get away with the murders. Louis Komer testified at one of the trials that Lonardo shot *him* three times up on the viaduct when Komer refused to shoot Sly and Fanner.

The last act in the Sly-Fanner tragedy finally played out in 1935. There had been persistent rumors that Angelo Amato had fled to Italy soon after the murders, and the Cleveland Automobile Club never relaxed its efforts to bring him to justice. It was reported in 1925 that Italian authorities had arrested him; this was later reported as a mistake. There were further erroneous reports in 1927 and 1929 that he had been apprehended. Finally, in 1930, he was tried *in absentia* before an Italian court. Just as the court was about to hand down a guilty verdict and a life sentence, Amato's lawyer, S. H. Lo Presti, moved for a mistrial on the grounds that his client was not present. The court agreed, on the understanding that Amato would eventually surrender himself to the authorities. Finally, on February 6, 1934, Angelo Amato turned himself over to the police in Palermo. His wife had died the month before, and he was ready to face his fate.

Because there was no extradition treaty in effect between Italy and the United States in the 1930s, Amato had to be tried in an Italian court, using depositions and documents translated into Italian. The documents and depositions were duly prepared, and George Matowitz, Charles Cavolo, and Assistant County Prosecutor Frank D. Celebrezze traveled to attend the trial in Agrigento, Italy. On April 11, 1935, Angelo Amato was sentenced to thirty years at hard labor for his part in the Sly-Fanner murders. An amnesty provision in Italian law automatically reduced it to twenty-three years.

With Amato's departure to prison, the Sly-Fanner tragedy came to a close. It had lasted fifteen years, spawned a trail that stretched across the continent and beyond, sent three men to the electric chair and two to prison for life, devastated several families, and put two decent, hardworking Clevelanders in their graves well before their time. And while it didn't stop crime in Cleveland, it was the wake-up call that signaled the end of its days as a "wide-open town."

Let that be the epitaph of its two innocent victims.

"They Call Me Mad and a Butcherer . . ."

Double Encore and Farewell, August 16, 1938

The days and months went by. The usual and unusual suspects were rounded up, often by the tireless Peter Merylo, and as often released by frustrated Cleveland police officials who could not connect any suspect with a largely anonymous collection of corpses. By this time, it is likely that Cleveland law enforcement officials hoped the elusive Torso killer would just go away and leave them alone. They were about to get their wish—but only after a spectacular, dreadful finale to Cleveland's long-running serial murder spree.

Today, the area just east of East Ninth Street opposite the Rock and Roll Hall of Fame and the Great Lakes Science Center is simply a highway access area, a grimy stretch of asphalt ribbons connecting the Shoreway with the Inner Belt, I-90, and East Ninth. In 1938, however, this area, extending from the Pennsylvania Railroad tracks to the Shore Drive was mainly an unofficial dump, an enormous acreage stretching east to East 26th Street that, since the turn of the century, had evolved into an unsightly and verminous junk pile of both private and public refuse. Clevelanders could—and did—dump whatever they wanted to there, and sometime in 1938 some person or persons took that license to the limit.

It was late in the afternoon of August 16 when three men found themselves at the East Ninth Street dump. James Dawson, 21, James McShack, 23, and Edward Smith, 50, were there in search of scrap iron, and sometime after 4:00 p.m. Dawson was on his way through the acres of rubble to retrieve a wheelbarrow he had brought to carry whatever metal he found. He saw what looked like a coat sticking out of the refuse and stopped for a closer look. He was standing about 200 feet east of East Ninth Street and nearly twenty-five feet south of the recently constructed Shore Drive. No—it wasn't a coat; he saw it was a patchwork quilt, covered with rocks. Dawson picked off the rocks and the quilt and found a female torso, wrapped in a threadbare blue suit coat and brown butcher's paper. Dawson immediately called the police.

By the time Cleveland lawmen arrived on the scene, pandemo-
nium was well under way. Hundreds of motorists on the nearby lakeside highway were already backing up to gawk at the crime scene,
and thousands of Clevelanders were converging to ogle the latest
Torso murder site. Even before the first remains were brought to the
county morgue, enough rubberneckers converged there to warrant a
special squad of patrolmen to keep them at bay.

The investigating police soon found more. The skeletal torso was
complete, unlike the dissected viscera of most of the Torso killer's
prey. And near by, underneath a concrete slab, was a makeshift cardboard container containing the arms and legs of the victim, again in
wrapping paper and with rubber bands around the remains. Soon,
police investigators found a matching head a few feet away, again
wrapped in brown butcher's paper. The total find was three neck vertebrae, seven dorsal vertebrae, twenty-two ribs, two pelvic bones,
and a skull. The remains seemed to be female but were in such of
state of decay that it wasn't clear whether the torso was badly
decomposed or had been disemboweled.

Among the spectators at the East Ninth Street dump that August
evening were machinist Todd Bartholomew and his wife. About 7:00
p.m., Todd noticed an awful smell coming from a heap of garbage
nearby. Removing some stones, Bartholomew gaped in horror as he
uncovered some skeletal remains. He summoned Sergeant William
Miller, who soon brought more police running to the new Torso site.

One of the first to arrive was Sergeant Hogan. As he strode to the
scene, Hogan bent down and picked up a can to retrieve some of the
suspicious remains. One can imagine his horror when he took a
closer look: inside the can was a human skull. By the time the sun
went down that Tuesday evening, searchers had found more than
forty bones of the second victim: twenty-two ribs, seven dorsal vertebrae, three cervical vertebrae, and two pelvic bones. By now the
police had recovered far more evidence than was the norm in Torso
victim discoveries, and Detective Peter Merylo sounded a note of
official optimism about the long-sought Butcher to a *Press* reporter:

> He's changing his technique. Why I don't know. But for the
> first time since the two bodies we found in September, 1935,
> he has left two victims together. And again, changing his
> method, he left heads of these last two. . . He's smart but he's
> gonna slip up. I know it.

Back at the county morgue, Sam Gerber and his crew examined

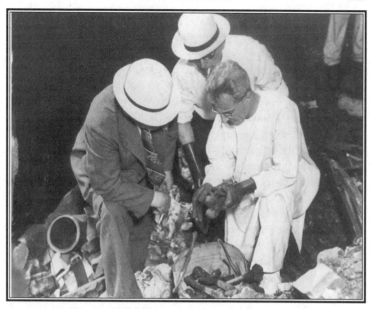

Looking at some of the remains of Torso victims No. 11 or No.
12, August 18, 1938. Left to right: Inspector Charles Nevel, Sgt.
James T. Hogan, Coroner Sam Gerber.

the two bodies. The first was a female, its head cut off between the
third and fourth cervical vertebrae. The victim's limbs had been
removed with "expert" cuts at the hip and shoulder joints. The left
leg was split at the knee, the right leg intact, while the right arm was
split but not severed at the elbow. The time of death was estimated at
about six months, and Gerber inferred from the hardening of the
remains that they had at some point been refrigerated. The pieces of
No. 12 had probably been dumped where they were found about two
or three weeks before.

Even with an intact skull, the twelfth victim was not going to be
easy to identify. The corpse was that of a healthy woman in her mid-
thirties, with long brown hair, size nine feet but small hands, five foot
four, and about 120 to 125 pounds. But even with some teeth to go
on and intact prints from the left thumb and three right-hand fingers,
no match with a missing person could ever be found for Torso victim No. 12.

The forensic implications for No. 13 were even more bleak. The
second corpse was that of a male, about five foot seven, 135 to 140
pounds, small-boned, and in his mid- to late thirties. He had long

wavy brown hair, good teeth, and a broken nose that bent leftward. He had been cut up at the neck, hips, shoulders, wrists, and ankles; and his hands, feet, and some miscellaneous vertebrae and ribs were never found. After looking at the corpses, Gerber announced that they were assuredly the work of the Mad Butcher.

The newspapers had their usual fun. A front page *Press* editorial demanded that a reward of at least $10,000 be posted by the city council, a step never taken because of its dubious legality. And some anonymous *Press* feature writer carried off the week's journalistic laurels with a breathless front-page study of the Mad Butcher's psychological makeup—largely drawn from the vivid imagination and expertise of Detective Peter Merylo:

> A cunning madman with the strength of an ox. That's the torso killer—the murderer who has ruthlessly slain 13 men and women, then dismembered their bodies and hidden the parts in lonely places. He's as regular, as coldly efficient and as relentless as an executioner when the mood to kill comes over him. Never has an intended victim escaped his relentless knife, never has a "friend" lived to tell the tale. . . Many of these acquaintances are from the lower walks of life. They are the sort of people whom nobody misses. . .The slayer doesn't harm men and women who have families, homes and friends. His victims are perverts; some of them probably penniless transients and some just drifters who had lost their friends and their standing in the community.

Eliot Ness, for one, had had enough of the Torso killer and, more particularly, of mounting public criticism of his failure to find the butchering fiend. Some unkind souls were even suggesting that the placement of Torsos No. 12 and No. 13—within sight of Cleveland City Hall and the safety director's office—had been intended as a deliberate taunt to the erstwhile "Untouchable" hero. It was time for one of Ness's dramatic, well-publicized strikes, and he began to orchestrate a surprise for both his critics and his elusive homicidal prey.

Just after midnight on Thursday, August 17, three fire trucks, two police vans, and eleven squad cars arrived in the Flats, in the area down by Canal Road in the shadow of the Terminal Tower. After six squads fanned out to block possible escape routes, the fire trucks' powerful lights were suddenly turned on. Ness, carrying an axe handle, and twenty-five other policemen charged into Cleveland's

Eliot Ness talking to hoboes rousted in burning of shanty jungle, August 19, 1938.

biggest hobo jungle, smashing apart the crude shanties and rousting the sleeping, often inebriated hoboes within. It must have been a terrible scene, filled with the threatening shouts of the cops, the screaming curses of the homeless men, and the barking of the numerous dogs who lived with their down-and-out companions in the shantyville. Some of the tramps resisted—Ness himself was almost decked by a shovel swung in anger—but by about 1:15 a.m. thirty-eight men had been arrested and were on their way to Central Station. A half hour later, another surprise raid on the hoboville underneath the Lorain-Carnegie Bridge—where Rose Wallace had been found—netted another ten transients. A third and final descent on a homeless encampment at the East 37th Street bridge—the site where Torso No. 6 was found in the pool—caught fifteen more men in the police dragnet.

Ness's logic in ordering the shantyville raids was obvious enough: since he couldn't find the alligator—the Torso killer—he had decided to drain the swamp. If he couldn't catch the predator, he could at least deprive him of a potential pool of victims by destroying their habitat. What Ness could not have anticipated was the angry, critical reaction to his raids, as Clevelanders viewed the col-

Burning the hobo shantyville near Commercial Road,
August 18, 1938.

lection of forlorn, stumbling, broken men his grandstanding effort
had bagged. Public shock at the callousness of the raids was intensified on August 18, when Ness ordered Cleveland firemen to burn
down the hobo encampments. They did so, using fuel oil and creating a spectacular blaze that was witnessed by hundreds. *The Plain
Dealer* denounced Ness's actions as "brutal," and the *Press* excoriated his rationale that the mass arrests might aid in either catching
the Mad Butcher or identifying his future victims:

> Director Ness himself did not believe that any of the tran-
> sients arrested in this raid . . . was the butcher who has slain
> and dismembered 13 persons. He said he was convinced that
> it was from such transients that the killer selected his victims
> and that he hoped that the finger-printing of those arrested
> might aid in the identification of possible future victims. . .
> To most of us, the arrest of the mad butcher would seem more
> important than the completing of arrangements for the iden-
> tification of a possible corpse.

Eleven of the sixty-three men arrested proved to have criminal records and were turned over to the FBI; those with families and jobs were eventually released and the remaining forty-eight men sentenced to terms in the Warrensville Workhouse.

Within two days it was obvious that the police could not identify the latest Torso victims, so detectives concentrated on the physical evidence found at the discovery scene. The two sections of the makeshift cardboard box were traced to the Central Market area and the patchwork quilt to an eccentric peddler named Elmer Cummings, but the police could not discover how they had ended up near the Shore Drive, filled with human guts. A secret house-by-house search of the Third Precinct's ten square miles in late August likewise failed to turn up the Mad Butcher's secret laboratory, which Ness and Sam Gerber were convinced must be somewhere near his stalking grounds. The arrival of a decomposed male corpse on the beach at Gordon Park on August 17 proved only a momentary distraction that Coroner Gerber immediately dismissed as a drowning victim.

No one knew it at the time, but the Mad Butcher's reign of terror was over. Although more headless corpses would turn up in Cleveland during subsequent years, none of them would be attributed to *"the"* Torso killer. But 1938 did produce one last, Parthian shot from the much pursued madman. It arrived in the form of a letter, addressed to Cleveland chief of police George J. Matowitz and delivered to Central Station on December 26. Mailed from Los Angeles, it was dated December 21, 1938, and this is what it said:

> Chief of Police Matowitz,
> You can rest easy now as I have came out to sunny California for the winter. I felt bad operating on those people but science must advance. I shall soon astonde [sic] the medical profession—a man with only a D. C. What did their lives mean in comparasion to hundreds of sick and disease twisted bodies. Just laboratory guinea pigs found on any public street. No one missed them when I failed. My last case was successful. I know now the feeling of Pasteur, Thoreau and other pioneers. Right now I have a volunteer who will absolutely prove my theory. They call me mad and a butcher but the "truth will out." I have failed but once here. The body has not been found and never will be but the head minus features is buried in a gully on Century Blvd. between Western and

Crenshaw. I feel it is my duty to dispose of the bodies I do. It
is God's will not to let them suffer.

(signed) X

There are those who believe that this letter was a genuine confession from the Torso murderer. This chronicler is not one of them; the
misspellings and oddities seem deliberate (what does Thoreau have
to do with Pasteur?), and intensive digging by Los Angeles police
failed to unearth a head in the gully on Century Boulevard. Steven
Nickel, the most knowledgeable Torso expert, is probably correct in
his theory that widespread public credence in the validity of the letter was the product of expectations created by the Cleveland media.
Journalists had worked so hard and so long at creating the legend of
a Forest City Jack the Ripper that Clevelanders fully expected—
indeed, demanded—that the Mad Butcher follow the Ripper model
exactly and write at least one letter boasting of his bloody deeds. It
was the least he could do.

Chapter 11

CLEVELAND'S BURNING!

A Trio of Catastrophic Fires, 1883–1914

It's an unkind irony that Cleveland's best-known fire is the 1969 Cuyahoga River blaze that made national headlines and was eventually immortalized in a Randy Newman song. It wasn't the first time the Cuyahoga caught on fire, and it certainly wasn't its most serious or expensive combustion. And it couldn't hold a candle to at least a half dozen fires that have actually threatened Cleveland's very existence as a city during its two centuries. Perhaps the most catastrophic were the great fires of 1883, 1884, and 1914.

The First Terror of Kingsbury Run: The 1883 Standard Oil Fire

As *The Plain Dealer* later remarked, 1883 did not augur well for the world. Zadkiel Tao Sze's *London Almanac*, which had been published since 1831, predicted "all manner of calamities by flood, fire, crime and war." Raphael, a London astrologer since 1821, also predicted unprecedented troubles, warning especially of catastrophes for "mercantile interests." Sadly, before the year was through, Cleveland was to get more than its usual share of such woes.

Cleveland was already in a state of emergency by Friday, February 2. Rising temperatures combined with torrential rains began to melt accumulated snow and ice that morning and by Saturday had produced the worst floods in Cleveland history. Most of the Flats and the Cuyahoga River Valley all the way from the Superior Viaduct south to Broadway were inundated with five or more feet of water. Much railroad rolling stock was under water, many bridges were badly damaged, and from twenty to twenty-five million feet of lumber from Flats lumberyards was floating out to Lake Erie and oblivion. Two men were drowned, and the total commercial losses from the floods alone were probably $1.5 million even before a more dangerous enemy—fire—struck on Saturday morning.

It began at the Shurmer & Teagle Refinery just west of Willson Avenue (now East 55th). Waste oil from a Standard Oil facility upstream on Kingsbury Run had been leaking for some hours, helping to swell the normally two-foot-deep Run into a raging, oily torrent. Surging past the boiler house of the Shurmer works adjacent to the Run, the oil was ignited by falling coals. Kingsbury Run burst into flames, and the greatest fire in Cleveland history was under way.

The first alarm was called in from Box 69 at 6:20 a.m. Saturday, and Engine Companies 7, 9, and 13, as well as Truck 3, responded. Within several hours, the blaze had spread to the Merriam & Morgan paraffin works downstream, at which point Box 56 called in Engine Companies 3 and 8 and reactivated Companies 7 and 13, and Truck 3. Despite the best efforts of the firemen, thousands of gallons of burning oil continued to pour into the Run. Just about the time firemen got the Shurmer & Teagle blaze under control, the stream of burning oil reached the main Standard Oil works, three miles downstream.

There was, undoubtedly, a terrible beauty to the destruction that waxed over the next twenty-four hours. Thousands of Clevelanders, estimated at half its 180,000 population, witnessed it, many of them vigorously obstructing the efforts of firemen. All streetcars to the area and the local saloons were jammed by the curious. The Standard Oil stills and tanks, filled with gasoline, coal oil, petroleum, and tar, began to explode and burn about 12:30 p.m. Through the still-driving rain, dense black smoke and arcing flames began to fill the horizon of Cleveland. One by one, nine enormous Standard Oil storage tanks, each containing from five to sixteen thousand barrels of oil, kerosene, or gasoline, blew up over the next twelve hours, adding thousands of additional, lethal gallons to the inflammable torrent rushing toward downtown Cleveland. At one point, no fewer than seven oil tanks were burning at once.

If ever Cleveland came close to the fate of Chicago in 1871, it was on the afternoon of February 3. Fire Chief James W. Dickinson, who arose from a feverish sickbed to orchestrate the smoke-eating heroics, later recalled waiting for one of the 16,000-barrel oil tanks to explode:

> Cowen [head of the Standard Oil safety forces] said to me that when it became necessary I should wave my hat and the Standard's fire department would open out on the tank. I looked up and saw that the tank was boiling over and all ready for the grand collapse, and said, "well, they had better begin now." At that instant the tank boiled over with a blinding flash, but the Standard firemen didn't wait to begin . . .

FOURTH EDITION.

FURIOUS FLAMES!!!!

THE FIRE-FIEND ATTACKS THE STANDARD.

Fast Floating Fire Followed by the Most Terrific Explosions.

TANK AFTER TANK, STILL AFTER STILL BLOWS UP, AND THE END IS NOT YET.

Cleveland Press headline, February 3, 1883.

You see a tank usually boils about five hours after it takes fire before the grand blow-out occurs, and one can tell pretty nearly when the explosion is to take place.

As at Gettysburg, the fate of the city turned on a simple railroad embankment, adjacent to an obstructed culvert by Broadway Avenue. As the flaming river of fire moved closer and closer to that culvert, Cleveland firemen realized that if they didn't stop it there it would jump downstream to ignite both sides of the Flats all the way to the mouth of the Cuyahoga. It was a time for heroes, and Cleveland's firefighters did not disappoint. The climax came early Sunday morning, as reported by the *Cleveland Leader*:

> As on Saturday, the great fight was to keep the fire from getting across or under the NYP & O bridge and into the purifying works [filled with gasoline] on the side of the Cuyahoga River. Yet the warfare was a triangular one. To the north of the flames stood forty ponderous tanks filled with crude oil, and standing so thickly together as to give that vicinity the name of 'Tanktown.' The fire was in momentary danger of reaching these great storehouses yet unharmed. To the east were the extensive Doan works that were guarded by three engines,

while the great objective point was the river. Had the fire once
jumped across the embankment that runs between Kingsbury
Run and the Cuyahoga, no one can estimate what it might
have done.

Concentrating their blasts on the embankment, Cleveland firemen
and Standard Oil's own safety forces battled for hours to keep the
flaming torrent of Kingsbury Run from jumping north of Broadway
and the New York, Pennsylvania & Ohio railroad tracks. Many of
them spent hours waist deep in the icy, oil-drenched waters of Kingsbury Run. At one point a flaming stream of naphtha did escape to the
other side—but it was beaten back by the exhausted, scorched, and
seared men. Many Cleveland firemen spent up to fifty hours battling
the three-day fire.

By early Sunday morning, the city had been saved, but exhausted
firemen continued to pour water on the various blazes well into Monday. By the time the conflagration was finished, late Monday
evening, February 5, nine large storage tanks, thirty stills, and other
Standard Oil facilities were in ruins, not to mention the hundreds of
thousands of gallons of petroleum products lost. The total losses to
Standard Oil were estimated between $250,000 and $300,000, with
losses to other businesses totaling about $500,000. Miraculously,
there were no fatalities, despite many fire-related injuries, especially
to Cleveland firemen.

Although some improvements were subsequently made to the
Cleveland Fire Department's equipment, later and yet more terrible
fires in 1884 would give evidence that the lessons of the 1883 Standard Oil fire had not been learned. As Chief Dickinson remarked,
just two days after the final flames were extinguished: "The citizens
of Cleveland will never know how near the city came to burning up.
But for the protection formed by the NYPO track the burning oil
would have run down the culvert and out into the river."

Burn Down the Town: The 1884 Flats Lumber Fires

Cleveland's most serious fire? Well, probably the East Ohio Gas
Company fire, if you're talking corpses and ruined lives. At 130, its
death toll edges out the Cleveland Clinic fire by at least five—and
only quibblers would insist on the Collinwood School fire, which
after all occurred outside Cleveland proper.

It's harder to make a choice if you're measuring property damage
or a threat to the survival of the city. The 1883 Standard Oil fire

(above) came within minutes and one jammed culvert of burning its way right up both sides of the Cuyahoga River all the way to the lakefront. The 1914 Fisher-Wilson lumber fire, too, threatened to consume at least the entire Flats in flames and even managed to *melt* away 300 feet of the Central Viaduct. My vote, though, would be for the twin 1884 Flats lumber fires, which not only threatened to burn down the whole city but were probably intended to accomplish just that.

Extending south along the Cuyahoga River from Whiskey Island, the Flats consists roughly of five peninsulas whose bulging projections sometimes leave persons on the east bank standing west of those actually standing on the river's west bank. In 1884, most of the third peninsula, including parts of Carter, Scranton, Girard, and Collins streets, and the CCC & I railroad tracks, was home to many of Cleveland's enormous lumberyards. This had been the case for some years. In February 1883, these yards had suffered terrible damage and losses when catastrophic floods had washed up to twenty-five million feet of lumber out into Lake Erie.

And then, in September 1884 someone decided to burn them down.

The initial arson was apparently committed in the Woods, Perry & Company lumberyards. Just before 7:00 p.m. on September 7, Frank Stepanek, a watchman for the Variety Iron Works, noticed a fire in a pile of shavings there and called in an alarm from Box 23. Chief James W. Dickinson got there within minutes with Engine Companies 1, 2, and 8 and Hook and Ladder Company No. 1, and he immediately called in four more companies and another hook-and-ladder unit. Cleveland's greatest fire was on.

For the first several hours it was no contest. With enormous lumber piles as high as sixty feet spread about in all directions and separated by narrow alleys that let in even more oxygen, the fire remorselessly advanced in all directions against the outmatched firemen and toward more waiting wood. Soon, the lumberyards and shops of the C. G. King Company, Potter, Birdsall and Company, Davidson and Howe, and the Novelty and Variety ironworks were enveloped in flames and smoke. The incredible heat generated by the burning of millions of board feet soon generated whirlwinds—mini-firestorms, really—that began to rain burning brands and sparks over downtown Cleveland, and even as far as East Cleveland. And as flames continued to blaze in a fifteen-to-twenty-acre triangle—1,100 by 1,300 by 1,300 feet—the fire jumped north across the river at about 10:00 p.m. and enveloped the Stanley Lard Oil and Candle Works, the Sherwin Williams Company, and the NYP & O freight depot. By now, two thousand feet of river docking was also well on its way to becoming smouldering ashes. As the fire reached its climax late on the night of September 7, a Cleveland policeman watching it turned to his companion and said, "Go and repent! There's as good a picture of hell as you can get on this earth!"

Within two hours, the situation had escalated into the most serious threat in the city's history to its very survival. Virtually all fire units were now committed to the Flats inferno, leaving the rest of the city defenseless from further arson or accidental fires. Even as his wearying men continued their fighting retreat from the ever-growing flames, Chief Dickinson appealed for help to neighboring communities. And his plea was generously answered: before the crisis was over, firefighters and equipment from many communities were rushed to Cleveland. Help came from Painesville, Columbus, Elyria, Youngstown, Sandusky, Akron, Lorain, Toledo, Ashtabula, Delaware, Norwalk, Oberlin, Clyde, Galion, Fremont, and from Erie, Pennsylvania. The train carrying the engines from Painesville made the thirty-mile trip in twenty-eight minutes; the engineer of the Youngstown fire train didn't even set his brake. As an added precaution, the Fifth Regiment was called out at the Armory. Its purpose was to help prevent looting, if necessary, but it ended up dispersing lumber piles in the path of the advancing flames.

It was a miracle the fire was contained mostly in the Flats. (One reason it may not have burned north all the way to Lake Erie was the proverbial "lake effect"; the heated Flats helped create southerly winds that pushed the flames away from the lake.) With hundreds of burning brands and sparks broadcast for miles over the city, many persons spent sleepless nights beating out flames as fiery debris came down on Cleveland by the light of a full moon. Sparks were reported "thick as snow" on Prospect Avenue, and the ghastly light from the Flats could be seen as far away as Hudson, Akron, Wellington, Oberlin, Shelby, and just about everywhere within a seventy-five-mile radius. The roof of the Handyside flour store on Ontario Street was set afire four times by sparks, and a two-story house on Wason Street burned down because there were no firemen available to put out the fire.

How hot was it? Well, workers cleaning up the wreckage later found kegs of nails completely melted together, barrels of broken glass fragments fused into one mass, and several tons of wood completely converted to coal that night. And the heat could be felt as far away as the upper windows of buildings on the eastern blocks of Superior Avenue.

As the long hours of September 7 gave way to September 8, the tide began to turn. The Cleveland fire forces couldn't do much to stop the holocaust in the Woods, Perry & Company area, but they succeeded admirably in preventing or putting out fires outside the critical region. The force's efforts were hobbled by a lack of adequate manpower—the entire force was only 150 men—and equipment. Access to the primary blaze was hindered by lack of a fireboat, and there was no firehouse in the area—despite Chief Dickinson's frequent prior pleas for both. And there is even some question as to the quality of the water supply: much of the water used on the fire was pumped directly from the river and was reputed to be so contaminated with grease and oil—probably from the Standard Oil works upstream, via Kingsbury Run—that firemen weren't sure whether their streams were aggravating the fire or putting it out. Anyway, much of the water available had to be sprayed directly on the firefighters to prevent the intense heat from overcoming them or setting their clothes on fire. Two engines, trapped by the enveloping flames, were pushed into the river by escaping firefighters.

As with most Cleveland disasters, the work of the safety forces was complicated and imperiled by the actions of the thousands of Clevelanders—acutely described by the *Cleveland Leader* as "adventurous loafers"—who came out to gape at the fiery, magnificent spectacle. One of them, at least, got his comeuppance. A male onlooker, apparently unaware that a nearby engine was pumping water directly from the Cuyahoga River, was seen greedily drinking with cupped hands from the spraying leak in a firehose. Minutes later, the same man was seen vomiting uncontrollably in the streets of Cleveland. The more fortunate qualities of Cleveland's populace were demonstarted by the dozens of old-time volunteer firemen from Cleveland's past who turned out unasked and unpaid to work side by side with their professional brethren. Another bright aspect was the report of a brigade of "motherly-appearing ladies bearing sandwiches and coffee for the firemen" who appeared in the Flats during that long night. It is said that Cleveland saloons did a roaring business all through the night and morning. One of them belonged to William Droge. Although his Canal Street saloon was in the path of the flames, he sold beer and whiskey even as a family at the rear of his building evacuated their belongings. He sold his last beer at 9:30 p.m. and announced with satisfaction, "Well, if this place goes up I won't have to move anything, as I am completely sold out."

When the morning of September 8 came the fire was under control. Over a million dollars of damage had been done, mostly to Flats lumber concerns, but also to CCC & I railroad tracks and rolling stock and Western Union lines and buildings. The main area of destruction probably took up twenty acres and as much as fifty million board feet of wood.

Unbelievably, there were no fatalities. A fireman named Dewey broke his ankle and Assistant Chief Rebbeck was knocked unconscious by falling lumber, which also smashed the foot of Frank Jennett of Engine Company No. 3 and the kneecap of No. 9's George Hemrich, and knocked out Jacob Beilier of No. 12. Many of the firemen were badly blistered by the heat: Chief Dickinson's face was said to look "like a bladder," while Assistant Chief George A. Wallace (Dickinson's future successor and Cleveland's most legendary fireman) "seems to have been boiled in wax, judging from his complexion, and his voice is *non est.*"

Chief Dickinson was angry in the wake of the fire, especially as his recommendations after the Standard Oil Fire of the previous year had gone largely unheeded:

> I say now what I said after the Standard Oil fire, and that is that this city don't know what to expect in the direction of fires. It might have been worse than it was. We are liable to just such conflagrations at any time. Suppose that another destructive fire had broken out in the center of the city, what could we have done? My object in obtaining aid from outside was more to be prepared for such an emergency than anything else. Do you know that three of those companies coming in here had more men than we have in the whole department?

For obvious reasons, arsonists love Sundays. Exactly two weeks later, another fire broke out in the fifth peninsula of the Flats (the present-day Tremont area). Shortly before 11:00 a.m., the watchman at Monroe Brothers & Company discovered a fire in the center of its lumberyard. He immediately turned in an alarm from Box 57 at the corner of Jefferson Street and Centralway, but the fire was well under way by the time firemen arrived. It was brought under control three hours later, but another fire—also deliberately set—sprang up in the Monroe dry house over 300 feet away. As firemen rushed to extinguish it, yet another blaze erupted nearby at the Browne & Strong yard. Chief Dickinson knew the routine by now, and calls for help went out to Columbus, Painesville, Delaware, Galion, Toledo, Bellevue, Clyde, Oberlin, Elyria, Painesville, Ashtabula, and Akron.

fire under control by 8:00 p.m. By then it had consumed property, mainly stacks of lumber, in a two-block area running over eleven hundred feet from east to west, six acres in all. The fire's last gasp was yet another arson blaze discovered at 6:50 p.m. at the Bell, Cartright lumberyard. The accelerant used was probably coal oil. The fire drew another estimated 50,000 spectators, many of whom improved the economy of the local saloons.

Neither of the catastrophic 1884 Flats lumberyard arson fires was ever solved. Tramps or mischievous boys were the most likely suspects, and rumors that impending wage cuts had prompted both the Woods, Perry and Monroe Brothers arsons were angrily discounted by officials of both companies. It is also possible that both fires were started by sparks from either a passing river tugboat or one of the many locomotives passing through the area.

It was rumored during the Monroe Brothers blaze that a "slouchy-looking man" was overheard to say, "There'll be another fire here pretty soon," a prophecy soon fulfilled in the Monroe dry house and elsewhere. Several hours later, a suspect was arrested in the vicinity of the fire by Patrolman McMasters and apparently interrogated during the following week to no avail. He boasted the improbable name of Christ Schweitzer and was reported by the newspapers to be a "dissolute person well known by the police." Schweitzer was very nearly lynched by the crowd that had come out to gawk and interfere with the safety forces. To add insult to injury, the *Cleveland Press* further defamed him as "a man who some time ago chopped off one of his hands so that he would not be obliged to work and support his family." Nineteenth-century Clevelanders, like their twentieth-century counterparts, apparently loathed arsonists, but they had it in for welfare cheats, too.

The Ultimate Fire: The 1914 Fisher-Wilson Inferno

Most catastrophic fires come without telltale warning signs. So it was with Cleveland's last city-threatening conflagration, the 1914 Flats lumber fire. Indeed, just three hours before it broke out, Cleveland Fire Department assistant chief Charles B. Whyler stated publicly, albeit injudiciously: "Cleveland's clean-up [of hazardous fire conditions] will decrease fire loss 50 per cent." Alas, his boast was not to be.

Whyler should have known and probably did know better. Although Cleveland fire losses were well below the national average, underlying conditions suggested an unwholesome fire profile for the Forest City. There were known water-pressure problems in the Flats area—the city's industrial core—and the 1912 National Underwriters' Report had severely criticized the shortcomings of Cleveland's fire department: "[It] is below the average, and the city [is] severely criticized as having a weak distribution system for its water supply and needing a higher pressure service."

The Flats were really just an accident waiting to happen. That accident happened on May 25, 1914.

It began in the extensive Fisher-Wilson lumberyards, adjacent to the Central Viaduct and the Nickel Plate trestle spanning the Cuyahoga River, near West Third and Stone's Levee. No one will ever really know how it started, but it was clearly arson. Cleveland authorities later flirted without result with the notions that mischievous boys threw matches into sawdust or that tramps hurled lit cigarettes into piles of wood shavings strewn carelessly about the Fisher-Wilson yards.

Whatever the cause, the blaze was first spotted at 8:30 p.m. by Engineer Frank Kaftan from his perch atop the "Big Four" railroad bridge near the Fisher-Wilson lot. He ran to end of the bridge and called in the alarm. It was already too late, as he subsequently recalled: "It was just a small blaze when I saw it first. But by the time I had turned in an alarm from tower KD at the end of the bridge it looked to be out of control."

And so it was: even as the words "North One!" went out to the fire department—indicating the origin of the fire—Cleveland's greatest twentieth-century fire was well on its way to burning down the entire city.

It was almost as if the Fates had conspired to create a perfect nightmare for the Cleveland Fire Department. Thanks to the congestion caused by railroad locomotives and rolling stock in the Flats, firemen found their access to the fire hampered and even blocked altogether for precious minutes at key points. And though fireboats were already steaming up the Cuyahoga to fight the flames, firemen on the scene battled inadequate water pressure, lack of coal to fuel their engines, wildly erratic winds, and ever-increasing heat. For at least three hours flames raged unchecked north and south of the Central Viaduct, consuming everything in their path, driving firemen ever backward, and raising fears that they would obliterate the entire city by morning. After burning up about four million feet of hardwood at Fisher-Wilson, the flames moved into the millions of board feet at the Martin-Barriss lumberyards. Unsatisfied, the fire next reached for the enormous Saginaw Bay lumberyards, the Nickel

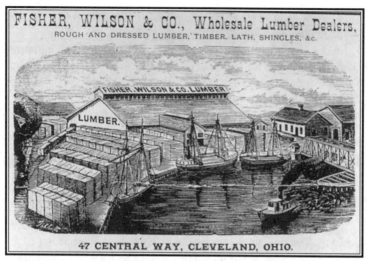

Fisher, Wilson & Company advertisement, 1890s.

Plate trestle, and the Central Viaduct.

As midnight neared, the fate of the city seemed dire. By now, a half-square-mile area of the Flats was in flames or ashes, and burning embers, cast by strong winds, were creating incendiary havoc as far away as East 40th Street. A six-story elevator of the Cleveland Grain Company was now afire, an adjacent nine-story elevator was threatened, and fire engines in the zone of maximum danger were shutting down for lack of available fuel. It must have seemed like a lost cause to Chief George A. Wallace and his beleaguered force of 225 Cleveland firemen, all of whom were in the Flats that night.

Somehow, at about midnight, the tide turned. This was partly due to sheer heroism on the part of Cleveland firemen: fighting with watery blasts from every vantage point—especially from perilous stations atop the flame-enveloped Central Viaduct and Nickel Plate trestle—they managed to prevent the fire from spreading beyond its lumberyard feeding grounds. At a critical juncture, the coaling ship *Pittsburgh* managed to steam up the Cuyahoga River with crucial fuel for the fire engines. More importantly, as Assistant Chief Whyler later admitted, the issue was decided by a change in the wind. About midnight, it shifted abruptly—and pushed the flames back toward their origin, thoroughly burning out whatever they had missed in the Fisher-Wilson and Martin-Barriss lumberyards. The fire was virtually under control by 2:30 a.m. and was officially declared so at 9:00 a.m. on May 26. Chief Wallace stepped down his force on the scene from thirty companies to twenty at 8:00 a.m., and then down to ten companies at noon.

By that time the fire had long since done its worst. Although firemen on both spans fought fiercely, both the Nickel Plate and Central Viaduct bridges were casualties of the blaze. About 350 feet of the Central Viaduct literally melted from the heat of the lumber fires below, and the fall of its fiery debris collapsed at least 200 feet of the Nickel Plate trestle below.

Clevelanders awoke to a smoking ruin at the center of their city on May 26, 1914. Up to twenty million feet of Flats lumber lay burning or in ashes. A good part of the Flats was covered with half a foot of the water Cleveland firemen had aimed at the flames. And one of Cleveland's main thoroughfares—the Central Viaduct—was ruined, as was one of its vital railroad arteries, the Nickel Plate crossing over the Flats. The Viaduct damage would have been worse had not Chief Wallace supervised the removal of much of its oil-soaked planking.

All in all, the Viaduct inferno furnished the most dramatic moments of the catastrophe. Despite the efforts of frantic firemen and repeated charges by Cleveland police, thousands of eager spectators thronged the south end of the Central Viaduct. Most of them would not leave even as the flames licked hungrily at their feet. The reward for their persistence eventually came when a crazed man broke through police lines at West 14th and ran toward the already collapsing Viaduct. He reached the core of the flames, recoiled from the burning metal of the bridge rail—and jumped over the side into the hot core of the Flats lumber fire. It was the only fatality of the 1914 Flats fire.

It could have been worse. The Ringling Brothers Circus was in town that fatal night, and, believe it or not, had pitched its big top in the Flats. Shortly after 8:30 p.m. several frightened men ran past the entrance of the filled tent crying "Fire!" It is recorded that shrewd, burly circus personnel instantly seized the criers and beat them into immediate silence with tent pins, fists, and whatever else lay at hand. Thereupon, the ringmaster calmly informed the audience that the circus was adjourning a half hour early—and admonished them to file out in order. They did, and Cleveland was spared an additional catastrophe of mass disorder to sully an already unfortunate night. Potential panic among the circus folk was averted by the soothing mien of Georgia Hartzell, the wardrobe mistress and unofficial "Mother" to the many young and unmarried females of the troupe. She moved among her charges, dispensing reassurance, even as twenty-five circus cars—worth $30,000—burned up in the night.

Photograph of burnt Central Viaduct. *Cleveland Press*, May 26, 1914.

Upcoming shows in Marion and Toledo were canceled, but new trains were already speeding westward to put the circus back on its feet and on the road.

Other than the unidentified suicide, no civilians or firemen were badly injured. But the disaster did not lack for terrible moments or heroic acts. Lieutenant Dittman of Engine Company No. 2 and six of his men were overcome by fire and smoke while fighting flames at an oil shed owned by the Big Four Railroad; they escaped, but Dittman was carried away unconscious. And tragedy was narrowly averted by the men of Hook and Ladder Company No. 6 and other firefighters as the fire reached its climax about midnight. Trapped by flames on all sides while up on the Central Viaduct, they made a desperate dash right through a wall of flames to safety on the east side. And firemen were not the only heroes that memorable night. Frank G. Hogen and W. H. Gray organized a battalion of fifty school custodians who manned a bucket brigade to keep the East 14th-Central Avenue neighborhood from being torched by the numberless embers and burning brands cast into the air by the inferno. Hogen and his men put out at least twelve fires that night. And T. W. Cannell, the superintendent of the city garbage department, labored successfully with several dozen of his men to save the department's Flats stables—and their 150 horses—from the hungry fires.

As always, the fire also kindled less heroic behavior. Many

tramps, rousted by the fire from their customary haunts in Flats lumber piles, groggily stumbled forward to beg or steal food and coffee intended for the firemen. Pickpockets, deprived of expected prey at the circus by its abrupt end, sauntered forth to find victims among the estimated 250,000 Clevelanders who came out to see the Flats burn down. A man named John Gladish was robbed and severely beaten by three men, while unlucky Charles Kammin was robbed and stabbed, probably by the same gang. Most Clevelanders present, however, behaved themselves by not getting in the way of the firemen any more than usual.

The final bill for damages totaled somewhere between a million and a one and a half million dollars. Because the costly damage to both the Viaduct and the Nickel Plate trestle was due to the immense piles of lumber stored *right underneath* them, irate acting Cleveland mayor John N. Stockwell loudly demanded legislation to prevent such conditions from occurring again. The Viaduct and the Nickel Plate were quickly repaired, and the city put its last truly life-threatening fire behind it.

Mad M.D.s and Frank Dolezal

1938–1939

History records that the Torso killer was never found. For all of the hundreds of arrests, thousands of perverts and derelicts rousted, and numberless clues searched out and sifted through, no suspect or suspects were ever arrested, indicted, and convicted of the dozen or so homicides attributed to the Mad Butcher of Depression-era Cleveland. But there *were* two serious suspects at the time, and their stories should be told. Both are inconclusive, both are pathetic, and both reflect very poorly on local law enforcement. These are the sad stories of Francis Edward Sweeney and Frank Dolezal. May God have mercy on their tormented souls.

It was never any secret that most serious Torso investigators were searching for a rogue doctor in the endless manhunt for a decapitating fiend. Coroner Gerber always had doctors on the brain (who can forget his later failure to identify or find the "surgical instrument" he claimed that Dr. Sam Sheppard used on his wife, Marilyn?), and he continually insisted that the Torso killer had a knowledge of anatomy likely to be found in someone with a medical background, such as a doctor, nurse, hospital orderly, or veterinarian. But Gerber wasn't the only sleuth convinced a physician was behind the Torso mystery: much time was spent by Detective Peter Merylo and others on the trail of other suspects with medical profiles: a beheading "voodoo doctor"; a surgeon who claimed he could graft human limbs like a tree surgeon; and an elderly physician who claimed he had invented an effective death ray.

A less ephemeral lead surfaced during the summer of 1938. A police acquaintance from Eliot Ness's Chicago "Untouchables" days alerted him to an alarming story told by an erstwhile hobo. The hobo, eventually apprehended and interrogated by Ness in Cleveland, was a man named Emil Fronek; his tale sparked hopes that the Torso killer was about to be caught. It seems that while bumming around the Kingsbury Run area in 1935, Fronek had been accosted by a man claiming to be a doctor. The "doctor" brought Fronek to his office on East 55th Street, promising him food and clothes. While eating, however, Fronek realized that his food had been drugged and just managed to flee out the door, pursued by the screaming doctor.

Fronek successfully escaped and eventually slept off the effects of his drugging over a three-day period. But the news of subsequent Torso murders prompted him to think about his chilling episode with the "doctor," and his apprehensions were further heightened when he heard about an identical experience from another Kingsbury Run hobo. Try as he might, though, Fronek was unable to point out to Ness the office on East 55th Street to which he had been led. So ended another "hot" Torso lead, as did Peter Merylo's pursuit of another "doctor," suspected of having bought Flo Polillo some drinks just before she died.

If a great number of Torso murder aficionados are to be believed, the most serious medical suspect surfaced in 1938. Although official suspicions about him went unpublicized at the time, he has, in the sixty years since the killing spree, become the favorite candidate for identification as Cleveland's Mad Butcher. His name was Francis Edward Sweeney, and he was everything Coroner Sam Gerber and like-minded theorists could have desired: a doctor, an alcoholic, a man with an office near the killing zone—and a man going downhill fast, in every sense of the phrase.

No matter how he is considered, Dr. Francis E. Sweeney was a sad case. Born in 1894 to a respectable Irish immigrant family, he grew up on the East Side of Cleveland. Graduating from Central High School, he enlisted in the army and served with the American Expeditionary Force in France, suffering a head injury. After the war he worked as a pharmacist's assistant to put himself through medical school and, after taking his medical degree from St. Louis School of Medicine in 1928, began his surgical career at St. Alexis Hospital. He married a nurse and had two sons.

Sweeney's upward professional and personal arc didn't last long, though. By the mid-thirties things had soured at St. Alexis, and Sweeney severed his association with the hospital. At the same time, in 1936, his wife divorced him on grounds of alcoholism.

It must have seemed like a perfect fit to Eliot Ness. Here was a potentially deranged physician with means, opportunity, and—if Gerber was right about the influence of drugs or alcohol in stimulating the Torso killer's murderous frenzy—circumstances that could link him to the trail of butchered corpses that was beginning to create a public relations problem for Ness. So, sometime in 1938, Ness had Sweeney picked up and taken to the Hotel Cleveland on Public Square (now the Renaissance), where the safety director confronted the distressed doctor.

It cannot have been a pleasant interview. Whatever the defenders

HUNT EX-DOCTOR AS TORSO KILLER

Could this be the week that Eliot Ness met with Dr. Francis Sweeney? *Cleveland News*, April 9, 1938.

of Eliot Ness may claim, there was no direct evidence to connect Francis Sweeney with the ghastly murders, however unsavory his reputation or persona. The Hotel Cleveland interrogation may have taken place in April of 1938; hence the *Cleveland News* headline: "HUNT EX-DOCTOR AS TORSO KILLER." But it is irrefutable that Eliot Ness did not bring charges against Francis E. Sweeney, then or at any subsequent time. Years later, when talking to Oscar Fraley, author of *The Untouchables* and the writer who immortalized his exploits, Ness apparently talked about Dr. Sweeney, disguising his identity as "Gaylord Sundheim" and voicing dark suspicions about his role as the probable Mad Butcher.

There is little reason to think that Ness was right, if he in fact said these things. It is true that Dr. Sweeney subsequently checked himself into the Veterans' Hospital in Sandusky and spent the rest of his life in like institutions until his death in 1964 at the age of seventy. And it is true that Sweeney was the probable author of a serious of crank postcards mailed to Eliot Ness from Dayton in the 1950s. Variously signed "The Sweeney Boy," "F. E. Sweeney M. D. Paranoidal Nemesis," and "The American Sweeney," these postcards were probably Sweeney's way of taunting his erstwhile accuser for his failure to capture the Torso killer. But none of that—alcoholism, surgical skill, proximity to the murder sites, and a grudge against Eliot Ness—makes Sweeney the Mad Butcher of Kingsbury Run.

Much the same could be said of Peter Merylo's pet theory, which fingered a male nurse at Cleveland Hospital as the fearsome Kingsbury decapitator. Proponents of either Sweeney or the unnamed male nurse as prime suspects often claim—without any solid evidence—that police officials knew who the *real* murderer was but declined to prosecute because of the social prominence of the suspect. If such conspiracy theorists lived in England, they would claim Prince

Eddie—Queen Victoria's oft-suspected grandson—was Jack the Ripper, but that doesn't make it true.

Lingering speculation about Francis Sweeney is mere historical defamation. But the circumstances of the Frank Dolezal case are outright shameful and a continuing blot in the annals of Cuyahoga County justice. No one will ever know the exact truth about Dolezal, or the full story of what happened to him in the fatal toils of the Cuyahoga County Sheriff's Department. All we can be sure of is that he was treated barbarically and that he was *not* the fearsome Torso killer.

The Cuyahoga County sheriff had largely avoided the Torso hoopla from the beginning, claiming lack of jurisdiction (the bodies were all found in Cleveland City proper—the Brooklyn corpse excepted) in an investigative embarrassment best conceded to Cleveland cops and Eliot Ness. But sometime in early 1939 a private detective, Lawrence J. ("Pat") Lyons, persuaded Sheriff Martin L. O'Donnell to hire him as a special investigator on the Torso case. Lyons was a legendary sleuth to Cleveland-area lawmen, and he convinced O'Donnell that he knew how to crack the case.

Lyons's method was simple enough. Since the identities of three of the victims were known to police—Edward Andrassy, Florence Polillo, and Rose Wallace—Lyons reasoned that the way to find their murderer was to hang around the joints, dives, and places of low repute they had frequented in the Roaring Third district. Soon discerning that all three victims had been habitués of a foul watering hole located at East 20th Street and Central, Lyons began honoring it with his custom in the late winter of 1938–39. His strategy was simply to listen to the prostitutes, perverts, alcoholics, and marijuana users who hung around there, and his patient eavesdropping eventually paid off as he heard more and more disquieting stories about a man named "Frank."

His full name was Frank Dolezal, and he was well known in the Roaring Third as a sullen, burly, hard drinker given to wild rages when in his cups and to boasting about his prowess with knives. Sustained and surreptitious observation by the police soon revealed that he was also a homosexual given to picking up strange men in Public Square and taking them back to his home on East 22nd Street.

The weeks of the spring and summer of 1939 went by, and Frank Dolezal looked better and better as a Torso suspect with each passing day. He had once worked in a slaughterhouse, presumably giving him the anatomical knowledge and dexterity with a knife useful to a Mad Butcher. He was much given to drink, which conformed

Frank Dolezal in custody. Left to right: Lt. Pat O'Brien, Joe Krupansky, Jack Gillespie, Frank Dolezal, Mike Kilbane, A. Burns, Charles King.

with the theory of Coroner Gerber and others that the mad killer did his bloody deeds while in a drug- or alcohol-induced frenzy. Better yet, Lyons learned from his neighborhood informants that Dolezal had actually been seen at one time or another *with all three identified victims and an unidentified tattooed sailor!*

Lyons had been around long enough to know he needed some corroborative physical evidence, so he began probing into Dolezal's past, especially his life during the mid-1930s, the years of the Mad Killer's prolonged spree. Eventually he identified Dolezal's former apartment at 1908 Central Avenue—only several hundred feet from where Flo Polillo's body parts had been found and virtually the epicenter of most of the Torso murder sites. There, in Suite No. 5, in some cracks in the bathroom floor, Lyons scraped out some suspicious-looking stains. Examined by Gerald V. Lyons, the detective's chemist brother, the stains were pronounced to be human blood. Lyons was convinced he had at last found the long-sought "laboratory" of the Mad Butcher.

Frank Dolezal was arrested by deputies of the sheriff's department at 6:00 p.m. on July 5, 1939. Searching his current apartment on East 22nd Street, investigators found four butcher knives (two of them suspiciously stained), female shoulders and heads from several mannequins, and a notebook with several dozen names in it. And within two days, Sheriff O'Donnell was able to announce that Frank Dolezal had signed a confession, admitting to the murder of Florence Polillo in January 1936.

Dolezal's "confession"—the full text of which O'Donnell refused to make public—stated that he and Flo had been drinking at his Central Avenue apartment on Friday night, January 24. They had quarrelled about money, and when Flo came at him with a knife, Dolezal hit her:

> Yes, I hit her with my fist. She fell into the bathroom and hit her head against the bathtub. I thought she was dead. I put her in the bathtub. Then I took the knife—the small one, not the large one—and cut off her head. Then I cut off her legs. Then her arms.

After dismembering the body, Dolezal said, he had taken parts of it to the back of the Hart Manufacturing Company building, where they were found the next morning. And then he had taken the head and the rest of Flo, walked to East 49th Street, near the Kirtland pumping plant, and thrown the remains in the lake.

Sheriff O'Donnell was ecstatic, as were the newspapers. Trumpeting a "Big Score For Sheriff," *The Plain Dealer* praised his investigative coup and rubbed salt in the psychological wounds of the Cleveland police and Eliot Ness:

> As the matter stands, however, it appears that Sheriff O'Donnell and his staff have performed a major task in crime detection. The Cleveland police, at work on the torso cases steadily for many months, seem to have victory snatched from under their noses.

Louis Seltzer's *Press* joined in the applause, also noting that it would only be "sportsmanlike" for the Cleveland police to join in congratulating Sheriff O'Donnell and his men for a job well done.

It was just as well that the Cleveland police withheld any compliments, as Sheriff O'Donnell's case against Dolezal began to unravel almost as soon as his capture was announced. Dolezal's "confession" had come after two days of almost nonstop interrogation, and the dazed, zombie-like Dolezal who stared glassily at reporters on

Friday, July 7, as his confession was announced, looked more a victim of the third degree than a terrifying multiple decapitator. Then there were the problems with the confession itself. Dolezal claimed that he had thrown Flo Polillo's head into the lake—yet Cleveland weathermen reported that the lake on January 26, 1936, was frozen all the way out to the breakwall. Confronted with this inconsistency, Dolezal admitted, after more vigorous questioning, that he had burned the head with a gallon of coal oil near the East 37th Street railroad bridge—the site of the September 1936 torso discovery in the stagnant pool. When detectives failed to find any evidence to support this scenario, Dolezal changed his story again, claiming that he had abandoned the rest of Flo's remains near a steam-shovel in the WPA project area near East 26th Street and the Shore Drive. Nothing was found there, either.

Sheriff O'Donnell didn't help his credibility by now bringing forward a young woman named Lillian Jones, who claimed that Dolezal had attacked her with a knife in his apartment in the week before his arrest. She claimed she had escaped by jumping from a second-story window, breaking the heel of her shoe. O'Donnell claimed Jones's story supported his picture of Dolezal as a crazed psychopath, but *The Plain Dealer,* for one, wanted to know just how Lillian Jones could have jumped out of a second-floor window without hurting more than the heel of her shoe. (Jones would later claim that she only made her improbable claim because O'Donnell and his deputies harassed her and got her "drunk as a monkey" on beer and wine.) In response to mounting criticism, O'Donnell had Dolezal submit to a polygraph exam on July 10 at the East Cleveland Police Station. The results of the exam indicated that Dolezal was lying when he denied killing Flo Polillo. The same day, two psychiatrists, Doctors K. S. West and S. C. Lindsay, pronounced Dolezal sane.

The situation deteriorated rapidly. Two suicide attempts by Dolezal on July 9—successive attempts at hanging himself with his shirt and his shoelaces—were thwarted, but they fueled suspicions that he was being mistreated. On July 11, *Press* writer William Miller summarized the increasing public and press skepticism about Sheriff O'Donnell's strong-arm methods:

> One of his eyes was black and swollen. Sheriff O'Donnell said Dolezal suffered this when he fell to the floor when he tried a second time to hang himself . . . This seemed unlikely in view of the instinctive and automatic reflex action which makes anyone falling forward throw his arms out before him

to protect his face. Dolezal also complained that his "ribs hurt" . . . [When Capel] McNash [a United Press reporter] ventured to ask Dolezal what was wrong with his ribs . . . County Detective Harry S. Brown yanked Mr. McNash backward by the shoulder and Sheriff O'Donnell told him, "You ought to have your jaw punched."

On July 12, East Cleveland police chief L. G. Corlett told reporters that Dolezal had told him he had been beaten, although Corlett disbelieved him. Meanwhile, the Cleveland chapter of the American Civil Liberties Union and the Cleveland Bar Association wanted to know why charges had not been brought against Dolezal—he was being held illegally—and why he did not yet have legal counsel. An attorney, Fred P. Soukup, was swiftly engaged, and under his counsel, Dolezal repudiated his confession on July 12. Two days later, Dr. Enrique E. Ecker, a pathologist at Western Reserve University, reported that his analysis of the "bloodstains" found in Dolezal's Central Avenue flat revealed that they were just "plain dirt." From that moment on, O'Donnell and his men would find no sympathy or quarter in the columns of Cleveland's three newspapers.

Two weeks after his arrest, on July 19, Frank Dolezal was finally bound over to the grand jury on a single charge of manslaughter. O'Donnell doggedly refused to try and connect Dolezal to any of the other Torso victims—much to the public scorn of Coroner Gerber and Detective Merylo—and as his case against Dolezal relied heavily upon the latter's three confessions, he was forced to go along with Dolezal's assertion that the killing of Polillo had been the unpremeditated result of a drunken argument.

Four weeks went by. Dolezal languished in his cell at the Cuyahoga County Jail, Cleveland newspapers heaped scorn on O'Donnell & Co., and the sheriff's department worked frantically to gather more evidence against Dolezal. By this time virtually no one outside the sheriff's department believed that Dolezal was the Torso killer, but the department was forced to go forward with its preposterous case. Then, on August 24, Frank Dolezal solved everyone's problems by hanging himself in the Cuyahoga County Jail.

Sheriff's deputies subsequently claimed that there was nothing they could have done to prevent Dolezal's suicide. Deputy Hugh Crawford's story was that he had left Dolezal alone for only three minutes at 1:45 that afternoon, while he escorted some visitors from the jail area. Returning to the cell block, Crawford found Dolezal

The Plain Dealer, April 2, 1939.

hanging from a hook in Cell No. 11. Opening his pocket knife, Crawford cut the noose while two other men lowered the five-foot-eight-inch Dolezal from the five-foot-seven-inch hook. The fire rescue squad got there at 3:00 p.m., but all they could do was take the dead man to the county morgue. Attorney Soukup was enraged when he got to the jail, shortly afterward. "I had a hunch something like this would happen before he ever came to trial," he shouted at Deputy Clarence Tylicki. "What kind of a jail are you running here, anyway? I thought you were keeping a twenty-four-hour watch on him." Soukup's anger was echoed by the next day's *Plain Dealer,* which summed up public disgust at the way Dolezal had been treated with the caption, "Hounded to Desperation."

Coroner Sam Gerber was not inclined to embarrass Sheriff O'Donnell, a fellow Democrat, but the general public outcry, and a more specific demand by William E. Edwards of the Cleveland Crime Commission that he hold an inquest, forced his hand. The inquest opened on August 26, and its testimony constituted a withering indictment of Sheriff O'Donnell's department. O'Donnell and his men vociferously denied they had ever laid a hand on Dolezal— but Gerber's own autopsy disclosed that Dolezal had recently suffered six broken ribs. As Dolezal had worked as a bricklayer right up until the day of his arrest, it seemed unlikely that he had broken those ribs before his incarceration, leaving witnesses to draw the obvious conclusion. Fred Soukup testified that Dolezal had reported that he was repeatedly blindfolded, gagged, bound, and beaten. Dr. L. J. Sternicki, who had been called to treat Dolezal in his cell on July 11 after his first suicide attempts, admitted under oath that Dolezal's chest had already been taped and that there were discolorations on his left arm and right eye. George Palda, an attorney, and Frank Vorell, a Cleveland policeman (and Dolezal relative by marriage), swore that Dolezal had told them of his beatings in the Cuyahoga County Jail. And a girl named Ruby Lee Jones took the stand to say that she had heard Detective Pat Lyons say these words to a woman in a Central Avenue beer parlor shortly after Dolezal's arrest: "Sure, we've got the right man. He'll get the hot seat. He'll never live to walk out of County Jail."

Jones went on to report that Lyons said "they'd beat him up to make him say he's the man, whether he did it or not." There was little O'Donnell could say in response to such damning testimony, except to insist, "We did all we could to keep him from committing suicide. We treated the man too well."

Gerber's discreet inquest verdict was handed down on September 5. His major conclusion was that Dolezal had committed suicide and that the evidence of his rib injuries involved enough ambiguity to let O'Donnell's men off the hook. The closest Gerber came to incisive criticism was in his finding that Dolezal might have lived if he had been cut down sooner; the coroner's conclusion was that Dolezal had been hanging for considerably longer than Deputy Crawford claimed, perhaps twelve to fifteen minutes.

And that was the end of the Frank Dolezal tragedy, except for a few sarcastic newspaper editorials. With no more Torso corpses turning up, no one was about to make much of an enduring stink about a man perceived simply as an alcoholic Bohemian homosexual loser, whose miserable life story resembled the biography of a Torso victim far more than that of the mythical, stalking, homicidal mastermind of newspaper and police reports. It probably makes the most sense to think of Frank Dolezal as the Mad Butcher's last victim. Better to blame *him* than to indict an entire Cleveland community, and the law-enforcement establishment that stood by while this miserable, pathetic wretch was hounded to death by Cuyahoga County's minions of the law.

Chapter 12

"YOU BETTER BE HOME BEFORE DARK"

The Beverly Potts Mystery, 1951–?

It's every parent's nightmare. We knowingly bring our children into a world of suffering and evil and then anxiously attempt to shield them from every conceivable or danger as they grow to adulthood. We tell them not to talk to strangers, not to accept candy or rides, always to let us know where they are, who they are with, and where they are going, and to be home before dark. We repeat every clichéd parental warning—and hope for the best. Usually nothing goes wrong. And why should it? All children have their cuts and scrapes, their scary moments that make a mother's or father's heart stand still—but most make it through childhood intact to begin protecting their own offspring. But once in a while, something does go wrong—terribly, obscenely wrong—and becomes yet another fearful parable for parents to tell their children as they go forth into the world outside their safe, sheltering houses. The tale of Beverly Potts is such a story, the most legendary in Cleveland history, and one of the most puzzling mysteries in the annals of the Forest City.

There have been other missing children in the Cleveland area over the years. The twentieth century's first decade saw the vanishing of "Sonny" Hoenig, an angelic three-year-old who disappeared right in front of his parents' store at 2822 Scovill Avenue—only to turn up dead several days later, just scant yards away. More recent years have brought us the highly publicized murders of Tiffany Papesh and Amy Mihaljevic. But the Beverly Potts case remains in a class by itself: puzzling, poignant, and still unsolved almost a half century later. She is the Judge Crater of Cleveland, the little girl who vanished into thin air in a crowd of people, many of them her own neighbors. As columnist Dick Feagler once wrote, she will always be ten years old, and her winsome face still stares out at us from yellowing newspaper clippings, beseeching us to find her at last.

August 1951 was an unremarkable time for most Clevelanders.

True, the headlines of the city's three newspapers chronicled unpleasant events in faraway places. The war in Korea dragged on, striking workers were paralyzing America's copper production, and a whiff of unspeakable fear could be sensed in public discussions of civil defense against the newfangled nuclear peril. But Clevelanders, like Americans everywhere, were mainly concerned with getting on with their lives in an epoch of postwar prosperity. They were concerned with their jobs, concerned with their children, and very concerned indeed with the performance of the Cleveland Indians baseball team, locked in a close race with the hated New York Yankees as the last days of August arrived.

Beverly Potts was not occupied, one suspects, with any such weighty adult concerns. Ten years old that summer, she was enjoying the last weeks of vacation before she entered the fifth grade at Louis Agassiz Elementary School on Cleveland's West Side. Every day she played with her friends, especially her next-door neighbor, Patricia Swing, 11, who often accompanied Beverly as she whiled away the golden summer afternoons with bicycle rides, card games, and the like with her school friends. And on this day, Friday, August 24, Beverly was particularly excited. She was already looking forward to tomorrow, when she and her older sister, Anita, 22, would accompany their parents on an all-day outing at Euclid Beach Park. Beverly's excitement intensified when she discovered, sometime Friday afternoon, that the Showagon was coming to nearby Halloran Park that evening.

Sponsored by the recreation league and the *Cleveland Press,* the Showagon had become an annual summer tradition by the early 1950s. A troupe of singers, dancers, magicians, and other performers, the Showagon traveled around Cleveland's neighborhoods during the summer months, giving free performances at local playgrounds and other public venues. It had already become one of Beverly's favorite summer activities, and she was anxious that Friday afternoon because her mother, Elizabeth Potts, had forbidden her to go to Halloran Park for two weeks after Beverly and a cousin had come home late from playing there earlier in the week. But Beverly begged winsomely, and Mrs. Potts, as is the wont of an affectionate parent, relented and said she could go that night. Her supper finished, Beverly helped her mother dry the dishes—she earned a nickel for her labor—and then went next door to get Patricia Swing. The two girls departed for the show at Halloran Park on their bicycles.

Located only an eighth of a mile away from the Potts house at 11304 Linnet Avenue, Halloran Park stretched south from Linnet for

Beverly Potts, 1951.

three blocks between West 117th and West 120th streets. Originally a vacant lot that had become an unofficial dump for neighborhood refuse, the land had been purchased by the City of Cleveland from the Cleveland Transit System and, by 1945, turned into a thirteen-acre civic recreational area boasting baseball diamonds, basketball courts, trapeze bars, and a shelter house. Named for William I. Halloran, a sailor killed on the *USS Arizona* at Pearl Harbor, it was the only major park facility in that part of Cleveland and was used by thousands of West Siders throughout the summer. Let us leave Beverly on her bicycle as she journeys toward her fate, and take a closer look at the girl whose name would become a Cleveland byword.

Everything known about Beverly before she stepped into forever was consistent with the picture of a normal, pleasant, likeable little girl. Four feet, eleven inches tall, she weighed ninety pounds and had recently had her blond hair cut. Her pigtails were gone, and she had bangs, which she frequently shook vigorously to keep them straight. She was quiet, rather shy, and got along well with her teachers and

Patricia Swing, 11, best friend of Beverly Potts
and one of the last persons to see her alive.

classmates. Norma Mazey, Beverly's fourth-grade teacher, remembered her as a girl she never had to discipline, a B student who
played the cello in the school orchestra. Her complexion was fair;
she had wide-set eyes and spaces between her teeth; and she walked
with her toes turned out—like a duck, her friends said.

Everyone also remembered later that Beverly was unusually obe-
dient and cautious. Patricia Swing would recall that Beverly never
went anywhere with her without asking her mother's permission
first. Virtually the only thing that made Beverly cry was a scolding
by her parents. And she never engaged in conversation with strangers
unless Patricia talked to them first. Beverly's mother had cautioned
her carefully and repeatedly not to talk to strangers, especially men,
and never to go anywhere with them. Patricia later summarized her
friend's wariness unequivocally: "I've known Bev since we moved
here about seven years ago, and she could scream louder than anyone I know. She wouldn't let anyone come near her."

And as another acquaintance recalled: "When boys talked to her,
she turned away."

Like anyone else, Beverly wasn't perfect. Patricia Swing recalled
the ups and downs of their friendship, particularly the fact that Bev-

erly "couldn't take a joke." Beverly had slapped Patricia's face several weeks before when Patricia hid her undershirt, but they had
made up afterwards, as they always did.

Beverly's close relationship with her family rounded out the picture of a normal, happy childhood. Beverly's father, Robert, 51, was
a stagehand employed at the Allen Theater on Euclid Avenue. Her
mother, Elizabeth Potts, 49, stayed at home, rearing Beverly and also
enjoying the company of older daughter Anita, 22, who still lived at
home.

It probably took Beverly and Patricia seven minutes to get to Halloran Park on their bicycles that Friday night. Lined with chestnut
and maple trees, Linnet Avenue was well shaded and disquietingly
dark after sunset, but it was still light out when Patricia and Beverly
got to the park shortly after 7:00 p.m.

The Showagon was in full swing by then, and the girls enjoyed the
performance of the numerous singers and dancers. But Halloran
Park was awfully crowded—later estimates put the crowd at 1,500
people—and Beverly and Patricia found it too distracting to keep an
eye on both their bicycles and the show. So the girls came back
home, ditched their bicycles, and were back watching the Showagon
by 8:00 p.m. It was hard for them to see because of all the tall adults
around, and Patricia got tired of standing on tiptoe to see the show.
And it wasn't much of a social occasion, either, at least as Patricia
remembered it: "We didn't talk to anyone. We didn't see anyone we
knew." About 8:40 p.m. it was beginning to get dark, and Patricia
told Beverly that she had to go home.

Patricia's parents had told her to be home before dark, while Mrs.
Potts had given Beverly permission to stay until the show was over.
And why not—she was in her own neighborhood, surrounded by
hundreds of people, many of them her own neighbors. So Beverly
stayed, telling Patricia that she would be along in a few minutes, and
Patricia started walking home. Her last memory of Beverly was of
seeing her standing and watching the show. A "plump, little woman"
stood behind her, with one hand on Beverly's shoulder and the other
holding on to a small child. Patricia thought she remembered the
woman saying that she had a child who was performing in the
Showagon.

There probably weren't a lot of people who saw Patricia Swing
on her journey home that August night. Although Linnet Avenue was
the kind of street where neighbors often sat out on their porches of a
pleasant summer night, many of them, like Robert, Elizabeth, and
Anita Potts, were inside this August 24, watching the Indians–Yan-

kee game on television. In any case, Patricia Swing got home safely by 9:00 p.m.

No one knows for sure how many people saw Beverly Potts again that night. A number of witnesses, many of them children and teenagers, later came forward with unlikely stories, some of which were proven to be deliberate lies manufactured to get attention. The woman standing behind Beverly was never identified in the subsequent investigation. Nor were the two young men whose green car a nine-year-old later claimed she saw Beverly Potts get into that night. Nor could an elusive convertible ever be found, upon the door handles of which, an out-of-town visitor later testified to police, she saw a playful Beverly Potts swinging at about 10:00 p.m. that Friday night. And there were hundreds of other stories like these of phantom cars and phantom individuals, none of which could ever be verified.

Probably the last person to see Beverly Potts on this earth—other than her presumed murderer—was Fred Krause, 13, of 11500 Linnet Avenue. It was about 9:30 p.m., the Showagon program was over, the park was emptying out, and he saw Beverly in front of him, walking diagonally across the park grass in a northeasterly direction toward her home. She was about 150 feet from the corner of Linnet and West 117th when Krause, who was riding his bicycle, beeped his horn, and Beverly stepped out of his way and continued walking. He clearly remembered it was Beverly, he said, because she was walking like a duck.

About 9:30 p.m., Beverly's family realized that she hadn't come home yet, and Anita called the Swing residence. Patricia's parents told her that their daughter had returned home alone, and so Robert Potts went to Halloran Park. After searching in vain with the help of neighbors, he returned home about 10:30 p.m. and called the Cleveland Police. They arrived soon afterward, and one of the greatest manhunts in the history of Cleveland was under way.

The police had a good description of Beverly, the details of which soon became hauntingly familiar to Greater Clevelanders. When last seen, the four-foot-eleven, ninety-pound Beverly was wearing blue jeans with a side zipper (no label), bright red cotton panties, plain green socks, a white cotton undershirt ("Honeylane"), a red sport shirt, a navy blue poplin jacket (both pockets torn, no label), size five or five and a half brown loafers ("Karrybrooke Sportshoes"), and a yellow gold ring. Within hours, dozens, then hundreds, and soon thousands of Clevelanders were searching Greater Cleveland for the missing girl. Within hours every postal carrier in Cleveland was

Elizabeth and Robert Potts, August, 1951.

given a description of Beverly, and posters with her picture were going up on utility poles, doors, and windows all over the city.

The hysteria surrounding Beverly's disappearance was unprecedented, and it was kept at fever pitch by Cleveland's three newspapers and the still-novel local television stations. Every possible theory and suspect was investigated, and every square inch of Cleveland covered during the weeks that followed—but to no avail. More than thirty suspects—most of them male deviates with child-molesting records—were jailed, questioned, forced to submit to polygraph tests, and ultimately released. And from the moment of her disappearance to this day, no solid evidence as to the fate of Beverly Potts has ever surfaced.

It wasn't for lack of trying that the Potts case remained unsolved. Thousands of Clevelanders quickly joined the search for Beverly, and soon platoons of Boy Scouts, off-duty police and firemen, union members, and just garden-variety volunteers were combing Cleveland's landscape for the missing ten-year-old. In addition, fifty Civil Air Patrol cadets began scanning hundreds of square miles of northeastern Ohio from airplanes. Louis B. Seltzer, the legendary editor of the *Cleveland Press*, his finger on the pulse of public opinion, characteristically struck the keynote that made all Cleveland parents feel a kinship with the heartsick Potts family. In a front-page editorial entitled "Let's All Join Hunt For Missing Child" on August 27, he evoked the fear of parents everywhere and demanded that his city's citizens enlist for the duration:

> This child, who played so happily through the day Friday and then vanished, left behind her a fearful mystery which brought to the minds of each and all a wish—and to the lips a prayer—that this nightmare shall pass and Beverly shall be restored to her parents. We must not yield in frustration to this deep sense of sympathy which a whole city feels for the parents. Instead, we should give it expression in a persistent search that will not end until the mystery is solved. Each parent knows that it might have been his own child. Let us unite and find Beverly. Let every person in Greater Cleveland, as he goes about his daily work, keep a sharp lookout for any bit of evidence, however small, that might lead to her discovery. The tiniest clew may lead to a solution of the mystery. And God grant that our urgent errand will be rewarded.

Clues to the fate of the missing girl poured into both the Potts home and Cleveland Police headquarters, eventually as many as fifteen hundred per day. Some of the tips were sincere and seemingly had great potential. New York Central Railroad engineer W. I. Gates told police that he saw a girl who looked like Beverly hitchhiking at Brookpark and Tiedeman roads on Saturday, August 25, about 10:00 a.m. The girl was with a teenaged boy, who sported a blond pompadour. Several witnesses reported seeing two men in a 1937 or 1938 black Dodge with a bad paint job and a noisy muffler at Halloran Park on Friday night—talking to a girl who looked like Beverly. All of these leads led nowhere.

Then there were the obvious cranks, malicious and otherwise, who inevitably gravitated to the Potts case in record numbers. A man who ended up in the Cleveland Police jail because he mumbled that he "knew all about the Potts case" proved to be merely a voluble drunk. A letter found in a postal box at East 93rd Street and St. Clair claimed that Beverly had been kidnapped, molested, and murdered, and that her body had been thrown into Lake Erie at East 71st Street. A false report on Tuesday, August 28, that Beverly was seen at East 13th and Chester Avenue brought thirty-four police to the scene at once. And creepier still was the tale that Beverly had been killed by a hit-and-run driver. This fiction surfaced on August 31, when it was reported that two boys who had borrowed a car from a female West Sider returned it to her with blood on the bumper and a warning that she had better not drive it because it was "hot." The story, initially bolstered by the arrest of nine "hot rodders," was that two boys in the borrowed car had struck Beverly while she was walking down darkened Linnet Avenue. Panicking, they had thrown her body in the trunk and subsequently buried it in Brook Park. The Cleveland police lab reported that a strand of blond hair found on the car door was like Beverly's—a "close match"—but the story proved to be completely untrue.

Harry Christiansen, veteran *Cleveland News* reporter, was memorably victimized by one of the many crackpots drawn to the Potts case. An old man walked into the *News* office and announced that he knew where Beverly's body was hidden. Harry took the man to his car, and, as he drove west, the man told him he had discovered the body by "using secret instruments in his room" that were stimulated by vibrations from Beverly's name. When they arrived at the Brookpark Road bridge over the Rocky River, the old man leaped out of the car and ran down into the park. Christiansen followed but lost the old man and ended up walking several miles back to his car, a sadder but wiser reporter. As one veteran newsman put it, the Potts case seemed to unleash an unprecedented deluge of "cranks, astrologers, dream interpreters [and] cultists of every hue."

The Cleveland Police did the best they could, considering there were virtually no clues and no apparent motive to an as-yet-undefined crime. (The Federal Bureau of Investigation refused to become involved in the Potts case because there was no solid evidence of a kidnapping, although the FBI did eventually distribute 22,000 posters of Beverly throughout the United States.) Chief of Detectives James E. McArthur, who headed the Potts investigation, was not known for his tact: the *Cleveland News* described him as "crisp and nervous," and reported he "often gets so irritable he throws reporters out of his office." But he gave his heart and soul to the Potts investigation, and he was candid throughout the sleepless manhunt of those frantic first weeks. While the *Press* was still calling loudly for an intensified public search, McArthur consistently voiced a frank pessimism from the start. On August 29, just a few days after Beverly's disappearance, he admitted: "I always thought she was dead. If she were alive I think by this time we would have heard something—with all the newspaper, radio and television publicity and the widespread attention given to the case."

McArthur's reasoning, based on his knowledge of Beverly's personality, has not been bettered since then. "I am convinced [that] Beverly," McArthur stated, "being the sort of child she was, would absolutely not have gone away with a stranger. Neither would she have run away. She was taken by force—everything points to it."

On August 29, McArthur expanded on his theory that Beverly knew her abductor:

> I think Beverly Potts was taken away in an automobile by a person or persons she knew well enough to talk to. . . That might be a young man, a middle-aged man or an old man. There may have been another or others in the car. But the one who first spoke to Beverly was not a stranger. Had he been, she would have run up the street.

But who? Although they questioned the members of the Potts family, their neighbors, and virtually anyone who might have knowledge of the case, the police could not turn up any evidence to explain Beverly's disappearance. So they did what they were expected to do, which was to round up the usual suspects.

Those suspects, of course, were any male Clevelanders known to the police as child molesters. The days after Beverly's disappearance saw an intensive roundup of Cleveland's pedophile population—a dragnet that proved as ineffectual as all other efforts to resolve the Potts conundrum. A twenty-six-year-old West Sider, "Bill," was arrested in Columbus after police traced an obscene call he made to a seventeen-year-old. Said to be a "motorcycle addict," Bill had a prior record for assaulting a child and he lived on West 116th—but he also had an alibi for the night of August 24. A fifty-six-year-old child molester who lived in the neighborhood was also rousted—but eventually released for lack of evidence, despite the alleged "nervousness" he exhibited during polygraph tests. A man said to have followed a girl around Halloran Park on Thursday, August 23, was jailed and put in a lineup to no avail. And a young male suspect from Amherst, Ohio, was likewise incarcerated, interrogated, and released for lack of evidence. Indeed, probably every pervert in Ohio and all adjoining states—especially deviates who worked in traveling carny shows and the like—was pulled in and given some form of third-degree treatment before the Potts investigation ran out of gas in early September.

The newspapers, especially the *Press*, fanned the public fears about sexual predators triggered by Beverly's disappearance. Headlines like "1000 Sex Offenders Are Free in City" were soon echoed by local and state government officials, who called for stiffer penalties and tighter supervision of convicted molesters. And, as always, Louis Seltzer both captured and amplified the increasingly angry public mood in a front-page editorial entitled "We Must Stay Aroused To This Peril":

> The very awfulness of it makes strong men shudder. Three innocent little girls—in three years. . . Each time—an aroused public. Each time—the soul-frightening question: "Whose little girl—or boy—next? Mine?" Each time—high resolves that something must be done. Each time—little, if anything accomplished. . . All the while a thousand potential molesters—and killers—of innocent little children, especially innocent little girls, roaming the streets. Infesting the neighborhoods. Luring children with candy, money, promises. Constantly endangering happy, playing, carefree children. . . This is a job for all of us.

The mood of both the hunters and their prey was deftly caught by a *Press* reporter in a story on August 27. Accompanying two Cleveland detectives, Patrick Lenahan and Ray Moran, to a West Side home, he recorded the somber scene that followed:

> An old man came to the door when they knocked. "You again," he said, his voice full of hate and accusation. "Some of you were just here." Could be, Moran and Lenahan thought, but they didn't really believe things were that crossed up at headquarters. The greatly agitated old man, with only a friar's fringe of gray hair, continued his abuse. "Can't you leave us alone? My son hasn't done anything wrong lately."

Day by day, the search went on, much as it had started in the late hours of August 24. Every inch of Halloran Park, Edgewater Park, the Big Creek area, and most of the West Side was searched and re-searched again both by organized units and thousands of amateur sleuths. Every boxcar of every train on every siding was opened and examined. Every sewer and utility line for about a square mile or more was searched—and searched again. There was even agitation to search some of the thousands of abandoned gas wells in the primary search area, until it was finally pointed out that the largest was no wider than eight inches in diameter. In a case lacking any real circumstantial evidence, virtually every possible shred of physical evidence was carefully examined.

And every shred of potential eyewitness testimony, too. Mayor Burke made a public plea for all who were at Halloran Park on the fatal night to talk to the police—but only a small percentage of the fifteen hundred spectators came forward. The Cleveland Police eventually interviewed several hundred students at Louis Agassiz School when classes resumed in September. Probably the only useful item of information turned up was Fred Krause's last sighting of Beverly. A more unseemly wrinkle was the story related by five of Beverly's schoolmates—four boys and a girl—that they had seen an old man who needed a shave driving a black Dodge around Halloran Park on August 24. They eventually confessed it was a lie made up to get attention. Meanwhile, Beverly's assigned fifth-grade teacher, Grace Michele, kept an empty seat waiting for her in the classroom.

Eventually, life returned to normal. The newspapers stopped writing about the Potts case—at least every day—about mid-September.

The rewards offered, totaling about $10,000, remained posted, most of the money put up by various unions, including the stagehands' union to which Robert Potts belonged. The police kept the case open—as it is to this day—but gradually redeployed the massive resources devoted to the Potts case elsewhere. This was only after they had searched the homes of neighbors in the Linnet Avenue area—when permitted by the owners—and interrogated both of Beverly's parents in an effort, cruel but necessary, to eliminate even them as suspects. And Clevelanders were left to ponder another unsolved mystery, another puzzling episode to put alongside the 1931 murder of William Potter and the Kingsbury Run Torso slayings.

Life, of course, did not return to normal for Elizabeth, Robert, and Anita Potts. Grief-stricken and sleepless for the first few days, Robert and Elizabeth Potts coped as best they could with the most unspeakable tragedy of parenthood. As Robert Potts said the day after his daughter disappeared: "You think you know how parents feel when you read about such things in the newspapers. But it's impossible." Only a few days into the investigation, the family had to be given an unlisted number, so great was the volume of crank calls that added to their torment. Early in September, both Robert and Anita Potts returned to their jobs. By then, Beverly's parents had lost hope of seeing their daughter alive, and made a poignant public plea: "We urge whoever did this terrible thing to write or telephone to us, or the police, the location of Beverly's body so that we can reclaim it, and give her a decent Christian burial."

Developments leading nowhere continued. On September 7, police converged on Middle Island, an obscure Lake Erie island twenty miles north of Sandusky, Ohio, and just across the Canadian line, on a report that an elderly man had been spotted walking with a little girl there. On September 28, the *Cleveland Press*, in a gesture demonstrating just how hopeless the case had become, offered a reward merely for any article of clothing worn by the vanished girl. On October 19, a fisherman angling ten feet off the mouth of the Rocky River snagged a bundle of clothing, hair, and possible human flesh. Nothing important came of either the Middle Island search, the *Press* reward, or the Rocky River fisherman's find.

A more macabre and odious episode occurred in November 1951. On November 9, Robert Potts received a telephone call while working at the Allen Theater. A male voice on the line asked Potts if he wanted to get his daughter back: "If you do, connect your phone tomorrow at 3:30 p.m. and raise $25,000," the caller said. "Don't tell the police or we'll cut the girl's throat. She's out of town."

More calls followed, and by the next week, arrangements had been made by Robert Potts—working with the police—to have Mrs. Potts deliver a ransom to Beverly's presumed captors at 5:30 a.m. on November 15. The delivery point was 750 Prospect Avenue, and Mrs. Potts was instructed to turn the money over to a "Negro man."

The denouement of this bizarre plot was a classic of criminal ineptitude. On the morning of November 15, "Mrs. Potts"—actually Detective Bernard J. Conley, very unconvincingly disguised in his mother's clothes—showed up at 750 Prospect to deliver the $25,000 (actually a bag containing one five-dollar bill and lots of newspapers). But, whether owing to the dubiousness of Conley's femininity or to other factors, the ransom pick-up man panicked before taking delivery of the money and started running away. No matter: within seconds, twenty-three Cleveland police and detectives surrounded him and put a shotgun to his head.

It turned out to be a pathetic, if simple, story, even with its undeniably farcical elements. The hapless "kidnapper," Frank D. Davis of 2530 East 33rd Street, had fallen into debt and decided to extort money from the Potts family by pretending to be Beverly's kidnapper. Davis's cruel plot ended in a prison term for him, a painful reminder for Beverly's parents of their continuing tragedy, and months of brutal teasing for Detective Conley from his police colleagues.

Life went on. Anita Potts eventually left home and got a job with

Bernard J. Conley, Cleveland
detective who impersonated Beverly's
mother on November 15, 1951.

the State Department, working for the Point Four Program in
Ethiopia. Elizabeth Potts never got over her pain, although she tried
to forget by giving Beverly's toys away and storing her pictures.
Described by her husband as "going downhill ever since Beverly disappeared," she died of a liver ailment on Thursday, May 10, 1956.
Robert said she had never given up hope that Beverly was alive, but
it was obvious to everyone that the loss of her daughter killed Elizabeth when she was just in her mid-fifties.

More days and months went by. In March 1953 a note found on
the floor of a Willoughby gas station washroom stated that Beverly
was buried in a nearby dump. The note turned out to be a hoax
hatched in the mind of an eleven-year-old Lake County girl with an
overactive imagination. A note found in a bottle in Lake Erie that
same year claimed Beverly was being held prisoner in a boathouse.

Then 1955 brought a seeming break in the Potts case. Warren J.
Tischler, a thirty-one-year-old house painter, convicted child molester, and father of eight, was held in Santa Ana, California, on suspicion of Beverly's murder. Tischler, it developed, had been working
at the National Carbon Company plant—close to Halloran Park—on

the night of Beverly's disappearance, and he seemed to know a lot of the details of the Potts case. But the Orange County sheriff's staff eventually decided that Tischler had gleaned all of his information from newspapers, and he wasn't even brought back to Cleveland for interrogation.

Four months later, Harvey Lee Rush, a forty-seven-year-old alcoholic drifter "confessed" to Los Angeles detectives that he had once killed a twelve-year-old girl in Cleveland, after luring her with candy from a West Side carnival in the early 1950s. Rush was able to pick Beverly's picture out of a group of six photographs, but his description of her appearance, especially what she was wearing the night of August 24, was highly inaccurate. Rush was ultimately taken back to Cleveland, where he attempted to find the spot under the Hilliard Road Bridge where he said he had buried Beverly's corpse. No body was found there, however, and *Plain Dealer* reporter Pat Garling eventually got Rush to admit that he had made up his story to evade California vagrancy charges and get a free trip to Cleveland. Rush, who had been arrested over 100 times for intoxication, was subsequently placed in a mental hospital.

The following year brought several new wrinkles, along with the passing of Elizabeth Potts. Just five days after her death, a thirty-five-year-old Cuyahoga Heights truck driver and child molester confessed to Cleveland police that he had "killed a girl near a playground" three or four years earlier. But his "memories" of that August night at Halloran Park were riddled with inaccuracies, and police dismissed him as a crackpot. The arrest that December of a West Side photographer on a charge of taking lewd pictures turned into something more exciting when one of his albums was found to contain a supposed photograph of Beverly. But Robert Potts finally decided the picture didn't really look like his daughter, and the search went on.

The Beverly Potts mystery was once again resurrected by the newspapers in 1958, when a Preble County gravel pit yielded some suspicious bones. Robert Potts, interviewed as part of the story, said, "I wish you'd forget about it. I'm trying to."

Three years later, a more promising lead developed in New Jersey. The wife of a mental patient at a state hospital became convinced that her husband knew something about Beverly's disappearance. And Cleveland police became very interested indeed when it was disclosed that the man had accumulated fifty charges of molesting young girls and was accused of exposing himself at a Lakewood park in September 1951. Hopes of solving the Potts case ended, however, after two Cleveland detectives interviewed the suspect at a Morristown hospital and concluded that he was not Beverly's killer.

Beverly would have been twenty-one years old in 1962, and Cleveland authorities got quite excited when they got a tip in April that Beverly Potts was living at a house on East North Street in Medina. Sure enough, when the cops got there, it *was* Beverly Potts: Beverly Ann Potts, 19, the daughter of John and Pearl Potts. One can imagine this Beverly's smothered annoyance as she explained to the detectives: "Every time I sign my name to something in Cleveland someone asks me, 'Are you THE Beverly Potts?'"

The Potts case was in the public eye yet again in early 1965 as a result of the brutal slaying of Beverly Jarosz in Garfield Heights. Although there really weren't that many similarities, *The Plain Dealer* insisted the cases were much alike: "In both cases, police have exhausted the primary and obvious leads, such as the questioning of friends, acquaintances and those suspected because of personality disorders." Which was really just another way of saying that both cases were unsolved and that no one had a clue as to how either crime was committed.

A whole decade later, and three years after Robert Potts died with virtually no media attention in 1970, Beverly burst back into the headlines again. In April 1973 Cleveland detectives got a hot tip from a former playmate of Beverly's that she was buried beneath an abandoned grease pit under Jim's Custom Body Shop at 1966 West 52nd Street. Sweating Cleveland detectives dutifully dug down five feet to the concrete floor, pierced that, and went a few feet deeper. Nothing relevant was found, although, curiously, Mrs. Amber Ware, Beverly's cousin, was living in a suite in the same building. She had lived there in the early 1950s, too, and Beverly had actually come to visit and play with her there.

In 1980, retiring Cleveland Police detective James M. Fuerst revealed that he and fellow detective James Shankland had "solved" the Potts case six years before. It seems that in 1974 Fuerst received a letter from the brother of a man who had fled Cleveland in 1966 after being indicted on a charge of abducting two young girls. The letter writer disclosed that his brother had told him that many years earlier he had kidnapped "a girl named Beverly" from Halloran Park in Cleveland. Fuerst and Shankland eventually traced the brother to Maple Heights and one night confronted him with their badges in his own driveway. Fuerst's recollection was that the man immediately blurted out, "You finally got me. I'm glad it's all over." After soliciting additional incriminating statements, the two detectives took their information to Cuyahoga County assistant prosecutor Joseph Donahue—who refused to prosecute the case because of insufficient evidence.

Did Fuerst and Shankland's still-shadowy Maple Heights suspect abduct Beverly Potts? If so, what are we to make of William H. Redmond, who died on January 2, 1992? In the aftermath of his death it developed that Cleveland police had long been interested in Mr. Redmond as a suspect in the Potts case. The likely killer of Marie Althoff, an eight-year-old from Trainer, Pennsylvania, who was found strangled on April 26, 1951, at the site of a traveling carnival, Redmond had a lengthy record of child molestation that began in the 1930s. Redmond never lived to be tried for the Althoff murder after he was finally arrested for it in 1985, but before he died he told another prisoner that he had killed three girls besides Marie. Given his record, Redmond remains at least as strong a suspect as the unknown molester from Maple Heights.

The Beverly Potts story is not over and will probably never be finished. But for sheer bizarreness, it would be hard to top the most recent episode in the Potts saga. On February 20, 1994, on Cleveland's West Side, Michael Vacha was ripping up the old carpet on the staircase to the second floor of his house on Midvale Avenue. Much to his surprise he found, under the carpet on the third step from the bottom, two tattered, yellowing pieces of notebook paper, along with some other papers and a man's shirt. The two sheets were pages of a letter, apparently written in 1960.

And in the letter, its writer, apparently a woman, blamed her husband for the abduction and murder of Beverly Potts.

The letter described how the woman had caught her husband burning Beverly's body in the coal-fired furnace of their basement. She went on to describe her husband speaking of how Beverly's "beautiful blue eyes" still stared at him, even after he had disposed of the cremated evidence—her clothes and bones—under seventy loads of dirt in his garden. And how he used to drive his family through Halloran Park and laugh maniacally about the "murderer returning to the scene of the crime." Weirder yet, she also stated in the letter that her husband told her he had raped Elizabeth Potts years before and that Beverly was actually his daughter.

Disclosure of the letter's contents, as one might imagine, reactivated the Beverly Potts investigation instantly. Real estate and other records revealed that the probable letter writer was Anna Haynik, who had lived at the house in 1960 and had been married to Steven Haynik. Further queries revealed that the Hayniks had been divorced in 1957, Steven had died in 1981, and Anna was now living in Bates City, Missouri. So Cleveland once again held its breath while Detectives Richard Martin and Edward Gray flew down to Bates City to interview eighty-three-year-old Anna Haynik.

The denouement of the Haynik letter proved a disappointment to the macabre minded, who had always hoped Beverly's demise reeked of such unwholesomeness. When interviewed, Anna Haynik admitted that she had made up the story as a kind of fantasy revenge against her husband Steve, who, she said, abused her terribly. The idea, one supposes, was Anna's hope that if her husband someday succeeded in killing her, he might—thanks to her letter, ticking like a time bomb under the stairway carpet—be accused of and pay the penalty for another awful crime: the unsolved disappearance of Beverly Potts.

Believe it or not, there are weirder stories in the Beverly Potts mystery subculture. The author has been regaled—by diverse Potts case enthusiasts—with theories which presume, if they do not quite prove, the guilt of virtually everyone in Beverly's family or anyone who knew her at all. One informant claims that Beverly ended up as a human sacrifice, served as a sacramental meal to drugged children by a West Side ring of cannibal killer pedophiles. And if all else fails, well, there's always *cherchez la femme*: many people still think Beverly must have been lured away by a female that night in Halloran Park. As Robert Potts put it: "We warned her consistently about talking to strange men but we never thought to warn her against women. She might just have been enticed by a woman."

Anita Potts probably got it right, right from the beginning. Her common-sense observation, made several days after Beverly vanished, still pierces through all of the rumors, legends, and just plain nonsense that has accumulated around the name of Beverly Potts for almost half a century: "She was the victim of a pattern. What happened, didn't happen because her name is Beverly Potts. She was in the wrong place with the wrong person at the wrong time."

The last word about the Potts case, of course, belongs to parents, especially those who reared the generation of Clevelanders that grew up during the late 1950s in the aftermath of the Beverly Potts tragedy. Parents like the author's, who, on many a summer night, after cautioning their children to be home before dark, would suddenly wince and whisper to their departing offspring: "Be careful— you don't want to end up like Beverly Potts . . ."

Farewell to the Mad Butcher

A Torso Finale, 1939–?

After the double torso discovery of August 16, 1938, the Torso killer phenomenon dissipated much the way it had started, with no announcement and no discernible pattern. For some years, hacked corpses had shown up every few months in Cleveland's wastelands; then, without warning, they stopped appearing. With no public body parts inventories to write about, newspaper scribes eventually turned to other matters, and the defensive Cleveland police and Eliot Ness—not to mention Sheriff O'Donnell—were happy to avoid the subject. There were, however, a few aftershocks of the Torso legend—and readers may make of them what they will.

On October 13, 1939, two railroad employees working a section of Pittsburgh and Erie Railroad track on the outskirts of New Castle, Pennsylvania, found the naked, headless, and badly decomposed corpse of a young man lying in some nearby weeds. Initial reports were that the body was that of a girl, but an autopsy disclosed it was a young man, twenty to twenty-five years old, with small hands and feet. The local coroner estimated he had been dead about two weeks, and all observers agreed that the decapitation was, well, a hack job, clumsily executed using a blade with a serrated edge. The body was badly charred and was found lying in a pile of burned newspapers. Police and reporters immediately connected the corpse to the bodies found in the nearby "Murder Swamp" some years earlier.

The missing head turned up on October 19, quite close to the site of the torso find and stuffed in the hopper of an empty gondola car, covered with leaves. The victim was never identified, although it was evident that he had had red hair, carefully combed and greased. Detective Peter Merylo, who journeyed to New Castle with other Cleveland officials to investigate this latest Torso find, returned to Cleveland convinced "beyond a doubt" that the Mad Butcher of Kingsbury Run had struck again.

And again and again and again. On May 3, 1940, railroad inspectors at the Pittsburgh & Erie Railroad yards in McKee's Rocks, Pennsylvania, were inspecting a string of ninety-nine boxcars in the Cedar Avenue yards, a desolate, nonresidential valley much like the Kingsbury Run area. Opening the door of a boxcar, they were

CLEVELAND NEWS   STOCKS SPORTS

Wirephotos—Exclusive Evening News of the Associated Press and International News—Wirephotos

DL 99—NO. 107   FRIDAY, MAY 3, 1940   THREE CENTS   Complete Stocks—Pages 16-17

FIND 3 HEADLESS BODIES, HUNT TORSO KILLING LINK

"The discovery of three dismembered men in a Pennsylvania boxcar in May, 1940, sets off a new round of Torso speculation." *Cleveland News*, May 3, 1940.

assaulted by a horrible odor. Inside they found a burlap sack containing seven decomposed pieces of a human being. The head was missing. Three cars away, they found another body, also missing its head, and with the word "NAZI" carved into its chest (with the "Z" reversed). In yet another boxcar, they found the remains of a woman, badly burned, cut into seven pieces at the neck, waist, hips, and shoulders, and placed in a burlap bag. Once again, the head was not found.

After careful autopsies, Dr. P. R. Heimbold of the Pittsburgh coroner's office indicated that two of the bodies (excluding the "Nazi" victim) had been mutilated "by an expert who had some knowledge of surgery or was a butcher." One of the male victims was eventually identified by the FBI as James David Nicholson, a thirty-year-old petty criminal and hobo from Chicago, but nothing more is known about his fate or about the identity of his two fellow victims.

The news from McKee's Rocks brought an anxious police contingent from Cleveland, a party that included Peter Merylo, Robert Chamberlin, Lloyd Trunk, and Martin Zalewski. They were unable to help solve this triple killing, but Merylo had somber words for a Cleveland reporter: "I think it's safe to say that the Mad Butcher's victims now total twenty-three."

Two years went by. On June 27, 1942, four boys playing in Kingsbury Run near East 69th Street and Sidaway Avenue found a trunk tied with rope. Opening the trunk, they discovered the head, arms, and torso of a young black woman. The legs, found seventy-five feet away in some weeds, and the head, discovered another ten yards away, were soon identified as the remains of Marie Wilson, 20, a prostitute who lived at 2395 East 100th Street. Police soon arrested her boyfriend, fifty-eight-year-old Willie Johnson, who quickly con-

Looking for the rest of Marie Wilson, June 30, 1942.

fessed to murdering Wilson after an argument. He had chopped her up and then disposed of the pieces in Kingsbury Run, hoping that she would be accounted a victim of the mysterious Mad Butcher.

Four months later Peter Merylo was finally taken off the Torso case, after seven years, 350 felony arrests (333 convictions), and 665 misdemeanor arrests (656 convictions). Seventy-seven of his arrests—the largest category—were for sodomy, owing, no doubt, to Merylo's long-standing characterization of the Torso madman he could not catch:

> I am of the opinion that the murderer is a sex degenerate, suffering from necrophilia, aphrodisia or erotomania and who may have worked in the pathology department of some hospital, morgue or some college where he had an opportunity to handle a great number of bodies . . .

Merylo further believed that the Torso killer was a railroad worker, a psychopath, and a marijuana smoker. Even after being officially removed from the Torso hunt, Merylo never stopped looking for the Mad Butcher, continuing his personal manhunt into his retirement years.

One last echo of the Torso years came in 1950. On July 22 Mike Jaratz and John Cooper, Lakeside Avenue residents, found a man's rotting left leg in a field on Davenport Avenue, near the Pennsylvania Railroad tracks. Shortly after the police arrived, employees of the nearby Norris Brothers Company mentioned a bad smell coming from the westernmost part of their property. In that area, underneath some steel girders, Cleveland police found the matching torso, arms, and right leg. With the pieces were some pages of a year-old *Cleveland News* and the "K" section of the Cleveland phone book.

The missing head was found on July 26, under some wooden beams only twenty feet away from the torso find. The male victim was six feet tall, with long brown hair and blue eyes; he was unshaven and had been dead for about six or seven weeks. Coroner Gerber pronounced the dissection skillful, allowing that it demonstrated the "Kingsbury Technique." The corpse was eventually identified as that of Robert Robertson, 44, an ex-convict, hobo, and suspected homosexual. Little more is known of him; by that time even the newspapers no longer cared to fan the flames of Kingsbury Run hysteria. The Mad Butcher era was over and virtually every interested party must have wished it good riddance.

So who butchered twelve, or thirteen, or twenty-three, or more victims in Cleveland, the New Castle "Murder Swamp," and the rail yards of West Pittsburgh and McKee's Rock, Pennsylvania, between 1934 or 1935 and 1940, or whenever? The answer should be pretty obvious, although it is not one likely to be accepted by the legions of Torso fanatics, who like all conspiracy addicts everywhere insist that horrific effects must have equally awful causes. The bald truth is that the Cleveland Torso victims proper—say twelve or thirteen victims—may well have had as many killers. There was never any convincing reason to think that one maniacal, surgically adept killer was responsible for the Kingsbury Run murders. Anyone who has read the files of any major American newspaper from the beginning of this century can tell you that headless victims are as common and as American as apple pie. They were showing up in Kingsbury Run itself as early as 1908 and appeared in most large cities with wide rivers or desolate wastelands on a fairly regular basis. Decapitation has ever been the convenient resort of even the most untalented and unimaginative killer with an embarrassing corpse on hand, and it has often proved to be an irresistible option to even professional assassins laden with a compromising stiff. Sam Gerber, Peter Merylo, and

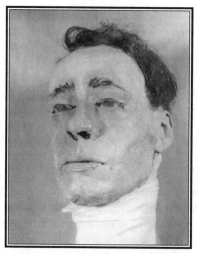

Artist's reconstruction of the head
of Robert Robertson, believed to
be the last Torso victim, August 8,
1950.

even the great Eliot Ness may have plumped for a mad, albeit gifted, surgeon, but the author is inclined to agree with the sentiments recorded by his father, Peter Bellamy, who wrote in 1939:

> There are some reporters and police who privately believe that there is no such thing as the Mad Butcher of Kingsbury Run, and that the murders have been committed by at least two, three or four different people. One, who is by way of being a "torso expert," told me that the mutilation of two of the victims resembles that which is commonly associated with Sicilians in their love-revenge killings, and not at all like the mutilation on the other corpses.

And Bellamy, with a wisdom garnered by the reality of working in a highly competitive journalistic environment, believed there were probably as many Torso killers as there were victims. He spoke volumes about the care and feeding of the legend of a single Mad Butcher:

> Personally, I have always looked coldly upon the suggestion that there is more than one torso slayer. If there were, it would

hurt circulation. Besides, think how complicated things would get if the story broke just before edition time and there were 12 killers instead of one to check . . . . While we will be irritated when the police get excited over a pile of ham bones found in Kingsbury Run and have to write shorts on silly tips and suspects, we won't complain about the Mad Butcher too much. My God, how that man can sell newspapers!

All of which is to say this: Clevelanders, especially those of a romantic cast of mind, can spend their lives thinking that there was one demented, Jack-the-Ripper-like demon who left a trail of a baker's dozen mainly headless corpses throughout Depression-era Cleveland. But the far more likely explanation is that the Torso phenomenon was simply a product of the law of averages aggravated by opportunism. Once Cleveland newspapers—the *News, Press*, and *Plain Dealer*—had built the legend of the lone Torso killer, it was simple logic and economy for anyone with an inconvenient corpse to have it chopped up by, say, an ex-slaughterhouse worker or even a reasonably skillful hunter—and have the remains dumped in Kingsbury Run or the Flats. "Tsk, tsk," the newspapers would say, "another victim of the fiendish Mad Butcher!" Those killed this way could rarely be identified and, given the marginalized nature of most of the victims, it was unlikely they would even have been noticed unless somebody literally stumbled across their remains.

The fact of the matter is this: There is virtually no evidence—other than the medical monomania of Sam Gerber and like-minded theorists—to indicate that the so-called Kingsbury Run Torso victims were murdered by one individual. The truth is that more than half the victims were not even found in Kingsbury Run—a telltale hallmark that reveals the carelessness of those who created the legend of the Kingsbury Run Torso killer. Cleveland has always wanted its own Jack the Ripper legend. As Hemingway might have put it, "Wouldn't it be pretty to think so?"

PHOTO CREDITS

For all newspaper reprints, the date of the featured headline is listed under the image.

Auth—Author's collection
CPL—Cleveland Public Library Photograph Collection
CSU—Cleveland Press Collection, Cleveland State University Archives.
CPHS—Cleveland Police Historical Society
PD—*The Plain Dealer*
Press—*The Cleveland Press*
News—*The Cleveland News*

If you enjoyed this book, try one of these other great books about Cleveland ...